CRITICAL THINKING
AND WRITING IN
PSYCHOLOGY

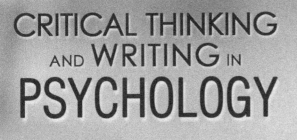

JANETT M. NAYLOR-TINCKNELL

CAROL PATRICK

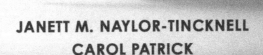

Kendall Hunt
publishing company

Cover image © Shutterstock.com

www.kendallhunt.com
Send all inquiries to:
4050 Westmark Drive
Dubuque, IA 52004-1840

Copyright © 2019 by Kendall Hunt Publishing Company

ISBN: 978-1-5249-7041-3

Published in the United States of America

Contents

Why Psychologists Write?

In Chapters 2, 3, and 4, you will read chapters from experts in the fields of Experimental, Clinical, Counseling, and School Psychology about the importance of writing in their educations and careers. Often students think, "I'm not going to write research papers; so why do I need to worry about my writing skills?" or "Why do I have to take more writing courses? I took composition classes." You will learn how important precise, objective, research-based writing is to psychologists, from researchers to practitioners. Scientific writing permeates their daily lives in numerous ways. The consequences of poor writing can vary by career. Poor writing can result in miscommunications, misperceptions, and misapplications, and even more importantly, misdiagnosis and improper treatments.

Mechanics of Quality Writing

Learning the skills of writing and writing well takes time and practice. Not only do you need to learn rules of grammar and language, but you must also adapt those basic skills when addressing different audiences by changing formality, tone, and purpose. What we write in short notes or text messages varies significantly from what we write in published works. In Chapters 5, 6, and 7, you will learn about types of writing, in particular persuasive writing, and the skills necessary for good writing. Although these chapters do not describe all the skills you will need to be a good writer, they are a good start on your path to becoming a competent writing psychologist.

Scientific Writing

Along with good, general writing skills, psychologists must know how to write scientifically. All psychologists use empirically grounded ideas to generate objective solutions to issues. You must investigate all sides of issues, rely on reputable sources, and then draw conclusions. Learning the mechanics of scientific writing involves learning the skills of brevity, conciseness, and precision, as well as discipline-specific style rules. In Chapters 8, 9, and 10, you will learn the skills of scientific writing and how to read scientific psychology articles, as well as an example of a student paper like you may be required to write for classes.

Finding, Reading, and Organizing Scientific Work

Now that you have learned the importance of writing, you will need the skills to find, evaluate, and organize empirical information. In Chapters 11, 12, and 13, you will learn key skills to be able to produce scientific work. Information literacy will help you understand the characteristics of quality scientific works. Once you know what types of scientific works to look for, you will need to know where to search for those works and how to narrow them down to what you need. Finally, you will learn several strategies to help organize the plethora of works, your time, and your ideas to begin writing.

Issue Chapters

The final chapters present controversial issues in psychology that have two opposing viewpoints. You will learn the empirically supported pros and cons for each issue. The authors are experts who have chosen a controversial topic that has no real definitive conclusion. You will use these chapters as the basis for your own research paper.

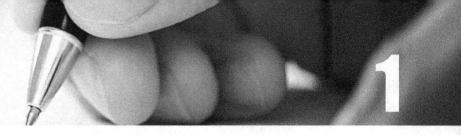

Introduction: Psychological Writing and Careers

by Carol Patrick, PhD

I don't know about you, but personally I feel I learn more effectively and with a higher degree of interest if I know beforehand what I am going to be learning, and the goals it will meet in my future development, both in the short term and long term. This chapter will address those issues for you up front, as we know not everyone thinks, "Oh yay! I am going to learn about writing in Psychology and APA style! I have been waiting my entire college career for this!!!" Hopefully, after this chapter, you will feel more excited about what we are going to learn, and if you already feel excited, "Yay!"

This book is arranged in five sections. First, the role of writing in the work of psychologists will be discussed. Then, we will describe types of writing and what is good writing. Next, we will learn about scientific writing and how to read it, and you will be given tools to help you do it well. Finally, a series of interesting issues in psychology, wherein the research supports both sides of the issues, will be utilized to develop your critical thinking skills.

In the short term, reading this book and participating actively in this class will teach you how to write scientifically, utilizing peer-reviewed, published research. In the past, and still now at many universities, psychology students learned these skills on their own, if at all, as they wrote research papers for different courses. As you might imagine, this is difficult to do, and most professors will tell you that students struggle with these papers and often receive lower grades than those who take a course like this one. The students then go on to graduate school or jobs and, well, trouble ensues. In my Ph.D. program, although the students admitted had high GPAs as undergraduates and very high entrance exam scores, many struggled with scientific writing due to the lack of experience. And one of employers' top complaints about college grads is that they just can't write, and it is an embarrassment for their companies.

So, although not too many students jump for joy to take a class like this, almost all indicate they are relieved that they didn't have to learn the information on their own, and some even enjoy it more than they thought they would. Certainly, feeling you are a more effective writer in psychology is encouraging to most, and worth the time. And getting better grades on research papers while in college is worth it, many former students indicate to us. Students also describe that it is more enjoyable to write papers in their topics of interest in classes like

Child Psychology, Social Psychology, Abnormal Psychology, or a variety of other classes, with the "how to write scientifically" information already under their belts.

In the long term, what you learn in this class is also important. Some students wonder, "If I'm not going to graduate school, why do I need to learn to write scientifically?" That is an excellent question, and my answer comes from my own professional background as a career counselor and job placement director for quite a few years. In this career, I helped students decide what they wanted to do occupationally, and I also had the opportunity to meet and talk with employers who hired college students for job openings in corporations and institutions, both big and small.

Often, employers have many more applicants than job openings; sometimes as many as hundreds of applications for a single job. Almost without exception, to narrow their field of candidates, the first thing they do is eliminate anyone with writing errors on their application, resume, or cover letter. You may think that is not very fair. However, employers may believe that the applicants are showing you their best work on these materials (or they should be), and that errors they make on job apps will only be worse in their day-to-day work. In other words, your writing will go to clients, customers, co-workers, and other institutions. Bad writing reflects negatively on their companies' images and could cause embarrassment for them. And although your teacher will edit your documents, your employer most certainly will not.

So our long-term goal for this course is to help you become more competent and confident writers, in all future settings. However, there are other skills you will learn in this class that are ones employers seek, and that former psychology students also agree are important in their career success. The top four skills are as follows:

The ability to:

1) work well with others, particularly in teams;
2) think critically;
3) have information literacy about the topics you research; and
4) write and present information well

Skill Set 1: Working Well With Others, Particularly In Teams

Four of the top ten skills employers want from new psychology graduates (and the top three) have to do with working with others in teams. They want you to have: #1) good listening skills, #2) ability to work with others as a part of a team, #3) get along with others, and #4) have good interpersonal skills (Landrum & Harrold, 2003). Employers, speaking to me informally about job candidates, have indicated that they believe psychology majors will have these skills, and sometimes like to hire psych majors for their businesses because of these perceived strengths. These may be one of your best selling points on the job market, so take advantage of it!

Also, take time to learn and perfect those skills. If you can, take courses that teach good listening skills (e.g., a counseling or therapeutic skills course), and learn to at least tolerate the most dreaded of college assignments, on which many critical memes are based, group work. Yes, I heard your screams. Group work frequently devolves into a situation where one or two group members take over or are forced to do all the work, with at least one person who doesn't turn their assignments in, and one person who magically disappears. Group work is not a student favorite, to say the least. But, when it comes to the world of employment, it is almost always a consistent reality you have to conquer. When psychology alumni were asked about the differences between college and their jobs, they describe the jobs as requiring more active participation with others, team effort, and dealing with people challenges more than intellectual ones (Hettich, 2004; as cited in Landrum, 2009). Another study of psychology alumni revealed that in jobs, important skills included needing the ability to receive and use positive and negative feedback from others, participating effectively in discussions, and giving direction and guidance to others as needed (Landrum, Hettich, & Wilmer, 2010). These alumni also indicated that the number one place where they learned these skills in college was . . . group projects. Now is the time for you to learn group work skills!

Skill Set 2: Thinking Critically

Hopefully, you are learning to think critically about different topics in all your college courses. By the time you finish this course, you should be able to argue convincingly two sides of a controversial topic, and then resolve which side is most correct; or at the very least, what the conflicting concepts are, and the factual argument for and against each. You will learn to separate opinion from fact, by reading the research literature available, considering the different sides and evidence for them, and creating your own reasoned point of view.

This skill area is used by clinicians to choose a therapeutic approach, and by experimentalists to read, understand, and suggest new avenues for research. Being able to think critically is rated by employers as important to success in the workplace (Landrum & Harrold, 2003). Psychology alumni also indicate that gathering information efficiently and being able to consider and evaluate alternative solutions, and their risks and benefits, are important (Landrum et al., 2010).

Skill Set 3: Information Literacy

In a world where information comes from so many directions at once, and much of it is not quite correct, or just plain wrong, it is an essential skill as a psychologist, and a functioning member of a society, to be able to discern what is the truth, and what is opinion. This course will focus on how to find the initial (or primary) research on which other articles and news media reports are based, and ascertain what are the true findings of that research. You know how sometimes you will read conflicting information: don't spank your kids, because this study says so. Then the next day, it's okay to spank your kids sometimes! Who is right? Who do you believe? In this course, you will learn the skills to be able to look up and answer that question. And social media? Don't believe a thing you can't verify through your own research.

Employers want you to have this skill set. Whether it is advising clients or writing papers or news briefs, the information that you put out as a professional needs to be factually correct . . . not just passed on from wherever you read it. Employers rate information gathering and processing as one of the top skills needed in their employees (Appleby, 2000). They are also not happy if you are too dependent on textbook knowledge, particularly if it is not recent. The American Psychological Association indicates that information literacy is one of the top 10 skills they expect you to learn as a student, as well as a thorough knowledge base in psychology and research methodology (American Psychological Association, 2007). You will be expected to keep up on your knowledge and make sure it is correct in any psychology job you have, so be ready.

Skill Set 4: Writing and Presenting Well

All psychologists write (See Chapters 2–4) and present in front of people. It is the main pathway, other than therapy, where we can use our knowledge to help others, and further the science of psychology. In this class, you will be expected to improve your writing and speaking skills. And if you are nervous when you speak to a group, talk to your instructor, who may have tips and may have suffered this too (after all, public speaking is feared even more often than death). Effective writing skills, writing proposals and reports, and public speaking are just some of the skills in this area that employers are seeking (Landrum & Harrold, 2003).

Conclusion

I'd like to make one final point before you start learning. Your book editors have developed this course and taught it many times. The topic area students struggle with most is probably the learning of APA style. All the details . . . a comma here, but not there; italicize this title, but not that one; capitalize this, but sometimes not . . . it is enough to make you scream. You may want to resort to those pre-canned programs that say they will put a reference in APA style for you, or just copying the citation off the source you find it on. Fair warning: rarely do those sources actually create a correct APA citation, and this can cause you to lose unnecessary points on papers in your classes. (So make sure you know enough yourself to spot when they are wrong!)

Slogging through the APA details also teaches you something else that is important in the long run: One of the most common reasons psych grads lose their first job is an inability to pay attention to and follow through with details (Gardner, 2007). If you return that assigned task in an incorrect format, at an incorrect time, or in an incorrect way, it won't be usable, or your super-busy boss will have to fix it for you. Too many of these and bye-bye job! A lack of follow-through with details may also be seen by your employer as poor work ethic, another reason new employees are let go.

As we move into the next section, psychologists (clinical, counseling, school, and experimental) will tell you about all the ways they use writing in their jobs. You will learn more about careers you may be considering for yourself, and also the writing involved!

References

American Psychological Association (2007). *APA guidelines for the undergraduate psychology major*. Washington, DC: Author.

Appleby, D. (2000). Job skills valued by employers who interview psychology majors. *Eye on Psi Chi, 4*(3), 17.

Gardner, P. (2007). *Moving up or moving out of the company? Factors that influence the promoting or firing of new college hires*. Research Brief 1-2007. Michigan State University Collegiate Employment Research Institute.

Hettich, P. (2004). *From college to corporate culture: You're a freshman again*. Paper presented at the Annual Meeting of the Midwestern Psychological Association, Chicago, IL.

Landrum, R. (2009). *Finding jobs with a psychology bachelor's degree*. Washington, DC: American Psychological Association.

Landrum, R., & Harrold, R. (2003). What employers want from psychology graduates? *Teaching of Psychology, 30*, 131–133. Retrieved from https://www.researchgate.net/profile/L_Epting/publication/285705167_Student_and_faculty_perceptions_of_effective_teaching_A_successful_replication/links/56b22f1308ae5ec4ed4b2c88.pdf

Landrum, R., Hettich, P., & Wilner, A. (2010). Alumni perceptions of workforce readiness. *Teaching of Psychology, 37*, 97–106. doi:10.1080/00986281003626912

2

Writing as Research/Academic Psychologist

by Alicia Limke-McLean, PhD

Follow the stylistic and editorial guidelines found in the 6th edition of the *Publication Manual of the American Psychological Association* (APA, 2010). I include this direction in almost every assignment in the classes I teach ranging from General Psychology (an introductory-level course) to Advanced Social Psychology (a graduate-level course). In response, students often ask me what I mean by APA style. Their difficulty understanding this sentence comes from a general lack of understanding of the importance of academic writing, as well as an under-appreciation of the complexity of APA style. Let me begin by addressing the latter issue first.

Students—specifically undergraduate students—often mistakenly reduce APA style to citations and references. Although an important piece, only two chapters (25%) of the current APA manual refers to crediting sources. Much of the remaining guidelines focus on the presentation of ideas, including the importance of writing with clarity, brevity, and precision (APA, 2010). To do this well, psychologists must understand how to organize their ideas, reduce bias in language, abide by guidelines of grammar and usage, reduce mechanical errors (such as punctuation, spelling, capitalization, and other errors), and follow other given rules to streamline psychologists' writing to increase accessibility and clarity.

Students' other major error—failing to understand the importance of academic writing—likely stems from lack of knowledge about the amount and variety of writing research/academic psychologists do. As a professor and researcher, writing is critical in almost everything I do, including disseminating original research findings, summarizing previous work, preparing for courses, corresponding with students, reviewing other professionals' work, communicating with non-psychologists, and applying for financial support.

Disseminating Original Research Findings

Outside of teaching courses (mostly in social psychology and statistics/research methodology), I spend most of my time at work in scholarship. In fact, tenure-track academic appointments at universities typically divide individuals' careers into three areas: teaching, scholarship, and service. For most psychologists, the scholarship component involves original scientific research contributing to the field. After proposing, conducting, and analyzing this research, psychologists disseminate their research findings to other academics who are interested in the field.

Most commonly, research psychologists disseminate their findings in peer-reviewed journals. In peer-reviewed journals, a panel of anonymous peers reviews the submitted article and determines whether the manuscript: (a) contributes to the content area covered by the journal; (b) communicates with clarity and brevity; and (c) follows the stylistic guidelines required by the journal (i.e., often APA style). This panel makes a recommendation to the editor (or an associate editor) regarding the disposition of the manuscript: acceptance, rejection, or required revisions.

Research/academic psychologists often also present their work at state, regional, or national/international conferences. These meetings (sponsored by professional organizations) allow psychologists opportunities to share their findings quickly and succinctly through poster presentations, paper presentations, and/or symposiums. These meetings also provide psychologists with excellent opportunities to involve undergraduate and graduate students in their dissemination efforts, allowing those students to participate in presentations by sharing information and answering questions.

Summarizing Previous Work

Sometimes, research/academic psychologists contribute to the profession by summarizing their own previous work or summarizing the work of others. Book chapters (such as this one) and literature reviews or theoretical papers do not present original research findings; however, they present ideas from multiple sources in one place, making an argument or proposing a new idea to be later tested. Often, authors of chapters in edited books go beyond a simple summary of previous research findings to synthesize research on a specific topic and present the previous findings in a new or creative way.

Preparing for Courses

I spend the majority of my time at work teaching. However, teaching does not just occur in the classroom. On average, each hour of class requires approximately 3 hours of preparation (especially for new courses). Although most of my classes include a "flipped" format (i.e., I expect my students to read the textbook before we meet so that I spend very little time talking at them and more time listening to them), I *do* spend time writing lectures before class (or even before the semester begins). I post lecture slides to my course websites to provide an additional resource to students to focus their study for exams.

After creating these lecture slides, instructors must prepare for their time in class with students. To do this, they identify important information to communicate, determine appropriate discussion questions or debate items, and create informative and sometimes entertaining in-class activities. Finally, instructors must determine ways to assess student learning effectively. Often, assessment includes exams, which requires instructors to write clear test questions that accurately reflect both the intent of the question itself as well as the knowledge of the student.

Corresponding with Students

Assessment of student work also includes grading/editing student work and providing feedback to students on work they submit. In graduate school, I remember writing papers and receiving the dreaded "awk" written in red ink in the margin. Although the instructor effectively communicated the idea that my writing was awkward, it was difficult for me to know exactly where the problem occurred or how to fix my writing. Thus, part of my job as an instructor is to provide efficient feedback to students. In addition to marking common grammatical and mechanical errors (such as mismatched subjects/pronouns, incorrect tenses, or use of the "universal we"), I also provide thoughts to my students about their organization of ideas, theoretical basis for scientific hypotheses, and overall feasibility of their proposed projects. It is my responsibility to be clear in my feedback and to provide a level of feedback that is both instructive in nature and non-destructive to the student's academic self-efficacy.

E-mail responses are another form of communication with students. Although students sometimes inappropriately send requests in text message or other informal format (e.g., "hey! r we having class today?") or ask inappropriate questions (e.g., "I ordered the book but it won't be here for another week. Can you send me screenshots of all of the pages we need until then?"), it is my responsibility to answer each message carefully and professionally. Both instructors and students should remember that electronic communication is still professional communication; therefore, messages should contain appropriate greetings and signatures, should be grammatically correct and free of errors, and should address all questions or issues previously identified.

Reviewing Other Professionals' Work

As part of the third portion of my job as an academic/research psychologist (i.e., service), I spend part of my time reviewing the work of other professionals in the field. Most often, I am part of the peer-review process for academic journals. As such, I review articles submitted by other psychologists. Reviewers receive copies of submitted manuscripts that editors mask to ensure anonymity. Reviewers make comments about the proposed manuscript and often provide recommendations to the editor regarding its outcome. It is important for this writing to be professional but also critical; that is, journal article reviewers are responsible for being the gatekeepers of research. It is their responsibility to ensure that research published is high quality in both research design and writing presentation. Similarly, journal editors often invite academic/research psychologists to submit reviews on newly published books relevant to the field of psychology. It is the responsibility of authors of these reviews to summarize the material concisely while providing an overall judgment on the quality and tone of the work reviewed.

Academic/research psychologists also serve as editors (or associate editors or action editors) of peer-reviewed journals. As such, they are responsible for securing individuals for the peer-review process (and communicating professionally with them regarding responsibilities, timelines, and other expectations), producing their own critique of the work, and determining the outcome of the submitted manuscript. They are then responsible for summarizing the issues noted by the selected reviewers, identifying the most common or notable issues authors should address, and communicating the decision of the manuscript outcome to its author.

Communicating with Non-Psychologists

One of the most exciting parts of my job (also part of the service component) involves communicating with non-psychologists. Most often, this includes describing my research to professionals at my university to obtain permission to conduct the research from the ethics board (i.e., the Institutional Review Board). However, this sometimes also includes briefs to other interested parties, both on-campus and off-campus. For example, lawmakers and other stakeholders often request summaries of topics from psychologists that will help enable them to make informed policy decisions. At the government level, these White Papers are often one-page briefs that quickly summarize research findings in an area of interest (e.g., the number of cases in which eye witness testimony led to wrongful imprisonment that was later overturned by DNA evidence), providing relevant (and easy to digest) statistics for the readers. Other private sector reports might also provide recommendations for action or other information.

Before my tenure-track appointment at my institution, I worked for three different government entities. As an undergraduate student/graduate student, I served as a Research Assistant and then as a Statistical Research Specialist for the Oklahoma Criminal Justice Resource Center (OCJRC; now part of the Oklahoma State Bureau of Investigation). Part of my responsibilities at the OCJRC included preparing reports submitted to the Oklahoma Sentencing Commission (part of the state legislature). These reports were often over 500 pages of tables and graphs but also included a one to two page executive summary of the findings. Because lawmakers used this information to make decisions about policy, it was important that we communicated these findings accurately and clearly. As a graduate student, I worked as an Interviewer and Assistant Site Coordinator for the Arrestee Drug Abuse Monitoring (ADAM) Project with the National Institute of

Justice. Part of my responsibilities included providing detailed notes about the research process to my supervisors and colleagues. Finally, upon the completion of my doctoral degree, I served as the Assistant Director in Special Education Services at the Oklahoma State Department of Education (OSDE). In this position, I oversaw all data collection, assessment, and finance in special education (approximately 90,000 students) each year. My task included providing reports about the services offered and compliance of school districts to federal law both to the public and to the United States Department of Education (USDE), which had the potential to affect federal funding decisions in subsequent years.

Research/academic psychologists also interact with the public through their writings. For example, one of my colleagues communicates regularly through a blog hosted in *Psychology Today.* His posts—written for the general public instead of primarily academic psychologists—are easy to digest and are relatively short in content compared to more academic types of writing. Similarly, psychologists also provide summaries of research findings through social media (e.g., the Society for Personality and Social Psychology posts on Facebook weekly about relevant news stories and exciting original research) and other mass media communication such as newspaper articles. In fact, the *Association for Psychological Science* supports a mission to use Wikipedia to deliver accurate information about psychology to Wikipedia users, asking psychologists and students to create and edit Wikipedia articles to better disseminate psychological information.

Applying for Financial Support

This research—disseminated to other psychologists, students, professionals in other fields, and the public—often does not occur free of cost. Sometimes, the studies that research/academic psychologists conduct are quite costly and require financial support inside or outside the university. For example, in one study, I wanted gamers in an online application to complete a study about their relationships both online and offline. However, I knew that it was unlikely I would get these gamers to leave their virtual environments for 45 minutes to complete the questionnaires I needed. Thus, I applied for financial support to pay them stipends in the form of in-game coins.

This grant process requires the ability to summarize the originality and necessity of the research question to investigate, the appropriateness of the design proposed to investigate it, and the potential of the contribution to the field upon its completion. The grant process (and documents involved) varies by institution and granting agency; however, each assumes that the applicant will write in a formal and technical tone, summarizing and synthesizing previous literature, and communicating ideas clearly. Applicants should also be sure to follow directions precisely and proofread continuously for errors.

Conclusion

Research/academic psychologists write. We write a lot. We serve different purposes and write to different audiences and this skill—writing to your audience—may be one of the most difficult writing skills to master. My advice in doing so is to determine who your audience is, what your audience needs to know (and what your audience likely already knows), and what you want your audience to think about you as the conveyor of information. Focus on your tone; for example, professional writing like that used for the dissemination of original research findings is very concise and technical, avoids first person (except for in discussions of methodology and analyses), avoids second person, and never includes creative writing devices such as metaphors. In contrast to these articles I write, I would never teach a course with that level of formality. My students learn best through personal examples, media highlights, and the small deadpan joke. Your audience matters . . . almost as much as the content you plan to deliver.

Reference

American Psychological Association (APA). (2010). *Publication manual of the American Psychological Association* (6th ed.). Washington, DC: American Psychological Association.

3

The Importance of Writing in Clinical and Counseling Psychology

Forward by Janett M. Naylor-Tincknell, PhD

Writing as clinical psychologists varies with the type of practice and the area of expertise. However, all applied psychologists write often and write with precision, clarity, and accuracy. As you will see in this chapter, applied psychologists rely on their writing skills to help their clients through the therapeutic process, to help their interactions with the community, and to help educate the next generation of psychologists. The authors in this chapter are all clinical or counseling psychologists who together have over 70 years of experience in the field. Each was tasked with describing the writing they do as therapists and how writing is important to their careers and successes.

As a Licensed Masters Level Psychologist (LMLP) and a Licensed Clinical Psychotherapist (LCP), Kenneth Windholz spent over 40 years providing therapeutic services to clients at a community mental health center, as well as about 4 years in academia educating future clinicians. His experience and reliance on his writing skills has helped thousands of people struggling with mental health issues. Dr. Carrie Nassif is currently in private practice after about 17 years in academia, private practice, and state run, in-patient agencies as a Licensed Psychologist. Her perspective on the importance of writing as a clinical psychologist mirrors the other authors and highlights the importance of writing in a private practice. Dr. Kimberly Stark, a Licensed Psychologist, discusses how writing has shaped her education and practice. She has spent two decades providing therapy in counseling centers and in academia. Overall, these three highly qualified clinical and counseling psychologists stress the importance of writing to their development as therapists and to their continued interactions with the individuals they help daily.

Foundations of Scientific Writing and Their Importance in Clinical Practice

by Kenneth Windholz, MS, LMLP, LCP

The ability to write well is a distinguishing quality in all professional fields, but particularly so in a psychology career. Because psychologists focus on behavior both in research activities, as well as in applied realms, psychology students are required to produce a significant amount of writing. Essays, reaction papers, case studies, and research reports are all part and parcel of psychology students' educational activities. By developing optimal writing skills, psychology students learn how to effectively communicate and support assertions, give clear descriptions of their observations, and describe the process by which conclusions are reached. These skills carry over directly to professional life and animate the work of psychologists in career practice.

As we shall see, skilled writing in the applied area of clinical psychology is a feature that may not be the first that comes to mind when we think about what clinicians do and what skills and qualities are needed to become well-rounded psychotherapists.

What Is Clinical Psychology and What Makes a Good Clinician?

Typically, when people think of Psychology, the clinical field might be among the very first to come to mind. But what actually is clinical psychology? Clinical psychology is described as ". . . the integration of science, theory, and practice to explain and understand, predict, and alleviate psychological problems and distress, as well as promote healthy human development." (Kuther & Morgan, 2013, p. 20). More generally, clinical psychologists are helping professionals who have been trained in assessing, diagnosing, and treating people with emotional and behavioral disorders that interrupt or compromise people's functioning and well-being. Clinical psychology is indeed a popular subspecialty of psychology, typically attracting those who might simply have a strong desire to help others in their times of distress.

The popularity of clinical psychology as a career path choice has evidentiary support. Kuther and Morgan (2013) report that in 2008, an American Psychological Association Center for Workforce Studies survey found that 61% of psychology doctoral graduates are found in the clinical, counseling, or school psychology subfields; that is, professional functions that require the application of helping skills. Further, within that 61% professional population, approximately 69% of those doctoral students eventually come to serve in a mental health related service position.

Since the early to mid-20th century in the United States, psychotherapy has come to represent a tried and true means of effectively treating mental disorders. Many people who are in distress find great value in "talking out" their problems and concerns, and about 40% of those seeking such support and assistance rely on psychotherapy as their resource of choice (Druss et al., 2007). Millions of Americans are recipients of psychotherapeutic services annually (Olfson et al., 2002). There is a distinct advantage to seeking out the services of well-trained, skilled helping professionals in time of distress in people's lives. Simply put, psychotherapy is effective. People in distress have a much greater chance of achieving problem resolution and distress reduction outcomes than people who do not utilize these professional services (Lambert & Ogles, 2004: Wampold, 2001, 2007).

A clear advantage of psychotherapy as a treatment modality is that it is often more effective than many other accepted but more expensive medical practices (Wampold, 2007). Further, some forms of psychotherapy are slightly more effective than others in relatively small ways in the treatment of specific disorders (Wampold, 2001, 2007, 2010). Although we know that psychotherapy works for treatment of individuals in distress, we might wonder why this is so, and more broadly consider what qualities and skills are important to those who apply the various therapeutic models' principles and interventions; that is, what is the skill set of the psychotherapists themselves? So if students want to be clinical psychologists and psychotherapists, what personal and professional qualities and skills should be cultivated? What of these qualities and skills result in the clinical interventions being helpful? In short, what makes a good and effective psychotherapist?

Bruce E. Wampold (n.d.) describes 14 qualities and actions of effective therapists that are based on research evidence (Anderson, Ogles, Patterson, Lambert, & Vermeersch, 2009; Baldwin, Wampold, & Imel, 2007; Duncan, Miller, Hubble, & Wampold, 2010; Lambert, Harmon, Slade, Whipple, & Hawkings, 2005; Norcross & Lambert, 2011; Wampold, 2007) that combines with evidence-based practice, policy, and theory (APA Presidential Task Force on Evidence-Based Practice, 2006).

The 14 qualities identified by Wampold and their brief, general descriptions are:

1) Interpersonal skills; for example, verbal fluency, interpersonal perception, affective modulation and expressiveness, warmth and acceptance, empathy, focus on other.

2) The ability to help clients develop trust, feel understood, and to believe that the therapist can help.

3) The ability to work with a broad range of clientele and form collaborative working alliances and important therapeutic bonds.

4) The ability to provide a plausible, well-informed, culturally sensitive, acceptable, and adaptive explanation for the client's distress.

5) Skill in providing a treatment plan that identifies the explanation for the presenting problem(s), and the effective, healthy evidence-based actions that will guide successful treatment outcomes.

6) The ability to be influential, persuasive, and convincing in a positive way so as to effectively and functionally explain the treatment plan and its strategies.

7) Authenticity in monitoring the client's progress; using assessment measures and truly wanting to know how the client is progressing with particular attention being paid to whether or not the interventions used are helpful and effective in helping to improve the client's condition.

8) Flexibility and the capacity to adjust to the client's resistance to therapy; the ability to make needed shifts in approach, treatment focus, or use of additional helpful services such as medication or bringing in another practitioner.

9) The ability to accept and effectively manage difficult material that the client might present; to be comfortable with strong affective interactions.

10) The ability to communicate hope and optimism to the client, especially through client relapse, lack of progress, and unexpected difficulties.

11) An awareness of the client's characteristics and context. That is, factors of client culture, race, ethnicity, sexual orientation, spirituality, age, physical health, support systems and available resources, cultural milieu, concurrent client services that are being provided by other professionals in the client's life.

12) Self-understanding; an awareness of one's own psychological processes, schemas, biases, reactions to client information and interactions.

13) An awareness of current research evidence about treatment, especially in terms of problems, social context, and of the important biopsychosocial factors and bases of client disorders.

14) A desire to continually improve in one's therapeutic skills and to rely on model-based feedback about client progress in order to make changes when needed, and to monitor the progress outcomes that are related to those changes.

The importance and value of optimal professional writing skills for the clinical professional and the relationship between these skills and any or all of the qualities and actions of the effective therapist might be subtle at first glance. However, the use of well-developed writing skills stand as an organizing and animating principle in people's therapeutic roles. For example, the evidence-based psychotherapeutic model Motivational Interviewing, also known as MI (Miller & Rollnick, 1991), has gained notoriety and value as a client focused, compassionate approach to treating and facilitating behavior change in a positive way across a range of diagnostic categories. Rosengren (2009) identified and described the spirit of MI as, ". . . the guiding philosophy that informs the principles, the use of 'microskills' . . . a special character or spirit . . ." (p. 12). These principles are central to psychotherapists' efforts to effect positive client behavior change and functionally mirror several of the qualities and actions that Wampold (n.d.) identified. In the MI model, partnership, acceptance, compassion, and evocation combine to represent this forming spirit of MI.

Although it is important that effective psychotherapists internalize these and similar forming principles, evidence of how these principles serve as aids to therapists in their clinical work often require an external expression; that is, they must be put into action. And evidence of the therapeutic action or demonstration necessarily takes the form of written expression as seen in client documentation, case communication, client treatment planning, and treatment outcome summaries among other written markers. Thus, the "tone" or "voice" of the therapy process as guided by therapists' own forming principles and related actions is revealed in the written expression and documentation of the pathway of the psychotherapeutic endeavor.

We will touch more specifically on this documentation process later. But first, let us consider where writing skills fall along the broad continuum of the clinical psychologist's toolkit. After all, are not being wise, compassionate, caring, strategic thinking, accepting, flexible, and well-trained individuals the most essential elements of the helping professionals? In many ways, yes. But there is more to be considered.

What Else Goes Into Making an Effective Clinician?   Thus far, we have focused on the high level of interest in the field of clinical psychology as a career path and on the prominence, value, and efficacy of the clinical subspecialty and the important applied qualities and skills of effective and helpful psychotherapists. In addition to the native interests that effective psychotherapists possess (e.g., interest in and compassion for others, self-awareness, trustworthiness, interest in mental illness and abnormal psychology, skill and interest in reading about research in mental illness, and ability to maintain confidentiality), Hayes (1996) and McGovern, Furumoto, Halpern, Kimble, and McKeachie (1991) further identify a range of skills that psychologists, in general, and psychotherapists, in particular, display.Among these are the ability to think critically and to use analytical skills, the ability to gather and evaluate information, to synthesize that information, and competence in speaking and writing.

An Overlooked but Important Clinical Skill   So, as we think about the essential skills needed to become effective and helpful clinicians, the importance of written communication skills must also be, but seldom is, considered as among the most foundational of those skills and must take a rightful place alongside those of compassion, warmth, abstract thinking, and social/interpersonal skills. In short, the importance of effective writing skills, those that are clear, lucid, and precise, stands as a singular and an essential component of the clinical psychologist's toolkit. Skilled written communication is central to clinical documentation and reports, case representation and description, and the explanation and communication of emerging evidence-based practices. For this reason, the importance of competent written communication skills in the clinical field will now serve as our focus of our attention.

Why and How Is Writing a Critical Part of Clinical Skills and Practice?   It is indeed conspicuous that writing as a professional skill competency is often found very near the end of most clinical skills priorities lists, if they are mentioned at all. Take another brief look at the list of 14 qualities and actions of effective therapists. Many undergraduate psychology students and students in clinical psychology graduate programs (and certainly the individual consumer of behavioral health and psychotherapeutic services) typically seem less likely to regard effective writing skills as a high priority requirement when considering a broadly based clinical skills set.

Beginning with undergraduate programs in psychology and continuing throughout the time spent in graduate programs, clinical psychology students are taught important writing mechanics and given practice opportunities to hone the writing skills that will serve students throughout a professional career. For example, at the graduate school application level, applicants' writing skills play an essential role in the evaluation of their candidacy for program admission and those skills are immediately on display in personal statements that describe students' background, interests, and talents in an effort to present themselves in the most flattering way. Additionally, exams may require students to display a range of psychology writing styles because students encounter essay writing more frequently than they previously experienced. Graduate-level research papers demand a level of writing skill that test students' ability to express their work in a concise, well-organized, and appropriately cited manner. The development, practice, and refinement of these essential writing skills serve as a foundation for the important clinical writing skills that will be required of psychotherapists throughout their professional careers.

How Is Documentation Used in the Clinical Setting?   Earlier, we identified the essential functions of competent and well-trained psychotherapists in terms of three factors: assessment, diagnosis, and treatment. Each of these clinical functions requires a high level of training and competence, especially including written communication.

Assessment.   As a part of the clinical psychologist's assessment function, report writing is among the most relevant and foremost representations of the assessment process and its outcomes. Client assessments are typically framed in the form of comprehensive written evaluations. Zuckerman (2019) notes that a typical psychological clinical report requires extensive documentation that includes elements such as the referral reasons, relevant background and problem history, behavioral observations that the clinician made, client responses to aspects of the examination, descriptions of the emotional and affective symptoms and disorders, abnormal signs, symptoms and syndromes, personality patterns, a description of the client's activities of daily living, social and community functioning, couple and family relationship factors, vocational and academic skills, and recreational functioning.

Psychological reports serve as vital documentation of findings that will ultimately influence treatment and treatment planning, as well as to clinically or medically justify the interventions and services that are to be provided. In addition, continuity of care across treatment modalities is greatly aided by clearly written, well-articulated clinical reports. Such reports are commonly regarded as essential to meeting important standards of care. The format for psychological report writing is organized in a sequence to include a summary of findings and conclusions, diagnostic statement and impression, recommendations, prognostic statements, and closing/concluding statements (Zuckerman & Kolmes, 2019). Clearly, competent writing skills are a central requirement for professionally written psychological reports.

Diagnosis. Turning our attention to the diagnosis function of clinical practitioners, it becomes evident that not only is a thorough and well-informed understanding of the spectrum of psychiatric presentations and psychopathology an essential requirement, but the documentation of the assessment and observations that yield the diagnostic impressions and conclusions is also a bedrock element in the treatment process. The diagnosis is based upon an objective, thorough, clear, and accurate description of the presented and observed signs and symptoms that meet the clinical criteria for a particular diagnosis. Given that some psychotherapeutic treatment models rely on the diagnosis as the crux of the application of that treatment model's interventions (Messer & Gurman, 2011), the client is best served when the diagnostic description and impression is presented in a clearly stated and well-justified manner.

My own clinical experience has provided important principles that serve as guidance when putting a client diagnosis on paper. Since treatment is frequently predicated on diagnosis, an ethically responsible clinician must be able to justify the diagnosis and do so through a coherent, logically derived accounting anchored on the evidence that illuminates the pathway from assessment to conclusion. Thus, optimal writing skills clearly advantage a skilled clinician who must show the evidence, describe it in a clear manner, and fit it to the observations made all in the best interests of meeting the client's treatment needs and goals.

Treatment. Finally, the treatment function in which the clinician engages often stands as the most identifiable of client care services. Although it is beyond the scope of this present subject matter to describe the innumerable treatment interventions currently available to modern clinical psychologists in the provision of psychotherapeutic services, it is vital to understand the major role that clinical documentation plays in psychotherapeutic treatment. The process of providing psychotherapeutic services requires documentation of those services be done at the highest possible level of professional standards. An axiom that seems to best describe the importance of the clinical record in the treatment process goes something like this, "Unless it's documented, it didn't happen." Thus, clinical documentation is one of the foundations of competent patient care. It provides continuity of communication among providers, details evidence-based practice and standard of care services, provides for a legal record as needed, allows for more efficient and effective clinical research, and serves the essential purposes of provider reimbursement. Important features of competent clinical documentation necessarily include the timely completion of the record, consideration of what should be included in the client record, a written trail of the client's situation/condition and ongoing condition changes and description of the clinician's actions, the client's progress as the result of the prescribed interventions, client need areas and ways in which they are being addressed, a summary of treatment, maintenance of confidentiality and provisions for sharing the clinical record, and treatment outcomes and treatment recommendations.

The Written Clinical Record Under Scrutiny   Inevitably, the client's clinical record that details the assessment, diagnosis, and treatment process will be reviewed. The review can occur across a variety of settings and for a variety of purposes. For example, as the client–clinician relationship and the success of treatment more often thrives in a collaborative setting (Zoellner, Roy-Bryne, Mavissakalian, & Feeny, 2018), clients increasingly ask to review their own clinical record. It is a client's right to do so. Secondly, when clients receive psychotherapeutic services as part of a "package" of service components or when multiple providers or agencies form a team with the aim of providing optimal client care, records are often shared among various providers or agencies after confidentiality and records release issues are fully articulated. A third reason for client record reviews may occur when clients are or may potentially become involved in a civil or criminal court matters. Attorneys may subpoena client records for their own purposes or those of the court. Clinical forensic reports provide a professional record in which information collected becomes evidentiary. Forensic reports provide organization to clinicians' data and information and also serve as a basis for preparation in direct and cross-examination (Melton et al., 2018). Further, "A well-written, articulate report may satisfy both parties to the degree that stipulations to the written findings and conclusions are entered. It may also serve as a basis for informal negotiations, as in plea bargaining or out-of-court settlements in civil cases." (p. 584). Given the importance of the clinical forensic document(s), optimal writing skills in the forensic functions of clinical psychologists cannot be overemphasized. Fourth, referring agencies and collaborating agencies and entities such as schools, physicians, disability services providers, certain employers, and social services agencies may request client records as part of their ongoing services with clinical clients. Finally, third-party payers and insurance reviews, as well as the service provider agency's internal records compliance and review systems, are standard practice in modern client care.

In each of these instances, all or part of the written client record can be the subject of review. Since the client record typically includes a great amount of detailed information about referral and treatment, diagnosis, treatment plan, descriptions of services, progress notes, progress reports, treatment summaries, psychological evaluations, treatment discharge summaries, frequency and type of client-therapist contacts, relevant financial information and services billing record, and treatment and confidentiality agreements, it is always the clinician's responsibility to act in the highest ethical manner in all matters involving the client record and documents. In each of these instances, it is essential that the written record reflects a clear, professionally recorded, accurate, appropriately detailed, and honest representation of clients' involvement with the clinician, services, and treatment outcomes. Clearly, a high level of competency in writing skills is as vital to the clinical psychologist's role as are any of the personal and professional therapeutic skills and qualities that clinicians strive to develop and employ in the treatment of all who seek psychotherapeutic services.

Issues in Psychological Writing: Private Practice Setting

by Carrie Nassif, PhD

As a clinician in graduate school, I was taught to write well; both clearly in style and including content needed to fulfill ethical responsibilities. This included using specific language to reflect the right intensity of symptoms in assessment reports, simplifying complex data to interpret research findings, and concisely documenting client symptoms, treatment plans, and interventions in progress notes. Much of the therapy-related writing was a tricky balance of conveying the requisite information while not intruding on clients' privacy or describing their concerns in insensitive ways. With a lot of practice and feedback, this became engrained, which I'm sure was the point of all of those writing assignments after all!

When I transitioned to building my own private practice, these skills were put to use, but with the added focus of marketing my services to the community at large. Some of this was outsourced; for instance, I worked with a graphic designer who helped me come up with a logo, a pamphlet layout, business cards, letterhead, and signage for my office space. I used these images to create a website, too; but I still had to write the copy, that is, the text to go in the website and pamphlet. I found it challenging to get into that mindset, though, because it involved me taking on a completely new relationship with my clients. I was not just their psychotherapist anymore, I was also trying to lure them in to my office so that I could earn a living. I found that writing letters of introduction to local referral sources (like physicians, schools, attorneys, and other mental health professionals) was a form of self-promotion even more uncomfortable to write than those cover letters my classmates and I tortured ourselves over for internship applications, and later, to be sent out to potential employers when trying to enter the job market. The difference was that back then, I had peers and supervisors to edit my work for free.

Now that I was solely responsible to represent my "brand", my words took on a heightened importance. Whatever I wrote would be potential clients' first impression of my practice. It was important to accurately and briefly describe the work I do in a way that would be understandable and welcoming to the population with whom I wanted to work. Even the extent to which I decided to use social media platforms, how much I personalized form templates, the layout and complexity of my billing invoices, what I said in my voicemail script, how I answered my phone, if and/or how I responded to client texts or emails—every one of these decisions reflected my business and clinical approach. Each typo, bad link, or thoughtless emoji would reflect poorly on me and the perceived standard of care I would provide a prospective client.

Another consideration for private practitioners is to determine an optimal balance of professionalism and approachability when promoting your services. In more rural or closed communities, an informal or down-to-earth writing style can help establish relatability and credibility, since stiff professionalism is likely to be seen as off-putting. On the other hand, many in more affluent communities, and those in forensic or medical settings, may view overt friendliness as inexperience or naiveté. This can be difficult to navigate in words on a page, but it ought to reflect a goodness-of-fit for your audience and who you are as a provider, too.

I live and work in a small city in a rural environment, and I am ever mindful that any time I go run errands I am likely to run into someone with whom I have interacted professionally. In small worlds like this, the way I dress and comport myself in public showcases who I am and broadcasts my competence (and my limitations!). Of course, this level of attention also extends to the care I take in preparing slides for presentations to peers or community groups, for guest lectures at the nearby university, in my interactions as a sponsor of a student club at the local high school, and to letters of recommendation I write for previous students or supervisees. These all generate potential clients and/or referral sources, and I always want to put my best foot forward.

The Importance of Writing in My Career as a Counseling Psychologist

by Kimberly S. Stark, PhD

As someone who teaches General Psychology (aka Introductory Psychology) on a regular basis, I am often shocked to discover how put off so many students seem to be by the notion that writing, and being able to write well, is an important skill for them to learn. Some students seem nearly outraged at the notion that I (a *psychologist*) would expect them to be able to *write*. After all, I am not an English professor (or so I have been told). My response to their outrage is to shake my head and explain that, although it might seem downright evil of me to push them to improve upon their writing, in the end, my ultimate motivation is to help them, not torture them. For instance, I point out that, when they eventually seek employment (presumably an end-goal of most undergraduates), they will need to be able to communicate well in writing via that all-important first impression to a potential employer: the cover letter for a job application. Likewise, I point out that any follow-up correspondence (including email messages) with potential employers should be free of any and all grammatical errors, with writing that demonstrates precision of word choice (i.e., the point should be clear to the reader, with no mechanical errors that might detract from the message). In addition to these basic examples that illustrate the importance of writing for *any* undergraduate major, in this chapter I will discuss why writing well is a particularly vital skill for *psychology* majors, especially those who aspire to someday do clinical work (i.e., those who wish to become clinical or counseling psychologists). As a counseling psychologist now in the third decade of my career, I can attest to the fact that writing well has been an essential component of my success every single day of my career, dating back to my undergraduate education.

The Importance of Writing as an Undergraduate Student   Without boring you with all the details of my undergraduate years, I would like to underscore the fact that writing well was vital to performing well in my undergraduate courses and to obtaining good letters of recommendation from my professors, which, in turn, was crucial to getting into graduate school. Being a good writer helped me to garner the attention of my professors who, upon noticing my aptitude for writing, invited me to collaborate with them on research projects. Writing well is crucial to the research process, as it involves synthesizing complex ideas and clearly conveying those ideas to the reader. Fortunately, my professors were pleased with my work and offered to write excellent letters of recommendation on my behalf when I applied to graduate school. In short, my strong writing skills helped me obtain opportunities as an undergraduate that made me a much stronger applicant when I applied to doctoral programs.

Making a Good First Impression When Applying to Graduate Programs   As with applying for a job, the application process for admission to graduate school (especially for those seeking admission to highly competitive doctoral programs in clinical or counseling psychology) requires the successful applicant to be able to write well. Programs typically require the applicant to submit a "Personal Statement" explaining why the admissions committee should even *consider* him or her for admission to the program. The personal statement essentially requires the applicant to "sell" him or herself through a brief written statement (typically one to two pages). The personal statement must be clearly and precisely worded (i.e., there is no room for "b.s." here), with no mechanical errors. Thankfully, my ability to write well helped me gain admission to a highly competitive doctoral program.

The Importance of Writing Well as a Graduate Student   The importance of being able to write well as a graduate student should be self-evident (think term papers), but I will highlight just a few of the many other reasons why writing well is essential to the success of graduate students in clinical or counseling psychology. Usually by their second year of graduate school, students in clinical or counseling programs begin working with clients/patients. Being able to communicate well in writing is an important skill for any mental health professional for a number of reasons. In addition to meeting with clients, clinicians (including students in training to become clinicians) are required to maintain records ("case notes" or "charts") of their sessions with clients (American Psychological Association [APA], 2007). Part of this record keeping involves developing a written treatment plan and documenting how the treatment plan is addressed in each session. Additionally, clinicians must sometimes contact other mental health professionals regarding their clients. For instance, if I were seeing a client who had recently been hospitalized following a suicide attempt, I would definitely contact the hospital staff to obtain records of the client's treatment. Although my first contact with the hospital staff might occur over the telephone, following up through written correspondence, along with documentation of this correspondence in the client's file, is an important part of good record keeping (Knapp, Younggren, VandeCreek, Harris, & Martin, 2013).

Maintaining good written records is an important (and inexpensive) risk-management strategy for anyone in the business of providing mental health services (Knapp et al., 2013). Those who do any form of testing/clinical assessment with clients, such administering IQ tests or neuropsychological testing, must maintain detailed written records of their assessment, including an assessment report, which is usually shared with others (e.g., other psychologists) at some point. The wise mental health professional maintains meticulously written records, keeping in mind that these records could someday be seen by others, perhaps even in court (e.g., in the event of a malpractice suit).

In addition to the types of writing described previously, most master's programs require students to write a thesis. A thesis is a fairly extensive research project, with some theses reaching 100 or more pages in length. Doctoral programs typically require the student to complete a dissertation, which is an even larger research project (mine was over 300 pages). Doctoral students must frequently pass a written "comprehensive exam" as well. The purpose of the comprehensive exam is to assess students' learning of all of their previously completed coursework and the exam usually consists of several essay questions. Most programs allot at least one full day, if not two days, to this process. In other words, students spend an entire day writing (completing the comprehensive essay exam) and a committee consisting of the programs' professors then evaluates the students' essay responses. Students must pass this exam to complete the doctoral degree, and most programs limit the number of times (three seems to be a magic number here) students can attempt the exam before being released from the program. In other words, students who do not pass the comprehensive exam after three attempts are "kicked out" of the program. Clearly, the ability to write well is vital here.

The Importance of Writing Well in Obtaining and Completing an Internship

Assuming successful completion of the thesis, dissertation, comprehensive exam, and all coursework, the next step for those aspiring to become counseling or clinical psychologists is to complete an internship. The internship application process is similar to the process of applying for graduate school. Thus, successful applicants must be able to convey their ideas well in writing, usually within a limited amount of space. Once again, this is a highly competitive process and there is no room for "b.s." here. (As a side note, I am frequently amazed when students lament that they do not know how they are going to "fill" 10 pages. Far more daunting, in my opinion, is the task of expressing all of the ideas I wish to convey within a limited number of pages.) The writing must be clear and precise, with no mechanical errors. During their internships, doctoral students engage in full-time clinical work, which involves similar kinds of writing as described in the previous section (e.g., maintaining detailed case notes, writing assessment reports, communicating with other professionals, etc.).

The Importance of Writing Well as a Clinical or Counseling Psychologist

Remember at the beginning of this chapter when I mentioned that writing well is a vital skill for any undergraduate who wishes to someday pursue gainful employment (i.e., the importance of the first impression cover letter)? Naturally, the same applies here when applying for a job in clinical or counseling psychology, regardless of the setting (hospital, private practice, university counseling center, etc.). Moreover, the importance of writing does not stop upon landing a clinical or counseling position.

As I have described previously, many aspects of clinical work require solid written communication skills. For instance, psychologists are legally and ethically obligated to maintain written records of their clinical work (APA, 2007). Maintaining good records is also crucial to providing high-quality services (Knapp et al., 2016). Reviewing clients' records prior to sessions helps psychologists to demonstrate consistency from one session to the next, thereby resulting in better quality service delivery and treatment outcome. Psychologists should also maintain their records in a manner such that another professional could comprehend them. In the unfortunate event that a treating psychologist were to die suddenly, the new therapist assigned to work with the deceased psychologist's clients would need access to records that clearly convey what has been occurring in therapy (APA, 2007).

As stated previously, good record keeping is a vital and inexpensive (i.e., free) component of risk-management (and doing therapy can be risky business indeed (Knapp et al., 2016). Psychologists, and particularly those who do any sort of forensic work (e.g., assessment and/or treatment of individuals involved in some way with the criminal justice system), should maintain records with the understanding that their records could someday be seen in a court of law. In the event that the psychologist is sued by a client, former client, or friends/family members of a client, well-maintained records could have a tremendous impact on the outcome of the case. One can imagine a scenario in which the prosecuting attorney convinces the jury that "sloppy" (unprofessional) records are a sign of "sloppy" (unprofessional) clinical work.

Thorough record keeping becomes even more important when working with potentially dangerous clients (i.e., individuals who are suicidal and/or homicidal). In such unfortunate cases where a client ends up taking his or her own life, the psychologist might have done an exemplary job of conducting a thorough assessment of suicidality and carrying out a well thought-out treatment plan. Unfortunately, however, if there are no records documenting such exemplary work, the psychologist could still be found guilty of malpractice. As noted by Knapp et al. (2016), in such cases, it is wise to remember that, "from a legal perspective, the general rule is 'if it isn't written down, it didn't happen'" (p. 46).

Another instance in which writing is integral to clinical work involves communicating with clients. Occasionally, clients will "no show" (i.e., fail to show up for an appointment without calling to cancel) for an appointment. If, after attempting to contact the client via other means (e.g., phone call or text), the client has not responded, it is usually prudent to send a follow-up letter, inquiring about the client's intentions of continuing treatment and offering to reschedule the missed appointment. In fact, as noted by Oordt et al. (2005), there is evidence to suggest that "simply maintaining contact with treatment-refusing patients through a follow-up letter or phone call" leads to a reduced risk of suicide (p. 212). This example illustrates how good writing could even have life or death implications.

In summary, good record-keeping, as well as solid communication with clients and with other professionals, are just a few examples of how writing continues to be an important skill throughout psychologists' careers. Psychologists who provide clinical services are obligated, both legally and ethically, to maintain records of their work, and good record keeping helps ensure high-quality service delivery. Maintaining good records, including communications with clients, can also help psychologists to protect themselves in the event of a lawsuit. These are just a few of the many ways in which writing is an essential skill for a counseling psychologist who provides clinical services.

The Continued Role of Writing in My Current Work as a Psychology Professor

It should be clear by now that writing is an essential skill for anyone who wishes to pursue a career in clinical or counseling psychology. The examples I have discussed in the preceding paragraphs describe how writing played a key role for me in pursuing and completing the education and training necessary to become a counseling psychologist as well as how writing is important for those who do any sort of clinical work. As I will discuss in the following paragraphs, writing continues to play a major role in my current work as a psychology professor.

Writing is so essential to my current job that it is almost impossible to think of an aspect of my job in which good writing skills are *not* important. After all, I am currently writing this chapter as part of my job. My workday typically begins and ends with a long series of email correspondence with students, faculty members, and other professionals. Sometimes the correspondence has to do with a simple matter, such as scheduling a meeting. Other times it might be a more complicated issue, such as responding to a student who is unhappy with his or her grade. The ability to write well helps convey competence and professionalism when engaging in such correspondence. Additionally, in the more complicated cases, such as a student submitting a grade complaint, it is incredibly helpful to have maintained good written records of all correspondence with the student.

A major part of being a psychology professor involves conducting research as well as supervising undergraduate and graduate student research. The end-goal of such research endeavors is to disseminate our research findings through some sort of peer-reviewed outlet, usually presentations at professional conferences and/or publications in professional journals. In these cases, we submit a written proposal, which is then reviewed by others in our field who decide whether to accept our work for presentation/publication. Being successful in this process requires mastery of the content area as well as exemplary writing skills.

I began this chapter referring to how students often lament over the various writing assignments required of them. In psychology, these writing assignments are usually much more technical, rather than creative, in nature. Gaining proficiency in this type of writing requires practice as well as guidance from someone who has mastered the art of technical writing. This (teaching students the skill of technical writing) is one of the job responsibilities that I take most seriously in my role as a professor. In my efforts to help students develop their technical writing skills, I provide extensive feedback on their writing assignments. Here again, my ability to write well is essential to helping others develop their writing skills.

Conclusion

In conclusion, the ability to write well has been vital to my success as a counseling psychologist at every stage of my career. My writing skills enabled me to obtain opportunities as an undergraduate student that helped me in the pursuit of my education as a counseling psychologist. Writing was essential to attaining my goals throughout my education and training, including applying for internships and numerous positions. Writing continued to be an important skill while working with clients in various clinical settings. In my current work as a psychology professor, I rely upon my writing skills to be successful in nearly every aspect of my job and have the opportunity to help others develop their writing skills.

After reading about the importance of writing in my career as a counseling psychologist, perhaps you have decided that counseling or clinical psychology might not be the thing for you. Why then should you even worry about all of this writing stuff? If I have not convinced you of the importance of writing yet, consider this: I would argue that being a good writer also helps you to be a better, more informed, reader and to be a smarter (and more interesting) person overall . . . and who could not use some of that?

References

American Psychological Association (APA). (2007). Record keeping guidelines. *American Psychologist, 48,* 993–1004. doi:10.1037/0003-066X.62.9.993

APA Presidential Task Force on Evidence-Based Practice. (2006). Evidence-based practice in psychology. *American Psychologist, 61,* 271–285. doi:10.1037/0003-066X.61.4.271

Anderson, T., Ogles, B. M., Patterson, C. L., Lambert, M. J., & Vermeersch, D. A. (2009). Therapist effects: Facilitative interpersonal skills as a predictor of therapist success. *Journal of Clinical Psychology, 65,* 755–768. doi:10.1002/jclp.20583

Baldwin, S. A., Wampold, B. E., & Imel, Z. E. (2007). Untangling the alliance-outcome correlation: Exploring the relative importance of therapist and patient variability in the alliance. *Journal of Consulting and Clinical Psychology, 75,* 842–852. doi:10.1037/0022-006X.76.6.842

Druss, B. G., Wang, P. S., Sampson, N. A., Olfson, M., Pincus, H. A., Wells, K. B., & Kessler, R. C. (2007). Understanding mental health treatment in persons without mental diagnoses: Results from the National Comorbidity Survey Replication. *Archives of General Psychiatry, 64,* 1196–1203. doi:10.1001/archpsyc.64.10.1196

Duncan, B., Miller, S. D., Hubble, M., & Wampold, B. E. (Eds.). (2010). *The heart and soul of change: Delivering what works* (2nd ed.). Washington D.C.: American Psychological Association.

Hayes, N. (1996). What makes a psychology graduate distinctive? *European Psychologist, 1,* 130–134. doi:10.1027/1016-9040.1.2.130

Knapp, S., Younggren, J. N., VandeCreek, L., Harris, E., & Martin, J. N. (2013). *Assessing and managing risk in psychological practice: An individualized approach* (2nd ed.). Rockville, MD: The Trust.

Kuther, T. L., & Morgan, R. D. (2013). *Careers in Psychology: Opportunities in a changing world* (4th ed.). Boston, MA: Cengage.

Lambert, M. J., & Ogles, B. M. (2004). The efficacy and effectiveness of psychotherapy. In M. J. Lambert (Ed.). *Handbook of psychotherapy and behavior change* (5th ed.). New York: John Wiley & Sons.

Lambert, M. J., Harmon, C., Slade, K., Whipple, J. L., & Hawkins, E. J. (2005). Providing feedback to psychotherapists on their patients' progress: Clinical results and practice suggestions. *Journal of Clinical Psychology, 61,* 165–174. doi:10.1002/jclp.20113

McGovern, T. V., Furumoto, L., Halpern, D. F., Kimble, G. A., & McKeachie, W. J. (1991). Liberal education, study in depth, and the arts and sciences major: Psychology. *American Psychologist, 46,* 598–605. doi:10.1037/0003-066X.46.6.598

Melton, G. B., Petrila, J., Poythress, N. G., Slobogin, C., Otto, R. K., Mossman, D., & Condie, L. O. (2018). *Psychological evaluations for the courts: A handbook for mental professionals and lawyers* (4th ed.). New York: Guilford Press.

Messer, S. B., & Gurman, A. S. (Eds.). (2011). *Essential psychotherapies: Theory and practice* (3rd ed.). New York: Guilford Press.

Miller, W. R., & Rollnick, S. (1991). *Motivational Interviewing: Preparing people to change additive behavior.* New York: Guilford Press.

Norcross, J. C., & Lambert, M. J. (2011). Psychotherapy relationships that work II. *Psychotherapy, 48,* 4–8. doi:10.1037/a0022180

Olfson, M., Marcus, S. C., Druss, B., Elinson, L., Tanielian, T., & Pincus, H. A. (2002). National trends in the outpatient treatment of depression. *Journal of the American Medical Association, 287,* 203–209. doi:10.1001/jama.287.2.203

Oordt, M. S., Jobes, D. A., Rudd, M. D., Fonseca, V. P., Runyan, C. N., Stea, J. B., . . . Talcott, G. W. (2005). Development of a clinical guide to enhance care for suicidal patients. *Professional Psychology: Research and Practice, 36,* 208–218. doi:10.1037/0735-7028.36.2.208

Rosengren, D. B. (2009). *Building motivational interviewing skills: A practitioner workbook.* New York: Guilford Press.

Wampold, B. E. (n.d.). *Qualities and actions of effective therapists.* Retrieved from American Psychological Association Education Directorate https://www.apa.org/education/ce/effective-therapists.pdf

Wampold, B. E. (2001). *The great psychotherapy debate: Model, methods, and findings.* Mahwah, NJ: Lawrence Erlbaum Associates.

Wampold, B. E. (2007). Psychotherapy: The humanistic (and effective) treatment. *American Psychologist, 62,* 857–873. doi:10.1037/0003-066X.62.8.857

Wampold, B. E. (2010). *The basic of psychotherapy: An introduction to theory and practice.* Washington, D.C.: American Psychological Association.

Zoellner, L. A., Roy-Bryne, P. P., Mavissakalian, M., & Feeny, N. C. (2018). Doubly randomized preference trial of prolonged exposure versus sertraline for treatment of PTSD. *American Journal of Psychiatry*. Retrieved from https://doi.org/10.1176/appi.ajp.2018.17090995

Zuckerman, E. L. (2019). *Clinician's thesaurus: The guide to conducting interviews and writing psychological reports* (8th ed.). New York: Guilford Press.

Zuckerman, E. L., & Kolmes, K. (2019). *The paper office for the digital age: Forms, guidelines and resources to make you practice work ethically, legally and profitability* (5th ed.). New York: Guilford Press.

Writing as a School Psychologist

by Jessica Feldhausen, MS, EdS

As an undergraduate student majoring in psychology, you expect to take fascinating psychology courses that demystify abnormal behavior and explore the etiology of mental health disorders. You may be surprised to know that being an undergraduate student majoring in psychology entails more than just learning about mental health. This course is a prime example. You are enrolled in a required course for your psychology major; however, surprisingly enough this course will teach you the importance of proper writing mechanics and APA format. You may be asking yourself, "Why is writing so important to me as a psychology major?" No matter the area of specialization you pursue in psychology, you will be expected to manage, interpret, and in some cases, share vulnerable information about people.

This chapter will briefly discuss the profession of school psychology, which is one area of specialization within the field of psychology. You will develop a basic understanding of school psychologists' professional responsibilities, including psychoeducational report writing. The intricacies of writing skills will be highlighted throughout the chapter to help you develop an understanding of why written composition skills are an important professional competency for undergraduates majoring in psychology.

What is School Psychology?

School psychology is an area of specialization within psychology, which is often not known about or fully understood. Many times, those who decide to pursue a graduate degree in school psychology learn about the profession late in their undergraduate career or even after completing their undergraduate degree. You may be asking, "What makes this profession so different?" Unlike clinical psychologists, school psychologists work primarily in educational settings (i.e., public or private schools) to provide support addressing the educational needs of children, including academic and mental health needs. School psychologists receive specialized training, including child development, cognition, intellectual and academic assessment, mental health supports, research design, inferential statistics, and professional ethics. School psychologists not only have expertise of child psychological and behavior constructs, but how such aspects can impact children's educational performance.

School psychologists have knowledge about appropriate instructional techniques, how to increase learning and motivation of learners, special education law, program evaluation, and disabilities that can impact learning. The marriage of psychology and education creates a very unique profession, known as school psychology.

At the onset of the profession in the 1970s, the role of school psychologists was known best for intellectual and academic assessment and special education eligibility determination (Merrell, Ervin, & Gimpel Peacock, 2012). The National Association of School Psychologists (NASP; 2014) currently defines school psychologists as:

> Uniquely qualified members of school teams that support students' abilities to learn and teachers' abilities to teach. They apply expertise in mental health, learning, and behavior, to help children and youth succeed academically, socially, behaviorally, and emotionally. School psychologists' partner with families, teachers, school administrators, and other professionals to create safe, healthy, and supportive learning environments that strengthen connections among home, school and the community. (p. 2)

Although assessment is only one component of the profession, it is a defining role. School psychologists are trained to administer standardized assessments, such as intellectual and academic assessments, and to interpret the assessment results to determine any underlying factors that may prevent children from experiencing educational success. School psychologists who conduct assessments gather sensitive information about children which can include, intellectual functioning, memory skills, academic performance skills, developmental and medical history, and even mental health information. The impact of assessments can be life changing for children and parents, especially if children are identified as having an educational disability and consequently, who may qualify for special education services. Ultimately, the culmination of the assessment is the development of the psychoeducational report (Wiener & Costaris, 2012).

Psychoeducational Report Writing: What's the Big Deal?

Purpose of Psychoeducational Report Writing.   Often the only communication about assessments, the psychoeducational reports, can be powerful sources for making decisions and/or influencing change about the individuals being assessed; therefore, care must be taken to ensure any written work is completed with competency and accuracy (Michaels, 2006). Reports are collections of information specific to children who have been assessed for special education eligibility. Useful psychoeducational reports should guide the reader through the assessment process and ultimately answer the referral question (Haas & Carriere, 2014). Likewise, Smith Harvey (2006) notes additional purposes of psychoeducational reports which strive to increase understanding of students' needs and functioning, as well as effectively communicates interventions to support students' needs. The findings of the assessment and recommendations are often given substantial weight in terms of decision making and program planning for students (Mastoras, Climie, McCrimmon, & Schwean, 2011), which only further propels the importance of psychoeducational reports. A report describing vulnerable information such as a students' intelligence, achievement, speech, behavior, or emotional functioning has potential for influencing the readers' perceptions of the students (Bradley-Johnson & Johnson, 2006).

Professional ethics and legal regulations are intertwined in the profession of school psychology, all of which impact the evaluation process and directly impact the psychoeducational report writing process. When creating psychoeducational reports, school psychologists may be governed by different federal and state laws, policies, regulations, or supervisor directives (Walrath, Willis, & Dumont, 2014). School psychologists are required to organize and write reports in ways that depict adherence to the previously mentioned demands while clearly articulating the assessment results and sharing the information in a format which is easily understood by readers. Haas and Carriere (2014) explain "it is essential for school psychologists to distinguish between what must be directly included in reports and what must be true of assessments" (p. 35). Within the ethical principles and guidelines for school psychology, NASP (2010) proposes that assessment results should be reported in language clearly understood by the consumers.

The psychoeducational reports serve many purposes, but one of the most important considerations is how the report conveys professional competence. The final products created by school psychologists are a direct reflection of professional competency. Seagull (1979) describes the importance of professional competency:

> People who have never met you nor heard of you will read it not only for the information it contains about a specific child, but as a way of judging your professional competence. The force of the content may be lost if the report contains errors in spelling or language usage which makes you look ignorant. Proofread it. If you are poor speller, buy a dictionary and use it. If you are unsure of your own ability to judge proper language usage ask the help of a supervisor, colleague, or literate student, or refer to a good manual of APA style. The way you sound on paper will affect the seriousness with which your recommendations will be taken, as well as whether you will get the next referral. (p. 40)

Who Is the Report Written For?   Psychoeducational reports are written to address the concerns of the individuals who initiated the assessment. Most often the referral sources are children's parents or teachers. There are a variety of consumers of psychoeducational reports, but the primary consumers are parents, students, teachers, and school support staff (Walrath et al., 2014). Other consumers who may have access to psychoeducational reports may include: social service workers, mental health providers, medical providers, and court officials. The levels of interest and background knowledge among consumers varies widely. Psychoeducational reports should be written with clarity in easily understandable language to broadly accommodate the wide variety of consumers.

Critiques of Report Writing

Although psychoeducational report writing is a key function of the school psychology profession, there is controversy around the effectiveness of psychoeducational reports. A review of the literature reveals common variables that affect the clarity of psychoeducational reports. Such variables include: readability, poor organization, generic interpretation, and report length (Groth-Marnat & Horvath, 2006; Mastoras et al., 2011; Smith Harvey, 2006).

Readability.   Psychoeducational reports have long been criticized for the lack of clarity due to the use of technical jargon and overall writing style. Most psychological reports are written at a 15- to 16- year educational level reading level (equivalent to some college education), which leads to comprehension difficulties among consumers (Smith Harvey, 2006). The use of technical terms and jargon leads to confusion and lack of understanding among parents, teachers, and other consumers unfamiliar with such terminology. The lack of understanding then impacts the usefulness of the report and fails to deliver important information to support the success of children.

Sentence structure, proper use of grammar, and correct spelling may seem like afterthoughts, but are of utmost importance. Not only is the written work a direct reflection of professional competence, but if the writing is fragmented and littered with spelling and grammatical errors, it decreases the value of the information and the readability. The consumers then begin to discount the reliability of the information.

Generic Interpretation.   The psychoeducational report serves the purpose of effectively conveying assessment results. Writing integrated psychoeducational reports may be challenging for early professionals because it requires knowledge transformation as opposed to knowledge telling (Scardamalia & Bereiter, 1987). School psychologists receive training on how to administer assessments and collect data from assessments, and how to appropriately interpret the data collected from assessments. The information collected from assessments should be directly related to the children. It is often more difficult for novice report writers to make assessment findings "meaningful" (Groth-Marnat, 2009). Why are assessments completed if the information is not thoroughly interpreted in relation with the children's functioning? All clinicians should aspire to complete thorough, in-depth interpretations that are connected to students' functioning.

Report Organization.   There is no single best practice or requirement for psychoeducational formats. NASP (2010) Standard II.4.3 states that "[s]chool psychologists include only documented and relevant information from reliable sources in school psychological records." Different sources all address the importance of good organization; however, all lack consistency with how to approach organizing psychoeducational reports

(Bradley-Johnson & Johnson, 2006; Groth-Marnat & Horvath, 2006; Mastoras et al., 2011; Seagull, 1979; Walrath et al., 2014). Report organization is wildly left up to professional judgement. Seagull (1979) notes the format of a report should follow the logical sequence of the completed assessment. Including information that represents the children's past, present, and future is a good standard of reference; however, this does not address organizational formatting. Bradley-Johnson & Johnson (2006) suggest creating an outline of the assessment data and grouping like data together to ease reading and increase comprehension of information.

Report Length.   The length of psychoeducational reports will vary. The length is dependent on how involved the assessment is, how many assessment measures were administered, and the detail provided by the school psychologists. School psychologists must be able to effectively integrate, synthesize, and organize assessment information so that is easily understood by the reader.

The process of assessment, interpretation of assessment data, and psychoeducational report writing all require a significant amount of professional responsibility. Given the controversies surrounding psychoeducational report writing and ethical duties, school psychologists should strive to perfect their psychoeducational writing practices. The critiques of psychoeducational report writing that dominate the literature include: readability, report organization, and report length all of which can be combated through writing mechanics. After reading the first section, it is apparent how important professional writing skills are to the profession of school psychology. The second section of this chapter will stress the importance of learning and practicing writing mechanics.

The Importance of Writing Mechanics

As a student who is currently completing their undergraduate degree, you have learned that you will never escape the requirements of written work. As you have progressed through your educational career from elementary, middle, high school and now post-secondary, the expectations of your written work only increase. This is a natural expectation given the continual progression of instruction throughout your educational experience. Let us take a moment to reflect on your educational instruction related to written language. In elementary school, you begin with very simple tasks such as spelling, spelling words in isolation, and then gradually spelling words correctly when writing sentences. As you progress through elementary school, language arts becomes a daily subject where you learn about sentence structure, verbs, pronouns, proper punctuation, all while learning how to convey meaning in your writing.

During middle school you refined your writing skills by integrating and applying what you learned in elementary school. You began to write essays all the while being expected to apply what you learned about sentence structure, verbs, pronouns, and punctuation. You were still learning advanced writing skills, but had more opportunity to put all your knowledge to practice, as teacher expectations of your written work increased. You were expected to spell words correctly, use correct punctuation, capitalization, sentence structure in your written work, while increasing your ability to convey meaning through your written work. There were probably times which you received point reduction because of misspellings or fragmented sentences. Although that may have been frustrating to you, the point was to teach you the importance and value of properly written communication.

Then you entered high school and you were required to write lengthy topic papers. Not only were the mechanics of writing assessed, but you were expected to appropriately convey meaning through your writing. Some of your written work required you to collect references or sources of data to help reinforce the topic about which you were writing. You were expected to integrate information from references to support the topic while adhering to the basic mechanics of writing. You might be thinking, "Yeah, and I didn't like writing at all. Why did my teacher(s) make me do such insignificant work?" There was a reason!

And now, you are in college. Are you still learning to write in college? Of course, you are! Not only are you are learning how to advance your research writing skills, but also you are learning different writing formats (i.e., APA, MLA, etc.). Even though there are required writing courses as an undergraduate student, you may be required to take additional writing courses for your major. You may have entered college expecting the requirements of written work or learning about writing to decrease, but what you have likely discovered is that the expectations have only increased.

You are reading this chapter because you are, in fact, taking a course that focuses on increasing your scientific reasoning skills and integrating information into written work. Wow! That sounds intense, but if you take a moment to reflect on what you have learned about writing, the expectations are congruent with the level of education you are pursuing.

So really, what is the big deal about writing? Why are you spending so much time learning about how to write properly? Why is it important to your major, Psychology? After reading the first part of this chapter, it is likely clear why it is important for a school psychologists to possess strong written language skills, but anyone who chooses to pursue a profession within Psychology must recognize the importance of strong written language skills. Writing is a method of communication about subject matter and has been one of the most valued methods of communication. Ways in which written work is used includes: entertainment, law and policy, specific subject matter, influencing change, news, and alternative communication methods (i.e., for individuals with hearing impairments). There are instances when writing is more formal than others, but nonetheless if the information is unable to be communicated effectively then the meaning is lost.

How To's for Improving Written Work

You may be wondering how you can improve your written skills in preparation for a profession in school psychology. Bradley-Johnson and Johnson (2006) suggest three ways you can improve writing skills which include proofreading, use of feedback, and clearly communicating information.

Proofreading.   The complexity of the writing process for school psychologists is often underestimated by students. Hayes and Flower's (1987) model of the writing process requires writers to plan, generate sentences, and revise work. Planning, collection of resources, and integration of sources to convey meaning can take a considerable amount of time. In addition, proofreading written work several times can increase the length of time until the final product is attained; however, it should help identify problem areas which require editing, such as grammar, word order, structural elements, organization, spelling, and sentence structure (Bradley-Johnson & Johnson, 2006). To help the editing process, writers are encouraged to put their work away for a several days and then resume the editing process to bring new perspectives to the report. Each school psychologist will approach report writing in a different way. Some may wait to begin report writing until all assessment data has been collected, whereas others may write sections of the report as data is collected. Either way, to be able to have time to write the report and then finalize edits after several days have passed, requires school psychologists to be well organized, efficient workers within required state and federal timelines.

Using Feedback.   Soliciting feedback from instructors and others to help proofread your work is a useful method for improving your writing skills. You may be hesitant to seek feedback and willingly open your work up to criticism; however, Bradley-Johnson and Johnson (2006) report using feedback can help improve clarity and organization of your written work, and in the long term will help improve your personal writing skills. Individuals who are unsure of their own writing skills are encouraged to seek help from instructors, literature students, supervisors, colleagues, or even a good manual of style (i.e., APA Publication Manual; Seagull, 1979). School psychologist practitioners are encouraged to seek feedback from immediate supervisors and/or colleagues to help protect confidentiality of the information within the report. Practitioners could also seek feedback from others who they do not work with; however, all personal identifying information must first be removed to protect confidentiality.

Clarity of Information.   The goal of any written work is to communicate information, therefore, the clarity with which the information is communicated is an important consideration. Bradley-Johnson and Johnson (2006) state, "a writer's credibility is established only when a report clearly communicates the assessment results and implications, and when readers are enlightened and not intimidated, by the material" (p. 4). Your written work should employ various writing techniques including, varied sentence length, multisyllabic words, and the use of transition words to clearly convey information and meaning. The following is an example of how a child's perceptual reasoning abilities may be interpreted and described within a psychoeducational report:

> When given tasks which require Billy to identify patterns and use abstract reasoning skills, he scored in the average range. His ability to use abstract reasoning skills to solve visual puzzles is similar to peers of his same age. Billy should experience success when completing classroom tasks which require the use of abstract reasoning skills.

Although creating a well-written document requires you to consider the basic mechanics of writing to help clearly convey information, it is the integration of information which ultimately establishes meaning. Scardamalia and Bereiter (1987) state the integrative writing process is a challenge for students because it demands *knowledge transforming* as opposed to *knowledge telling*. As you learn to write well-written APA research papers, you will come to know it is not just about the information you collect from your sources, but how the information from the sources is integrated to support your topic or research project. How well you integrate the information and align supporting details determines how effective your written work will communicate your goals and findings.

Conclusion

Since beginning to read this chapter, you have learned a little bit about the profession of school psychology, what psychoeducational reports are, and the importance of psychoeducational reports to the profession of school psychology. Lastly, you have learned why developing and refining appropriate writing skills is important.

There are many roles school psychologists serve, but psychoeducational report writing is one of the most important functions of the profession. Psychoeducational reports can serve a variety of purposes some of which include reporting assessment scores and sharing diagnostic impressions. The information included in psychoeducational reports is very personal and vulnerable relating specifically to individuals' level of cognitive and academic functioning. School psychologists are ethically responsible to share information in a competent, meaningful, clear, and understandable manner. Doing so allows individuals to make informed decisions about eligibility and educational programming. Therefore, it is the duty of school psychologists to use proper writing skills when disseminating information through psychoeducational reports.

If you think writing and writing skills are not important, think again!! You may now realize the magnitude writing composition and mechanics can have within the profession of school psychology. You may also be personally assessing your writing skills and thinking about how to improve your skills to become a better writer. You are in luck! Like with anything else, writing skills can be improved through practice. Consistently using strategies such as proofreading techniques and soliciting peer feedback can help improve your writing over time. Consistently striving to improve written composition will ultimately lead to positive student and family outcomes and collegial respect.

References

Bradley-Johnson, S., & Johnson, C. M. (2006). *A handbook for writing effective psychoeducational reports.* Austin, TX: Pro-Ed.

Groth-Marnat, G. (2009). The five assessment issues you meet when you go to heaven. *Journal of Personality Assessment, 91,* 303–310. doi:10.1089/00223890902935662

Groth-Marnat, G., & Horvath, L. S. (2006). The psychological report: A review of current controversies. *Journal of Clinical Psychology, 62,* 73–81. doi:10.1002/jclp.20201

Hass, M., & Carriere, J. A. (2014). *Writing Useful, Accessible, and Legally Defensible Psychoeducational Reports.* Hoboken, N.J.: Wiley and Sons.

Hayes, J. R., & Flower, L. S. (1987). On the structure of the writing process. *Topics in Language Disorders, 7*(4), 19–30.

Mastoras, S. M., Climie, E. A., McCrimmon, A. W., & Schwean, V. L. (2011). A C.L.E.A.R. approach to report writing: A framework for improving the efficacy of psychoeducational reports. *Canadian Journal of School Psychology, 26,* 127–147. doi:10.1177/0829573511409722

Merrell, K., Ervin, A., & Gimpel Peacock, G. (2011). School Psychology for the 21st century: Foundations and Practices. New York, NY: Guilford Press.

Michaels, M. H. (2006). Ethical considerations in writing psychological assessment reports. *Journal of Clinical Psychology, 62,* 47–58. doi:10.1002/jclp.20199

National Association of School Psychologists (NASP). (2010). *Principles for professional ethics and guidelines for the provision of school psychological services.* Retrieved from https://www.nasponline.org/standards-and-certification/professional-ethics

National Association of School Psychologists (NASP). (2014). *Who are school psychologists.* Retrieved from https://www.nasponline.org/about-school-psychology/who-are-school-psychologists

Scardamalia, M., & Bereiter, C. (1987). Knowledge telling and knowledge transforming in written composition. In S. Rosenberg (Ed.), *Advanced in applied psycholinguistics. Vol.2: Reading, writing and language learning* (pp. 142–175). New York, NY: Cambridge University Press.

Seagull, E. A.W. (1979). Writing the report of the psychological assessment of a child. *Journal of Clinical Child Psychology, 8,* 39–42. doi:10.1080/15374417909532880

Smith Harvey, V. (2006). Variables affecting the clarity of psychological reports. *Journal of Clinical Psychology, 62,* 5–18. doi:10.1002/jclp.20196

Walrath, R., Willis, J. O., & Dumont, R. (2014). Best practices in writing assessment reports. In P. L. Harrison & A. Thomas (Eds.), *Best practices in school psychology* (pp. 433–445). Bethesda, MD: National Association of School Psychologists.

Wiener, J., & Costaris, L. (2012). Teaching psychological report writing: Content and process. *Canadian Journal of School Psychology, 27,* 119–135. doi:10.1177/0829573511418484

5

Types of Writing

by Cheryl Duffy, PhD

Informal versus Formal Writing

You have likely done plenty of informal writing in your life, even in college. Of course, text messages to friends and notes jotted to roommates can be extremely informal, but even some essays you've written for certain classes might have been somewhat informal, especially personal essays or reflections based on your own experience or opinions. To make the transition to writing like a professional psychologist, however, you will need to shift to a more formal tone. Just as jeans and a t-shirt might be fine for certain occasions, you know that some circumstances call for more formal attire. The same is true for your writing style. Think of *informal* writing as the blue jeans and t-shirt option: It's not necessarily wrong, but it's not always appropriate. Most of the writing you will do for psychology should reflect a formal tone.

What's the difference between an informal tone and a formal tone?

Informal writing often:

- uses contractions like *don't, you'll,* and *can't* (instead of the more formal spelled-out versions: *do not, you will,* and *cannot*)
- uses short, simple sentences—even fragments sometimes
- uses slang words and casual diction like *kids, cool,* and *yup*
- uses short, easy-to-read paragraphs
- uses personal examples and stories
- uses first-person pronouns such as *I, me, my, we, us, our,* etc.
- uses second-person pronouns such as *you, your, yourself, yours,* etc.
- begins sentences with coordinating conjunctions such as *And, But, So,* or *Or*
- uses exclamation points
- uses humor

Formal writing typically:

- avoids contractions (Write *do not* instead of *don't*, for example.)
- uses longer, more complex sentences
- avoids slang and casual language (Write *adolescents* instead of *teens* or *kids.*)
- uses longer, more fully developed paragraphs
- relies on outside sources for support (cites studies and quotes experts—and uses a recognized system like APA to document those sources)
- uses third-person pronouns such as *he, she, one, they, their,* etc.
- avoids first-person pronouns such as *I, me, we, our,* etc.
- avoids second-person pronouns such as *you, your, yourself, yours*
- avoids beginning sentences with coordinating conjunctions such as *And, But, So,* or *Or* (opting instead for more formal transitions such as *Additionally, However, Therefore,* or *On the other hand*)
- avoids exclamation points
- maintains a serious tone

No piece of writing is completely informal or completely formal. It will fall somewhere along a continuum like the one below (See Table 1).

Table 1   Range of Formality

More Informal			More Formal
text to a friend about an exchange you had with a teacher	English Comp. I essay profiling an effective teacher from your past	undergraduate term paper analyzing styles of discipline in the classroom	master's thesis over a controlled study of preventative discipline

The point is, you have choices when you write. In fact, you *must* make choices when you write, and those choices affect how your readers respond to you. To be taken seriously in a scholarly setting, you should make choices that lean toward the formal end of the spectrum.

Which of the two sentences below is more formal and is, therefore, better suited for the kind of writing expected in psychology? What specific language choices helped you decide one sentence was informal and the other was formal?

A teacher who does not clearly specify his or her expectations and policies will discover that students misbehave at a higher rate than they would otherwise.

I believe that as a teacher, if you don't spell out to your kids what you expect, they're bound to mess up and get into a ton of trouble.

The first sentence, of course, is the formal one. It avoids contractions (*does not*), relies on third-person pronouns (*his or her, they*), and uses standard vocabulary (*students, misbehave, higher rate*). You can tell that the second sentence is too informal because it uses contractions (*don't, they're*), uses first- and second-person pronouns (*I, you*), and uses casual vocabulary (*spell out, kids, mess up, a ton of*). For most of the writing you'll do as a psychology major—and later as a psychologist—you should write in a formal tone. Write as if you are having a serious, professional discussion with another professional, not as if you are chatting with a friend. When in doubt, lean formal.

(By the way, you might have noticed that much of this textbook is written informally. In this chapter, for example, we often use contractions, the first-person pronoun *we*, and the second-person pronoun *you*. That's because we're opting for a friendly, helpful persona rather than a strictly serious, official persona. As we said earlier, informal writing isn't necessarily wrong; it simply is not appropriate for all writing circumstances. Student textbooks are one of those writing circumstances that often lean toward the informal end of the spectrum.)

General Modes of Writing

Beyond the challenge of maintaining a formal tone, students sometimes struggle to develop and organize their ideas. What follows is a brief refresher on the general modes of writing, which can help you expand your thinking on a topic. These basic modes of writing can prompt new ways of thinking about your topic, giving you strategies to flesh out your ideas and give them some structure. If you're struggling for something to say about a topic, revisit these modes for inspiration. Keep in mind that you might write an entire paper using one of these modes of writing, or you might simply use one or more of these modes to develop a section of a larger piece of writing. The basic modes are Description, Narration, Exposition (with its subgenres Cause/Effect, Comparison/Contrast, Definition, Division/Classification, and Process Analysis), and Persuasion.

Description.   At times, it might serve your purposes to describe people or places. For example, a writer might use description to illustrate a problem such as unsanitary housing conditions or injured participants in a contact sport. Specific details can engage your readers as though they themselves are there to experience the scene firsthand. That being said, descriptive writing is not typical in formal, research-based writing.

When you do describe something or someone, use the five senses: sight, sound, smell, taste, and touch.

- **Sight**—Think color, size, age, condition, brand, placement, etc.

  Don't write, "The room was a mess." Write, "Discarded gym socks and worn-out Nikes covered the floor, and the coffee table was crowded with empty beer bottles half full of cigarette butts.

- **Sound**—What do you hear? Think of background noise, the quality of someone's voice, the exact verb (*blared, whispered, screeched, clicked, hummed, chanted, echoed,* etc.). Also, remember the power of onomatopoeia (i.e., words that sound like the sound they represent: *buzz, beep, click, murmur, splash, crack, whiz, whoop, swish, boom,* etc.).

  "The creaking floorboards echoed down the length of the hallway."

- **Smell**—What smells are in the air—good and bad?

  "The musty odor of damp towels was overpowered by the smell of cat urine."

- **Taste**—This one doesn't always come into play, but sometimes just your descriptive adjectives alone can hint at taste—e.g., *bitter* cough syrup.

- **Touch**—Again, adjectives can pull their weight here—*soft, rough, coarse, fine, smooth, rigid, clammy, humid, warm, hard, cold, scaly, bumpy,* etc.

When you describe places or people, you can organize the details *spatially*: from near to far, from left to right, from top to bottom. Or perhaps it makes more sense to organize *chronologically*, starting with what one might notice or encounter first and then moving on to what one might notice or encounter later. You could also organize in order of *importance*, either starting with the most important feature and then moving on to less significant features—or vice versa, starting with an insignificant feature and then progressing toward the most significant feature. Your transitions will reveal the form of organization you're using:

- **To signal transitions of space (spatial organization):**

near (or nearby)	next to	adjacent to
farther	under	farther down (or up)
to the left (or right)	underneath	across
in front of	above	across from
behind	on top of	

- **To signal transitions of time (chronological organization):**

first (at first), second, etc.	later	at the same time
at the beginning (at the start)	next	simultaneously
initially	then	while
to begin	after	when
sooner than	before	as
as soon as	meanwhile	finally

- **To signal transitions of importance:**

more (or less) important/significant	less	worse
even more important	least	worst
most importantly	better	
greater	best	

Narration.   A narrative is simply an account in chronological order that tells what happened. Like description, you can use narration to demonstrate that a problem exists—or even to speculate about a solution by narrating the best possible outcome. For example, in a paper arguing for preventative discipline in the classroom, you could open with a real or hypothetical narrative about a disruptive class period, from start to finish—and you could close that same paper with a narrative that illustrates how that class period might have unfolded more positively if the teacher had implemented preventative discipline. Psychologists also incorporate narrative elements when they write up case notes about what happened during a session with a client.

Of course, you'll organize a narrative section in chronological order, using the transitions listed above under "To signal transitions of time." Depending on your writing situation, you might include descriptive details in your narrative as you relate not only what happened but also who was there and what the setting was like. (See "Description" above.)

Most narrative writing includes direct quotations/dialogue as well. Ask yourself, "Who's saying what?" Then include quotations to add interest and convey meaning. <u>A word of caution, though:</u> Sometimes a strong verb can bolster a quotation (the coach *bellowed*, Marci *whispered*). But be careful. Sometimes a simple *I asked* or *Anna said* is preferable to an overdone *Josh questioned menacingly in a hoarse voice*. Also, for case notes and other writing situations when objectivity is critical, be sure to use unbiased language. (For example, "yelled with a frown" would be more objective than "bellowed angrily.") Finally, be sure to check the APA style chapter in this writing guide to ensure that you're punctuating your direct quotations correctly.

Exposition.   Several familiar types of writing fall under the umbrella of expository writing: Cause/Effect, Comparison/Contrast, Definition, Division/Classification, and Process Analysis.

Cause/Effect.   A common form of analytical writing is cause/effect—that is, writing that analyzes the possible causes of something and/or the possible effects of something.

As you analyze causes (reasons), you ask, "What makes X happen?" "What causes X?" Note that there can be immediate or obvious causes as well as distant or systemic causes. An immediate, obvious cause for someone being homeless might be a recent eviction. But a distant, more systemic, underlying cause (sometimes called the "root cause") might be the lack of federal funding for residential-care institutions for those with severe mental illness.

To connect an immediate cause (eviction) to a more distant root cause (lack of federal funding) typically requires something called a "**causal chain**"—that is, an analysis that links one cause to another and then to another until the root cause is linked via intermediate causes to the most obvious or immediate cause. In the case of homelessness, it might look something like this:

> **Root cause:** Federal funding is cut for residential-care facilities.
>
> ↓
>
> **Intermediate causes:** Individuals with severe mental illness are turned out of residential-care facilities.
>
> ↓
>
> These individuals turn in large numbers to underfunded community service organizations, which are unprepared to serve this large number of individuals in need.
>
> ↓
>
> Being essentially forced to spend limited funds on food and other immediate necessities, such an individual falls behind on the rent.
>
> ↓
>
> **Immediate cause:** Individual is evicted.
>
> ↓
>
> **EFFECT:** Homelessness

When analyzing causes, then, the bottom line is that you must delve deeply enough to get beyond the surface causes to reveal the less obvious underlying or root causes leading to a particular effect—and you must connect those causes when necessary.

Analyzing effects is no simple undertaking, either. When you ask, "What happens as a result of X?" you need to look for both positive and negative effects, weighing their potential impact. In other words, a negative effect might be offset by a more significant positive effect—and vice versa. You also need to consider both short-term and long-term effects. And, of course, you must consider what other factors or variables beyond the cause you're exploring could be leading to the effects you're considering. Cause/effect thinking is complex!

In fact, one of the most important lessons you will learn from all of the thinking and writing you do as a student of psychology is this: Most issues worth discussing are more complicated than most people realize. Be wary of the "simple solution," and be willing to delve deeply into an issue, considering it thoughtfully from all angles.

When you begin to draft your cause/effect analysis, you'll need to ORGANIZE your discussion of causes/effects. Don't make it a discussion like this: *Here's one cause. Here's another one. And here's a last one.* That approach is random and boring.

Here are some ideas for organizing a cause/effect paper:
- Trace the causal chain from immediate/surface causes back to the root cause(s).
- Trace the causal chain from the root cause(s) forward to the more intermediate and surface causes.
- Organize from short-term to long-term effects.
- Organize from positive to negative effects—or from negative to positive effects.
- Organize from least to most (climactic order)—e.g., from the least positive to the most positive effect, or from the least impactful cause to the most impactful.
- Organize by first exploring causes and then the resulting effects.
- Organize by first exploring a particular circumstance and then the likely causes that have led to that circumstance (as an effect).

Comparison/Contrast.   To compare is to look for similarities, and to contrast is to look for differences. In your writing about a topic, you might simply do comparison, or contrast, or both. For this type of analysis, you might ask questions such as these:

- "How does X differ from Y?"
- "How is X similar to Y?"
- "What are the advantages and disadvantages of X and Y?"
- "Why would you recommend X over Y?"
- "What does X seem better suited for than Y?"

To organize comparison/contrast writing, you will use either the **Block Style** or the **Point-by-Point Style**, both of which are explained in the "Comparison/Contrast Structure" segment of the *Writing the Persuasive Research Paper* chapter of this textbook. In addition to that discussion of organization, it will be helpful to keep in mind the following transitions when writing about similarities and/or differences.

Useful transition words:

Contrast	Comparison
on the other hand	similarly
yet	in the same way
unlike X, Y . . .	also
while X is . . ., Y is . . .	like
but	likewise
while both X and Y are . . ., only Y . . .	as well
nevertheless	and
on the contrary	
though	
although	
despite	
however	
conversely	

Definition. Precise writing often hinges on the clear definition of terms. This statement is especially true for a new or unfamiliar term; a term that is often misused or misunderstood; a term that has various definitions, depending upon the context in which it is used; or a term that has a contested meaning (i.e., people debate what the term means and/or how it should be used). Sometimes you will need to define a term (or terms) early in a piece of writing. At other times, when a term is not introduced until later in your paper, you will wait to define it then. You have many options for defining a term, as you'll see below.

- **Synonyms:** Explain what other words this term might go by.
- **Analysis:** Divide whatever this word stands for into its separate elements, and then define each element separately.
- **Classification and Differentiation** (similar to a dictionary definition): What class does the subject belong to, and how is it different from other subjects in this class? For example, preventive discipline (the term being defined) is a classroom management technique (that's the classification) that relies on setting clear policies and explaining expectations and consequences up front (that's the differentiation—what sets this classroom management technique apart from other forms of discipline such as punitive discipline).
- **Comparison/Contrast:** Define a word by showing how it is like something familiar or how it is different from it.
- **Details:** What physical characteristics or other distinguishing attributes could you use to describe what this term represents?
- **Exemplification (Examples):** Provide examples that can *show* what is meant by your chosen term.

- **Negation:** Explain what it is *not* in order to better illustrate what it *is*.
- **Origins/Causes:** Where did this term come from? What is its etymology? What is the background information? What is its history? How has its meaning or use changed over time?
- **Results/Effects:** Discuss the consequences of the subject of this term.
- **Uses:** How is this term used—or how is whatever this term represents used?

Division/Classification.   You'll often see division and classification discussed together, but they really require two different thinking processes. *Division* means taking something apart—breaking it down into its individual parts. *Classification* means sorting types of something into separately labeled classes.

Division. If you write a paper explaining the many required elements of an IEP (an Individualized Education Program for a student receiving special education services)—in other words, if you take that one type of program and break it down into its individual parts—then you're writing a division paper. Those parts of an IEP would include, for example, a Statement of present levels of achievement/functionality, a Statement of goals, and so on. The same type of thinking would be required to explain the key elements of a successful romantic relationship, as S. Degges-White (n.d.) did in a *Psychology Today* article entitled "The 'Big 3' Keys to Relationship Success." That article is a *division* article because the author divides a successful relationship into its three key elements.

Classification. On the other hand, if you were to classify the *types* of individuals in a romantic relationship according to their communication styles—perhaps Open communicators, Closed communicators, and Non-communicators—then you would be writing *classification* because you'd be sorting individuals into categories (or classes) that you have labeled separately. Note that when you classify, it is important to classify by a common basis of classification: in this case, communication styles.

To organize a paper—or a segment of a paper—using division, you'll begin by providing a rationale. That is, what's to be gained from breaking X into its component parts? Then, as you discuss those parts, organize them logically. Three common forms of organization (and not just for division and classification) are "least to most," "chronological," and "spatial." Let your topic guide you to the most appropriate organizational strategy.

- *Least to Most*—For example, organize from the least important part to the most important part—or the least relevant to the most relevant—whatever. You can also switch the order and organize from most to least, such as from the most familiar to the least familiar.
- *Chronological*—For example, organize from the first part one would encounter to the last part—or from the earliest developed part to the most recently developed part—and so on.
- *Spatial*—If your topic takes up physical space in some way, organize by that principle—for example, from top to bottom, from outside to inside, from near to far, from smallest to largest, etc.

The same organizational strategies will work for classification. Begin with your rationale for classifying—why is it important or useful to group individual types according to the basis of classification you've chosen? Then organize your labeled types in some organized way, perhaps using one of the three common forms of organization introduced above.

- *Least to Most*—For example, organize from the least communicative to the most communicative, from the least restrictive to the most restrictive, etc. It will depend upon whatever basis of classification you've chosen. (In those first two examples, the bases of classification are communication styles and levels of restriction, respectively.) Again, you can also switch the order and organize from most to least, such as from the most communicative to the least.
- *Chronological*—For example, you could organize your romantic-relationship communicators according to the types that are typical in an early relationship, to those typical in a well-established relationship, to those typical in a fully mature relationship. Any pattern that moves chronologically through time will work.
- *Spatial*—Again, it might be possible to organize by moving through physical space. You could, for example, organize geographically, from rural settings to small cities to large cities—or from one region of the country to another.

Process Analysis. With process analysis, you will explain either

1) how a process happens

or

2) how to perform/complete a process

A well-known example of the first type is E. Kübler-Ross' (1970) analysis of the five stages of death and dying: Denial, Anger, Bargaining, Depression, and Acceptance. This type of process analysis helps a reader understand an often complex or misunderstood process.

The second type of process analysis—the "How To" type—guides a reader to complete a specific process. An example of a how-to process analysis would be an explanation of the chronological steps necessary to establish a trusting relationship with a client.

In either case, a key requirement is presenting the stages or steps *in chronological order*. If you merely discuss the various emotions experienced while dying—but not in chronological order (from first to last, or early to late), you have not written process analysis. Likewise, if you merely offer tips to keep in mind while establishing trust with a client, but you don't offer steps in chronological order (for example, what to do before the client arrives, when first meeting a client, during the session, at the end of the session, and then after the session), then you are not writing process analysis. To belabor the point: Process analysis must be written in chronological order.

To organize process analysis, you will begin by emphasizing *why* it is important to understand this particular process. If you are writing the how-to version, you will next list any supplies, materials, or conditions necessary for completing the process. From here, the beauty of this particular mode is that the overall organization is straightforward: It will always be chronological. In the "Description" section above, we listed words to signal transitions of time. You will use those transitions as you write process analysis.

Persuasion   The fourth overall mode of writing beyond description, narration, and exposition is persuasion. Because persuasion is so vital to the critical thinking you will do as a college student and as a psychologist (and, we might add, as a citizen), we have devoted an entire chapter of this book to the topic. Please refer to the *Writing the Persuasive Research Paper* chapter for guidance on how to write persuasively.

Specific Types of Writing Common in Psychology

Two specific types of writing within psychology—the scientific paper reporting on original research findings, and the persuasive research (or "term") paper—are covered elsewhere in this textbook. The section that follows here will cover a few additional types of writing you might find yourself doing as you settle into the role of professional psychologist: the book review, abstract, annotated bibliography, and literature review. For each of those, we will discuss the audience you'll be targeting, the purpose you'll be trying to achieve, and the persona you'll be trying to project. Then we'll offer some specific Do's and Don'ts to keep in mind as you write.

Book Review.   A book review is just what it sounds like: a brief discussion of a book's contents along with an evaluation of its merits and/or faults.

- Audience: Other psychologists who might be interested in the book you're reviewing.
- Purpose: To give potential readers of the book an overview of its content and structure. A book review is a combination of summary and critique—what's in the book, and how useful/effective it is.
- Persona: You want to come across as a thoughtful, informed reader with an overall positive, professional tone.

Do:

- If given a choice, choose a book that you care about—that you truly *want* to read and remember.
  - Check the author's credentials so that you select a book with some credibility. You can review a scholarly book (from a professional or academic publisher) or possibly

even a book from what's called the "popular press"—books published for non-experts. Just be sure that the book's author has the necessary credentials—such as a parenting book written by a licensed child psychologist.

○ Underline, write in the margins, and take notes as you read.

○ Ideally, you'll read the book twice—but that might not be realistic in a student's universe.

○ Determine the overall point/purpose of the book.

○ As you take notes, try to capture the main point/purpose of each chapter.

○ Also, try to step back and see if the book has an overall arc—that is, a clear path that it takes from beginning to end. What is that arc? If it doesn't seem to have one, that might be something to comment on, too.

○ Evaluate the book's strengths and weaknesses.

Questions you might ask as you brainstorm before starting to write:

• Who might find this book especially useful—and why?

• What might readers look for—but not find—in this book?

• What gaps does this book fill—or not fill?

• How broad or how narrow is its scope?

• Does this book offer any special features—like a glossary or helpful appendices?

• How is the writing? How readable is it? What is the author's tone (e.g., serious, helpful, dry, engaging, lively, straightforward)?

• If you have enough background, compare this book to similar books of this type. How is it similar—and how is this book different (in good and/or bad ways)?

Here is one possible organizational strategy:

• Start with a paragraph introducing the book and its author.

• Summarize the book's content and structure: Describe the book.

• Discuss the book's strengths.

• Discuss the book's weaknesses.

• Conclude with a paragraph giving your overall assessment of the book, including recommendations for who might find this book valuable.

Don't:

• Don't make the mistake of trying to say too much in a book review. Reveal the essence of the book and its contents—but save something for readers to discover on their own when they read the book for themselves. Book reviews are typically 600 to 1,000 words.

• Avoid lapsing into emotional language, whether you love or hate the book. Be clear and objective—neither too gushing nor too hostile.

Abstract. An abstract is a brief summary of the whole document. The abstract appears at the beginning of a paper, article, or book.

> - Audience: Anyone who might consider reading the full work. This audience, therefore, might be a fellow psychologist or simply someone interested in your topic.
> - Purpose: To summarize the larger document well enough that someone reading the abstract will have a good idea of the essential elements in that document—and can, therefore, decide whether or not to read it for more in-depth information.
> - Persona: As with most writing in psychology, you will (again) adopt a clear, direct, and professional tone.

Do:

- Include this key information in your abstract of a research study: 1) the question posed by this work, 2) the methods used to answer that question, and 3) the results/findings.
- For other types of writing, include the work's thesis in your first sentence and then follow it with sentences that support that initial main idea.
- Typically, you will follow the same organizational pattern of the larger work as you write your abstract.
- Keep your abstract at around 100 to 250 words.

Don't:

- This is not the place for opinion/commentary on the work you are summarizing.

Annotated Bibliography. An annotated bibliography is a list of sources you've located on a particular topic, along with a description of each source and a brief evaluation of that source's relevance/quality. Students will sometimes complete an annotated bibliography as a step during the process of writing a term paper—or they might construct an annotated bibliography on a topic *instead of* writing a full paper on that topic. In the professional world, annotated bibliographies are sometimes in scholarly journals or books for other psychologists interested in a given topic.

> - Audience: You/Your Professor/Other Psychologists
> - Purpose: Depending on the circumstances, an annotated bibliography can serve one or more of the following purposes:
>   - To force you to get an early start on your research.

- o To help you sort through your sources to determine which ones are the most relevant/valuable.
- o To demonstrate to your instructor your ability to conduct research, write APA citations, and read with analytic understanding.
- o To provide fellow students or colleagues with a useful overview of sources available on a given topic.
- Persona: You guessed it: clear, direct, and professional.

Do:

- Begin each entry with the APA citation for that source, followed by your annotation—a paragraph of about 150 to 300 words (closer to 150 for shorter works, and closer to 300 for longer works). Your instructor might have length requirements different from these general guidelines, of course.
- Use a hanging indent when you type your citation so that all lines of the citation after the first line are indented.
- Unlike an abstract, an annotation should include not only a *description* of the source but also an *evaluation* of its quality and relevance.
- To *describe* the source, you can follow the suggestions given earlier for writing an abstract.
- For the *evaluative* portion of each annotation, consider these questions:
  - o What's your overall reaction to this source?
  - o What are its strengths and weaknesses?
  - o How relevant is it to your topic/research question?
  - o Who seems to be the target audience for this source?
  - o How's the readability—geared more toward a novice or an expert?
  - o How strong are the author's credentials?
- Arrange your sources (and their accompanying annotations) in alphabetical order.

Don't:

- Don't limit yourself to just one kind of source—for example, articles. Consider a wide variety of sources such as articles, books (or book chapters), websites, podcasts, videos, blogposts, transcripts, government documents, speeches, poster sessions, conference proceedings. . . .
- Do not simply copy and paste a published abstract for your annotation of a particular work. Each annotation needs to include your original summary and evaluation; otherwise, you'd be guilty of plagiarism.

Literature Review.   A literature review is similar to an annotated bibliography in that both types of writing compile and discuss sources—but the differences are significant. While an annotated bibliography is simply an alphabetical list of sources with separate, individual annotations, a literature review is a comprehensive and integrated discussion of the important sources surrounding a research topic you're considering. It has an introduction, body paragraphs, and a conclusion. In essence, a literature review builds a case for a research project you are proposing. Your literature review, ideally, will convince your readers that within the existing literature, there is a gap to be filled—or perhaps a controversy to be resolved. You will discuss sources in whatever logical order helps to build a case for your own research project, and helps to place your project within the context of what has already been discovered in the field.

- Audience: Your audience could vary. It might be a course professor (or in graduate school, a member of your thesis or dissertation committee)—or it might be a member of an IRB review board or an agency from which you're seeking approval/funding for your research.
- Purpose: To convince readers that your proposed research project is original and necessary.
- Persona: Informed, well-read, professional.

Do:

- Start with an introduction that identifies the topic and explains why it is important. You should also include your thesis: What readers, in a nutshell, will discover from reading your review of the literature on this topic—especially as it relates to the specific research project you are proposing. Your introduction should typically be just one to two paragraphs.
- Follow with body paragraphs organized to build a case that your research project will fill a gap or resolve a controversy in the existing literature.
- Discuss how these sources have shaped current thinking.
- Look for similarities and differences among the sources you're reviewing.
- Your conclusion should sum up your main points and drive home your thesis (the gap you'll attempt to fill and/or the controversy you'll attempt to resolve).
- Again, to emphasize—your key purpose is to show that within the existing literature, there is a gap that you hope to fill with your research, or a controversy that you hope to resolve. Make this point clear in your introduction, body, and conclusion.
- After your conclusion, begin a new page and type "References" at the top (centered and without quotation marks). Then list in alphabetical order and in APA format every source you cited in your literature review.

Don't:

- For the body of your literature review, do *not* merely write a paragraph or two about each of your sources. Instead, incorporate your sources into your discussion of the themes/categories/theories/methods surrounding your topic. You will likely mention a source more than once, and you will possibly mention more than one source in any given paragraph.
- Don't include any sources on your References page that you merely read but did not actually cite within your literature review.

References

Degges-White, S. (n.d.). The 'Big 3' keys to relationship. *Psychology Today*. Retrieved from https://www.psychologytoday.com/us/blog/lifetime-connections/201509/the-big-3-keys-relationship-success

Kubler-Ross, E. (1970). *On Death and Dying*. New York, NY: Macmillian Publishing Co.

6

Writing the Persuasive Research Paper

by Cheryl Duffy, PhD

One of the most common types of writing you'll be asked to do in college is the persuasive research paper. Writing persuasively demonstrates your ability to delve deeply into a topic, think critically about it, take a stand, and provide your reader with evidence supporting that stand. Through this messy, challenging process, you will develop as a thinker and a writer. We've designed this chapter to guide you on that journey, striving to make it a little less messy and a little less challenging.

Choosing a Topic

The best advice we can give is to *start early*. That means you should start thinking about a possible topic as soon as you know you'll be writing a persuasive research paper in any given semester. Have your antennae up during class, and when an interesting topic strikes you, jot it in your notes and write "PAPER TOPIC?" next to it. Sometimes professors even say something obvious during class like, "That would make an interesting paper topic." Don't just smile and nod—write it down.

Do the same as you read for class: Be alert for paper topics and jot them down. If there's a "References" list at the end of a chapter/article you're reading, peruse the titles listed there, looking for intriguing topics. If you do find a topic among that list of sources, you will also have the bonus of having found a potential source for your paper. Look ahead in your textbook for intriguing chapter titles and subheadings within those chapters. Get your wheels turning early in the semester.

Google *Psychology Research Paper Topics*. You'll be surprised at all of the lists out there. Just keep in mind that not all topics you encounter will be relevant for your particular course or narrow enough for your paper (more on those concerns later in this section). Look for topics that are especially meaningful for you—perhaps because of your own experience, family background, friends, or career goals. Feeling a strong connection to a topic will likely make you especially motivated to do the research and thinking required for an effective paper. If your younger brother is out for football, maybe you'll want to explore the risks/benefits of contact sports. If you're planning to be a school psychologist, maybe you'll want to explore the possible effects of divorce on a child's academic performance. One caveat, though: Be careful that you're not so closely tied to a topic that you are unable to step back and be objective. At the very least, be aware of the potential for that kind of bias, and consciously guard against it: Be sensitive to key weaknesses in your own perspective, and consider the possible strengths in competing perspectives.

Once you have a topic you're considering, ask yourself these questions: Is it relevant? Is it a topic directly related to the course content? Does it take up a topic covered in class but dig deeper into that topic, or look at it from a different angle? Does it take a theory or concept studied in class and apply it in a new way? When in doubt about a topic's relevance, check with your professor.

Is it controversial? To be a persuasive topic, it has to be one about which there is some disagreement—some difference of opinion. Do reasonable people debate both sides of this issue? If so, it meets the "must be controversial" criterion. Keep in mind that you are not being asked to write a "report" or an informative paper similar to the kind of paper you might have commonly done in high school. In other words, for example, you will not be writing a paper that simply describes the different types of romantic relationships in the United States—but you might write a paper arguing that a certain type of romantic relationship does (or does not) provide a healthy environment for raising children. Now you have a controversial topic suitable for a persuasive paper.

Is there sufficient research available? Do a bit of research before you commit to a topic. (That's one reason to *start early*!) Can you find appropriate sources—sources that are current, credible/scholarly, relevant? Sometimes a topic is so new or so unique that not much research has been published about it. Keep in mind that you don't necessarily need to find sources that directly support your claim. You might find related research that you can connect to your topic, or you might find opposing viewpoints that you can nonetheless cite and then challenge or refute. Also, don't give up too soon. If you hit a brick wall, ask a librarian for help. Typically, that means actually going to your campus library and asking a reference librarian for help. (They won't think you're an idiot or a nuisance—it's their job to help students conduct research and make good use of the library's materials and database subscriptions!) In many cases, your library will even offer a "live chat" or an "ask a librarian" online option if you can't physically make it to the library. If you simply cannot find useable sources, it might be time to tweak your topic—or find a new one altogether.

Is it narrow enough? Granted, it's possible to have a topic that's *too* narrow ("bulimia among Latina sixth graders with divorced parents in rural Kansas")—but most college students have the opposite problem. They choose topics so broad that whole books could be written on them—topics like "sports," "divorce," "cancer," or "computers." It's fine to start broad, but do yourself a favor and narrow your topic sufficiently so that you will have a specific *focus* to guide your research and shape your argument. If your topic is too broad, you'll flounder around and end up saying a whole lot of nothing. You can try brainstorming to narrow a topic, and you can also do a bit of research to uncover a particular angle or focus for your topic.

Maybe you're interested in "sports" as a topic, and because you're planning a career as a counselor specializing in adolescents, you narrow your topic to "the effects of sports participation on high school athletes." Doing a little research, you find an article about "contact sports and their negative impact on the developing adolescent brain." Bam. You've found a workable topic.

way too broad:	"sports"
getting there:	"effects of sports participation on high school athletes"
narrowed topic:	"negative effects of contact sports on the adolescent brain"

Finding a Thesis/Claim

Once you have settled on a topic, it's time to start moving toward your thesis, sometimes called your "claim" in persuasive writing. What is it, exactly, that you are going to be arguing? What's the main point that you're hoping to persuade your readers to consider? The answer to those questions is your thesis.

A workable thesis is a complete statement that has two parts: a subject and a focus. The subject is *the topic* you're writing about, and the focus is *what you are claiming about that topic*. Consider this thesis statement:

Body Mass Index (BMI) alone is not a reliable indicator of overall health.		
The subject	=	Body Mass Index (BMI) alone . . .
The focus	=	. . . is not a reliable indicator of overall health.

For a persuasive paper, your thesis should be debatable or controversial. It needs to be a statement that has not been proven beyond any doubt—a statement with which not everyone would agree. Granted, a statement of fact might lead you to a thesis, but it cannot itself be a persuasive thesis. Consider this movement from factual evidence to a debatable thesis:

Fact #1: According to a recent survey by the Pew Research Center, "[S]martphone ownership has become a nearly ubiquitous element of teen life: 95% of teens now report they have a smartphone or access to one. These mobile connections are in turn fueling more-persistent online activities: 45% of teens now say they are online on a near-constant basis."

Anderson, M., & Jiang, J. (2018). *Teens, social media & technology 2018*. Retrieved from http://www.pewinternet.org /2018/05/31/teens-social-media-technology-2018/

Fact #2: In a study reported in *Educational Psychology*, some students were allowed to use their electronic devices during class. The study found that "divided attention reduced long-term *retention* of the classroom lecture, which impaired subsequent unit exam and final exam performance."

Glass, A. L., & Kang, M. (2018). Dividing attention in the classroom reduces exam performance. *Educational Psychology*. doi:10.1080/01443410.2018.1489046

Resulting Thesis: The subject of this thesis is "electronic devices during class," and the focus is the claim that "teachers should limit the amount of time students are allowed to use them."

> *Teachers should limit the amount of time students are allowed to use electronic devices during class.*

Note an extreme version of this thesis, which would likely be less convincing:

> *Teachers must never allow the use of electronic devices during class.*

The use of *must* and *never* in that second thesis would make the writer sound inflexible and unreasonable—and it would also make the writer's claim harder to prove. Such a claim ignores the possibility that there might, in fact, be some circumstances when electronic devices in the classroom would be advantageous.

When you're working with a controversial thesis, chances are good that you're not going to be proving your point beyond the shadow of a doubt. In such cases, you will sound more reasonable if you use wiggle-room qualifiers such as these:

may	typically	much
might	rarely	likely
can	often	possibly
could	many	probably

instead of absolute words such as these:

will	always	certainly
would	never	
must	all	

Bottom line: Qualify your claims to keep your tone reasonable and your thesis workable.

Here's something else to keep in mind: Contrary to what many novice writers believe, you don't necessarily *start* with a thesis once you've chosen your topic. In fact, if you start with a thesis—say, "Having divorced parents negatively affects a child's emotional development"—and then start looking for research to support that thesis, you're guilty of a critical thinking flaw called confirmation bias. Under the influence of confirmation bias, you might overlook key information simply because it does not support (or confirm) your pre-conceived thesis.

It's better to start with a research question (which your thesis will later attempt to answer):

- Are electronic devices in the classroom conducive to learning?
- Is gender binary?
- Is divorce bad for children?
- Does tracking sex offenders make us safe?

Such a question will guide your research and lead you to evidence supporting a specific claim—and that claim becomes your working thesis. It's known as a "working thesis" because it may well change slightly or significantly as you continue researching, thinking, and writing. But for now you have a focus for your paper, and that focus will lead you to the material that you will use to support—or prove—that thesis. To be especially clear and direct, you can introduce your thesis by writing something like "This paper will demonstrate. . . ." or "In this paper, I will argue that. . . ."

Persuasive Structure Options

Some people prefer to do as much research as possible on a topic and gather as much material as possible before they even start to think about how they might organize all of that potential content into a paper. A problem with that strategy is that it can be overwhelming. You could end up with so much material that you're essentially buried by it, or at the very least confused by it.

Instead, it might help to think *first* about some possible ways to structure a persuasive paper, and then, as you conduct your research and gather material, you'll have a better idea of what you're looking for—what information/evidence slots you might be trying to fill, what sections of your paper you'll end up writing. Start by looking at some common structures for a persuasive paper (covered below). Then, as you research and compile notes/sources, you'll begin to get a sense of how those notes/sources could naturally plug into whichever persuasive structure best fits your material.

Problem–Solution Structure.   This common structure calls for describing a problem and then arguing for a particular solution to that problem. Depending upon the length requirement for your paper and the amount of material you uncover in your research, you might begin by describing the problem and then propose just your one recommended solution, arguing why it's a feasible solution—and addressing any possible arguments against it. For a longer paper, you might describe the problem and then discuss multiple solutions that have been tried and/or proposed. You will explain why those solutions are less than ideal: Perhaps they solve only part of the problem, perhaps they are too expensive or impractical, perhaps they solve the initial problem but then create new problems of their own—whatever. Finally, you will fully introduce and defend *your* solution. Here, then, are the obvious slots to fill in this kind of structure:

- Description of the Problem. Be as specific as possible, using statistics, quotations, examples, narration, historical context, and/or other forms of evidence to demonstrate that a serious problem exists.
- One or More Solutions beyond the One for Which You Will Be Arguing (Optional). This section will also need to include evidence and reasoning to demonstrate why you do not recommend this solution or these solutions.
- Your Proposed Solution. Provide evidence supporting it, and address any possible opposition to your solution (more on dealing with the opposition later in this chapter).

Pro–Con Structure.

In this case, *pro* means "arguments for your thesis," and *con* means "arguments against your thesis." You will begin with an introduction that concludes with your thesis—and then you will present the pro arguments supporting that thesis, followed by any con arguments opposing your thesis. It's best to arrange those pro arguments (probably devoting a paragraph or more to each pro argument) in a "sandwich" fashion: Start with your second-strongest pro argument, and conclude the pro section with your strongest pro argument, sandwiching your weaker pro arguments in between those two strongest arguments. Don't feel a need to bring up every possible pro argument—just the most significant or convincing ones. Follow the pro section with the con section. What arguments might a reasonable person raise against your thesis? What evidence have you uncovered that contradicts your thesis? In the con section, you raise these concerns and then address them somehow, demonstrating the flaws in their reasoning, perhaps, or otherwise discrediting them. If an opposing viewpoint seems valid, concede that point but explain why you still argue in favor of your thesis. Again, don't feel compelled to dredge up every possible opposing point in your con section, just the most prominent ones. Here are the obvious slots to fill in a pro–con structure:

- Introduction with Your Thesis. Your introductory section might include background or context for the issue you will be analyzing, and you will build to your thesis.
- Pro Arguments Supporting Your Thesis. Include all the significant evidence you can assemble to prove the strength of those arguments, and arrange them so that you begin and end with your strongest arguments.
- Con Arguments Opposing Your Thesis. Sometimes novice writers include the opposing viewpoints but then neglect to address/refute them. Don't make that mistake! Raise the opposition—but then address it effectively before moving on.

Con–Pro Structure.   You can probably guess that this common strategy has the same elements as the pro–con structure—but in a different order. As before, you will start by introducing your topic and providing your thesis; however, before launching into the arguments supporting your thesis, you will first deal with the opposition. Once the con arguments have been effectively swept aside, you are in a good position to drive home the convincing arguments supporting your thesis. Again, an effective strategy is to begin this pro section with your second-strongest argument and to end it with your strongest argument, sandwiching any weaker arguments in the middle. Your structure, then, will follow this pattern:

- Introduction with Your Thesis.
- Con Arguments Opposing Your Thesis. Be sure to address these effectively before moving on to the pro section.
- Pro Arguments Supporting Your Thesis. Organize these in a "sandwich fashion" with your weaker arguments sandwiched between your stronger arguments.

Comparison–Contrast Structure.   With this structure you look at two or more subjects (i.e., theories, approaches, lifestyles, studies, policies, whatever) and compare (look at similarities), contrast (look at differences), or do both (look at similarities *and* differences). Keep in mind that you're writing a persuasive paper, so your purpose in comparing/contrasting will be to show that one is better than the other(s)—and this opinion will be your thesis. Let's say you'll be comparing/contrasting two subjects, which we'll label X and Y. You have two options for structuring such a paper: Block style has you presenting all the information about X and then all the information about Y. Point-by-point style has you discussing one point (or characteristic) about X and Y, and then another point about X and Y, and then another point about X and Y, and so on.

Assume, for example, that you are comparing/contrasting soccer and football as contact sports. In *block style*, you might first analyze soccer in terms of a variety of points like injuries to limbs, brain damage, and emotional impact, and then you would analyze football in terms of those same three points. In other words, you would have a block of your paper where you discuss soccer, and a block of your paper where you discuss football. Within each block, it will be important to discuss your points of comparison (limbs, brain, emotion) in the same order. In *point-by-point* style, you might first analyze injuries to limbs for both soccer and football, and then brain damage for both soccer and football, and finally emotional impact for both soccer and football. As you research for comparison–contrast structure, you will need to uncover information to fill these slots:

- Points of Comparison—Similarities—Among the Subjects You're Researching.
- Points of Contrast—Differences—Among the Subjects You're Researching.

Historical Structure.   Here you will trace the evolution of your topic over time. This structure can serve a variety of purposes. For example, if you demonstrate that over time attitudes have deteriorated or that a certain practice has changed for the worse, perhaps you will then argue for a remedy or a solution (see Problem–Solution Structure above). Or maybe you will demonstrate that social norms have changed over time—and then argue that certain policies or laws should therefore be amended to reflect those changes. The structural slots are obvious; it's just a matter of deciding how far back you want to start:

- Events/Attitudes/Theories, Etc. From the Distant Past. You would include, of course, your own analysis and commentary on these subjects at this and every chronological stage in your historical approach.
- Events/Attitudes/Theories, Etc. From the Not-So-Distant Past.
- Current Events/Attitudes/Theories.
- Proposed Action/Solution as a Result of Changes Occurring Over Time. As with any proposed action/solution, you'll need to address any resistance or opposition to what you propose.

Methodological Analysis Structure.   This persuasive structure is especially common within scientific disciplines. With this approach, you will examine a study (X) to demonstrate flaws in its method, thus discrediting its results. You would do this if you wanted to persuade your readers that an alternative study (Y) with contradictory results from study X is superior—and its conclusion(s) should therefore be accepted over the conclusion(s) of study X. Or you might conduct a methodological analysis in order to persuade readers that a new study needs to be conducted—one that corrects the flaws you've identified in study X. Your analysis need not be limited to just one study; often this approach examines multiple studies in order to prove a writer's thesis. Key elements of this paper will examine the method of each study under review:

- Analysis of Participants.
- Analysis of Materials.
- Analysis of Design/Variables.
- Analysis of Procedure.

As you draft your paper—perhaps one of the common persuasive structure options listed above, or some combination/adaptation of those structures—keep in mind that it is often necessary to include some background material toward the beginning of your paper. This background could provide context for your reader and could describe your issue before you launch into your persuasive argument.

As you develop the body of your paper, use headings/subheadings and transitions to guide your reader through whatever persuasive structure you're using. APA style prescribes five different levels of headings and subheadings, so refer to the later chapter in this book that covers those levels to ensure that you get the formatting correct. Chances are, you won't use all five levels—probably just the first two or three. Essentially, though, you ought to be able to remove everything but the headings and subheadings from your paper, and a reader would have a basic idea of your paper's structure. (Tip: Don't use an "Introduction" heading to begin your paper. Readers will already know that the beginning of your paper is the introduction; they don't need to be guided in that direction.)

Beyond headings and subheadings, you can guide your readers by using transitional words and phrases common in persuasive writing.

To add or expand upon a point:

in addition	moreover	likewise
additionally	also	to pursue this point further
furthermore	even more important	to follow up

To provide an example:

for example	specifically
for instance	such as
to illustrate	

To introduce or address a *con* (opposing) argument:

granted	one (perceived) downside	yet
admittedly	an opposing view	instead
some have argued	regardless	even so
(or contended)	still	nonetheless
while	in spite of	nevertheless
even though	despite	

To emphasize a point:

clearly	obviously	of course
indeed	again	
undoubtedly	in fact	

To discuss similarities:

similarly	in the same way	in a similar manner
like	along those same lines	(or fashion or way)
likewise	as with	also
too		

To shift your line of reasoning:

however	in contrast	yet
but	nevertheless	
on the contrary	on the other hand	

To signal a summary or a conclusion:

in other words	in short	thus
in summary	as noted earlier	therefore
to sum up	as we have seen	
to summarize	on the whole	

Addressing Your Opposition

More than once already in this chapter we have mentioned that you should consider opposing points of view in your persuasive paper. You might be wondering, "Why would I want to bring up opposing points that go against my claim/thesis?" Here are several good reasons for doing just that:

- It shows that you have a thorough understanding of the topic—not just a narrow understanding of only your own point of view. If you fail to address the opposition, then you're taking an oversimplified view of the topic and failing to appreciate its complexity. Astute readers will spot that weakness and will be less likely to accept your claim.

- If you can raise opposing points and then address them effectively—perhaps by showing how those opposing arguments lack evidence or relevance—then you can strengthen your own argument. Even if you end up conceding an opposing point (that is, you agree that the opposition has a valid point), you can nevertheless go on to argue for the greater strength of your own view. And making that concession shows you to be a reasonable thinker and writer.

- Just because you don't raise opposing arguments, that doesn't mean that they are not lurking somewhere in the minds of your readers. Opposing arguments are out there, so ignoring them does your own claim no favors. You're far better off raising those arguments yourself and addressing them effectively.

- Considering the opposition is a key way to develop your paper. If nothing else, you might be facing certain word-count or page-length requirements for your paper, and considering the opposition is one way to expand your thinking—and expand the length of your paper (without padding, wordiness, or repetition, which are all ineffective strategies students sometimes resort to in order to meet length requirements).

The Three Persuasive Appeals

Trying to persuade someone to consider your viewpoint is a practice that has been around for centuries. Back in the 4th century B.C., Aristotle proposed three types of appeals one could use to persuade an audience:

- Pathos (the appeal based on emotion)
- Ethos (the appeal based on the credibility and integrity of the person trying to do the persuading—that is, the speaker or the writer)
- Logos (the appeal based on logic/reason)

Pathos.   That first one, pathos, does not apply much to the kind of scholarly writing involved when writing a persuasive research paper for psychology. Stirring up a reader's emotions—whether they be feelings of fear, joy, compassion, anger, patriotism, jealousy, love, or whatever—is an approach better suited for other types of writing, like an editorial or a political speech. Do not rely on the emotional appeal when writing your persuasive paper for psychology.

Ethos.   Ethos, however, is critical when writing a persuasive research paper for psychology. If you write in such a way that readers trust you and believe you to be reasonable, intelligent, and fair, then you stand a much better chance of being persuasive than if you come across as careless, uninformed, and biased. So how do you convince your readers that you are, indeed, someone worth listening to? In fact, we have already made recommendations that will bolster your character in the eyes of your readers. For example, qualifying your claims by using words such as *some, usually,* and *rarely* instead of extreme words such as *all, always,* and *never* will help you to sound reasonable. Considering the opposition will also help you to project an informed and reasonable persona. Citing credible sources, organizing your ideas clearly, proofreading your sentences carefully, following APA format accurately—all these steps will increase your reader's opinion of you and will, therefore, make your writing more persuasive.

Logos.   Logos—appealing to your reader's sense of logic and reasoning—are especially important when writing persuasively. Your argument must be *sound*: It must be based on statements that are true. And it must be *valid*: It must follow logically from those statements. What follows is a crash-course in logic designed to help you construct logical arguments—and to recognize faulty logic when you encounter it in others' speech or writing.

Two Types of Reasoning

Inductive Reasoning is a form of argument based on evidence, on probability. When arguing inductively, avoid overstating or speaking in absolutes.

- NOT: All college students binge drink.
- BETTER: Many (or Some) college students binge drink
- BEST: According to a study reported by the National Institute on Health, 40% of college students aged 18 to 22 binge drank within a given month. https://pubs.niaaa.nih.gov/publications/CollegeFactSheet/Collegefactsheet.pdf

Inductive reasoning shows trends and suggests probability, but it does not *prove* anything. It demonstrates only the likelihood that something is true. Also, be sure that any inductive conclusion is drawn from a large enough sample of evidence so that you avoid making a faulty generalization (see "Logical Fallacies" below). If the sample size (i.e., the number in the subset of a given population under study) is too small to represent the larger population fairly, any conclusions drawn will run the risk of being invalid.

Deductive Reasoning is a form of argument based on absolutes (all, none, every, always, never) and on an arrangement of premises leading to a logical conclusion—known as a syllogism. (Note that this instance—that is, when constructing a logical syllogism—is one time when absolute language is acceptable.) Below is a sample syllogism:

- Major Premise: <u>All childhood trauma</u> can lead to PTSD.
- Minor Premise: *Spanking* is a form of <u>childhood trauma</u>.
- Conclusion: *Spanking* can lead to PTSD.

Here's the structure of a deductive syllogism arranged as a sentence:

- If <u>MAJOR PREMISE</u>, and if **MINOR PREMISE**, then *CONCLUSION*.
- If all childhood trauma can lead to PTSD, and if spanking is a form of childhood trauma, then spanking can lead to PTSD.

For your conclusion to be true, you must prove that your major and minor premises are true. For the syllogism above, the minor premise—"Spanking is a form of childhood trauma"—will probably be the more difficult premise to prove true. It will likely hinge on how you define *spanking*. By *spanking*, do you mean a single swat on the bottom with an adult's hand? Multiple swats with an adult's hand? Multiple hard swats with a flyswatter? With a wooden paddle or a belt? With a 2x4? Clearly, defining your terms can be a vital part of any argument.

Note also that the elements—the parts of the syllogism—have to be distributed properly throughout the syllogism, demonstrated in the PTSD syllogism with the <u>underlining</u>, bold-face, and *italics*:

- Major Premise: <u>All childhood trauma</u> can lead to PTSD.
- Minor Premise: *Spanking* is a form of <u>childhood trauma</u>.
- Conclusion: *Spanking* can lead to PTSD.

Note this illogical syllogism below (illogical because the elements are not distributed properly):

- Major Premise: <u>All childhood trauma</u> can lead to PTSD.
- Minor Premise: *Military service* can lead to PTSD.
- (Illogical) Conclusion: *Military service* is a form of <u>childhood trauma</u>.

Here's a more logical conclusion because the elements have been distributed properly:

- Major Premise: <u>Military service</u> can lead to PTSD.
- Minor Premise: *The Army National Guard* is a type of <u>military service</u>.
- Conclusion: *The Army National Guard* can lead to PTSD.

Logical Fallacies.   Aside from the logical missteps we've already covered, be on the lookout for any of these logical fallacies, which are common examples of faulty reasoning.

Ad hominem.   You're guilty of this fallacy if you attack an irrelevant aspect of someone's personal character rather than focusing on the issue at hand. *Ad hominem* means, literally, "against the man."

> "Being divorced, he can have no authority as a marriage counselor."

Bandwagon appeal. This is the "everyone else is doing it" appeal. The majority view is not necessarily the right or appropriate view. Further evidence is needed.

> "Many high schools in the U.S. issue electronic devices to their students, so those devices must be conducive to learning."

Circular reasoning. Circular reasoning happens when you assume what you're trying to prove, so you essentially talk in circles:

> "Cellphones are bad for a child because they have such a negative impact." (Essentially, you're saying they're bad because they're bad.)

Either-Or. Rarely are there just two options. This fallacy overlooks the existence of other realistic possibilities.

> "Either parents spank their children or society becomes plagued with irresponsible and potentially criminal adolescents."

False analogy. An analogy (a type of comparison) can help to illustrate a concept, but it does not *prove* anything.

> "Eliminating football from high school athletics would be like eliminating apple pie from the American diet."

False authority. False authority relies on a celebrity's opinion or testimonial when that celebrity, in fact, has no real expertise on the topic under discussion.

> "Denzel Washington has taken a stand against same-sex marriage. As a respected actor, he is someone whose opinion we should heed."

Faulty generalization (or sweeping generalization or hasty generalization). This is simply an inductive argument drawn from a sample that is too small or is not representative.

> *"All five of the high school girls surveyed about stress reported that it did not have a negative impact on their sleep. Clearly, stress does not disrupt sleep."*

Non-Sequitur. A non-sequitur means that you have not demonstrated a logical connection. The term literally means "it does not follow." You need to make the logical connection before your claim can be considered valid.

> *"If more parents spanked their children, we would have fewer juvenile delinquents."*

Faulty causal argument (post hoc). Just because occurrence Y happened after occurrence X, we cannot necessarily assume that occurrence X *caused* occurrence Y. Much more research would be needed to demonstrate a causal link. (Note: This fallacy is often called *post hoc* because it comes from the Latin phrase *post hoc ergo propter hoc*, which means, literally, "after this, therefore because of this.")

> *"Two students in Weber Hall have reported dating violence that occurred after a home football game. Clearly, the violence associated with football is spilling over into student relationships."*

Slippery slope. Sometimes this fallacy is also called the *Domino Effect* or the *Snowball Effect*. Essentially, it means you're assuming without sufficient evidence that one relatively small step will lead to a chain reaction that will result in a (usually negative) outcome; therefore, that first small step should be avoided.

> *"If we legalize marijuana, what will be next? Legalized methamphetamine? Legalized heroin?"*

Straw man. If you paint the opposing view in an exaggerated, distorted, or misleading way in order to make it easy for you to knock it down, you're guilty of the straw man fallacy.

Be sure that you truly understand the opposing viewpoint, and present it clearly and fairly, before you begin to address it.

> *"Smith argues that women should not engage in frontline combat. Clearly, he believes women should stay in the kitchen or the bedroom, where they belong."*

Persuasive Writing Rubric

A rubric is simply a chart that displays the criteria (running down the column at the far left of the rubric) that your instructor could be using to evaluate your persuasive paper—and the standards (running horizontally across from each criterion) that determine how well you've met each of those criteria. You can use the rubric displayed in Figure 1 as you work on your persuasive paper to be sure that you're covering all your bases. You can also use it during peer review—and be sure to take it with you if you visit your campus writing center. It is designed to help you during the drafting and revising stages of your persuasive writing process.

Figure 1 Persuasive Writing Rubric by Fort Hays State University Writing Across the Curriculum

	Not Proficient=1	Developing Proficiency=2	Proficient=3	Exceeding Proficiency=4	Points
A clear and debatable thesis	No clear thesis.	Writer has a thesis, but it is too broad or too narrow, is not obviously debatable (more a statement of accepted fact), and/or is poorly worded.	Clear and debatable thesis (is neither too broad nor too narrow, is obviously debatable, and is clearly stated).	Significant and debatable thesis is exceptionally clear and well stated.	
Fully developed and supported ideas	Little or no development. Ideas are often stated and then dropped. Repetition/Restatement is confused with support.	Some evidence of development and support (examples, explanation, analysis, evidence, quotations, and the like), but important claims still lack full development/support.	Sufficient evidence of development and support throughout (examples, explanation, analysis, evidence, quotations, and the like).	All ideas are richly developed in exceptional depth.	
Clear organizational structure	Disorganized and hard to follow throughout.	Somewhat easy to follow with logical, persuasive organization and clear transitions—though at times the reader might be confused and/or the transitions might be lacking or inappropriate.	Easy to follow the writer's logic and overall arrangement of ideas. Writer uses clear transitional devices such as transitions, effective repetition of key words, clearly labeled sections, and pronouns (e.g., this study).	Polished organization and coherence make this essay effortless to read.	
Effective consideration of opposing arguments	No opposing arguments are raised—or if they are, they are irrelevant and/or inconsequential.	Relevant and consequential opposing arguments are raised but are not adequately developed, not adequately addressed, or both.	Relevant and consequential opposing arguments are raised, adequately developed, and adequately addressed.	The most important opposing arguments are raised, thoroughly developed, and masterfully addressed.	

	Not Proficient = 1	Developing Proficiency = 2	Proficient = 3	Exceeding Proficiency = 4	Points
Use of credible sources	No use of outside sources.	Use of outside sources, but with problems of quantity, quality (credibility), and/or presentation (clumsy handling).	Good use of sufficient credible sources (scholarly/expert, peer-reviewed, unbiased). Quotations are handled with skill. Paraphrases are accurate and focused.	Extensive and thoughtful use of highly credible outside sources—smooth incorporation of quotations and paraphrases.	
Appropriate documentation of sources	Either no documentation or seriously inadequate documentation. Plagiarism might be evident.	APA documentation style is applied, but with many errors.	APA documentation style is applied with reasonable accuracy.	APA documentation style is applied with near perfection.	
Consideration of a target audience	No evidence of audience consideration: word choice, sentence style, and content are possibly too informal or formal for the audience—or too jargon-filled or simplistic for the audience. Bottom line: the language and/or content seem inappropriate for the audience.	Some evidence of audience consideration: appropriate word choice, sentence style, and content overall—with many lapses.	Consistent evidence of audience consideration: appropriate word choice, sentence style, and content overall—with minor lapses only.	Style and content are exceptionally well tailored to the needs and interests of the target audience.	
Conventional grammar and mechanics	Frequent and serious errors keep pulling the reader's attention away from the essay's content.	Essay contains some errors, but readers are still able to focus on the writer's meaning without much trouble.	Essay might contain a few errors, but they don't significantly distract.	Masterful command of the conventions of standard written English—minor errors only, or perhaps no discernible errors whatsoever.	

Total Score: _____

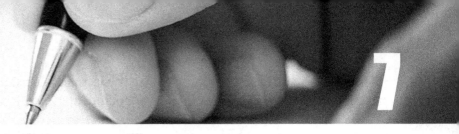

Good Writing

by Cheryl Duffy, PhD

What is "good writing"? Unfortunately, there's no simple answer to that question—unless you'll accept the answer "It depends." It depends upon a consideration of the audience, purpose, and persona. Who will be reading what you write? That's your audience. What do you hope to accomplish—what effect do you hope to have on your reader? That's your purpose. How do you want to come across—what kind of voice, personality, or image do you hope to project? That's your persona. You can imagine that a piece of "good writing" intended by a comedian to make college students laugh might look quite different from a piece of "good writing" intended by a psychologist to make other psychologists change their minds about an accepted therapy practice.

Audience, Purpose, and Persona in Writing for Psychology

Audience.   Of course, your audience might vary. As a student, your audience will, of course, be your professor, but that professor will often expect you to write as if your audience were members of the profession you're hoping to join soon—i.e., an audience of fellow psychologists. In either case—a professor or fellow psychologists—you can see that a polished, formal tone will serve you best. (The chapter on "Types of Writing" opens with a helpful discussion of informal versus formal tone.) At times, your professor might even have you specify your (hypothetical) audience: for example, high school guidance counselors.

> As you think about your audience, ask yourself these questions:
> - What does my audience know?
> - What does my audience believe?
> - What biases might my audiences have?
> - What does my audience need?
> - What does my audience expect?
> - Is my audience friendly or hostile?

The answers to those questions will help you make decisions about everything from word choice to examples to organization to documentation format.

Purpose.   Most writing for an outside audience falls under three general purposes:

- To entertain
- To inform
- To persuade

A piece of writing might accomplish just one of those purposes or some combination of the three. A piece of satire written for *The Onion*, for example, will sometimes make readers laugh while also persuading them to change their behavior. A term paper for a psychology class might inform readers of a problem and then persuade them which solution is best. The vast majority of the writing you do in psychology will not aim to entertain but to inform and/or persuade. If you consider those two purposes combined with your professor/ psychologist audience, you will see the need for writing that is clear, direct, and professional.

Persona.   When you write, the last thing you want to sound like is an uninformed, biased novice. We designed this book, in fact, to keep that from happening! If you read these chapters carefully and make an honest effort to apply the principles covered in these chapters, you will develop a persona that is intelligent, professional, clear, and fair—even though you are, most likely, still a novice.

NOTE: See the "Specific Types of Writing Common in Psychology" section of the "Types of Writing" chapter for more examples of audience, purpose, and persona.

Handling Quotations

The smooth handling of quotations is one sure way to enhance the credibility of your persona and meet audience expectations. To illustrate, we'll start with material from page 420 of an outside source:

"Additionally, the type of presence used in the previous research has also been inconsistent."

Source: Claypoole, V. L., & Szalma, J. L. (2018). Facilitating sustained attention: Is mere presence sufficient? *The American Journal of Psychology, 131*(4), 417–428.

Let's look at some ways you might incorporate that material into a paper you're writing:

Signal Phrase + Comma + Quotation.

Claypoole and Szalma (2018) note, "[T]he type of presence used in the previous research has . . . been inconsistent" (p. 420).

If you provide the names of the authors in the signal phrase—"Claypoole and Szalma (2018) note"—be sure to put the year of publication in parentheses after the author(s). Put a comma after the signal word (*note*) if you use a quotation that is a complete sentence (as this one is).

Use brackets [ ] whenever you add something to a quotation that was not in the original. In this example, the capital T has been added because in the original it was a lower-case t—but we need a capital T to start the sentence.

Use ellipsis dots . . . to indicate that the writer has left something out in the middle of a quotation. In this case, the word *also* was omitted. To type ellipses, place a space before, between, and after the dots. If you're quoting from two or more sentences and the material you leave out includes the end of at least one sentence, then you'll use four dots: one for the period and the other three for the ellipsis. Don't type a space before the first dot whenever you're typing four dots.

If there's a page number to cite, put it in parentheses after the quotation. To cite the page number, put "p." and a space before the page number. If you have more than one page to cite, you'll use "pp.": for example (Smith, 2016, pp. 32–33). Save the period for your sentence until after the parenthetical page number.

Authors Not Mentioned in a Signal Phrase.

> Researchers have found that "the type of presence used in the previous research has also been inconsistent" (Claypoole & Szalma, 2018, p. 420).

If you don't mention the authors in a signal phrase, you will list them in parentheses following the quotation. In the example above, note that you, again, save the period until after your parenthetical citation. Also note that within that citation, you separate the items with a comma after the author(s) and after the year.

When the word *that* precedes your quotation, you do not capitalize the first word of the quotation—even if it looks like a complete sentence. The reason? Using *that* automatically converts your quotation into part of a noun clause beginning with *that*, so it's technically no longer a complete sentence that would need to start with a capital letter. For the same reason, you do not include a comma before the quotation when you use *that* to introduce the quotation.

Quoting Just a Word or Phrase.

> Claypoole and Szalma (2018) found inconsistencies in "the type of presence used" in studies that preceded their own (p. 420).

In the above example, note that sometimes it might be preferable to quote just part of the original sentence, in which case you do not use commas on either side of the quotation.

Handling Long Quotations (more than 40 words)

If you have a quotation that is longer than 40 words, you handle it a little bit differently from a short quotation:

- Introduce a long quotation with a colon : rather than a comma.
- Indent *every line* of your long quotation as a block of text ½ inch from the left margin (i.e., the same amount that you would indent the first line of a paragraph). An easy way to do that in Word is to hit Ctrl+m before typing the first word of your quotation. This will indent your margin one tab. When you're done, hit Ctrl+Shift+m to return to the original left margin.
- Do <u>not</u> use quotation marks for this indented long quotation. Indenting already tells your reader that this is a direct quotation, so you don't need the quotation marks.
- If you have a parenthetical citation after your long quotation, you will put the period *before* the parenthetical citation, unlike with short quotations, when you put the period *after* the parenthetical citation. In other words, with a long quotation, you will not have a period after the final parenthesis.

Paraphrase to Avoid Quoting Too Much

As a final suggestion, try not to fill your writing with too many quotations from outside sources. Remember that paraphrasing—putting the information in your own words—is perfectly acceptable and sometimes even preferable to all of the trappings of quotation marks and indentations. Just remember, you still must cite your source even when you paraphrase:

> Claypoole and Szalma (2018) faulted earlier research for inconsistencies regarding the kinds of performance measured as well as the kinds of presence applied.

Style

To repeat a common refrain: Be clear and direct. Clear and direct writing is professional writing that readers easily understand. Part of being clear and direct is adopting a formal tone rather than a conversational, informal tone.

Be careful, though, not to swing so far away from a familiar writing style that you end up producing a style of writing that Ken Macrorie (Nordquist, 2019), a composition theorist, once labeled as "Engfish." Engfish is student writing that is convoluted and awkward, full of phrasing that just doesn't sound natural and contains unnecessarily "big" words. Use language that is *natural* without being too *informal*. Your goal is to sound professional and scholarly—but that does not have to mean stiff and wordy. Below are three sentences that illustrate what we mean. Each one says essentially the same thing, but the first one comes closest to the style of writing you should aim for in your writing for psychology.

Clear and Direct.   A psychologist's first step is to determine what is causing a client's anxiety.

Too Informal:

I believe that Job One for a psychologist is trying to get to the bottom of what's causing your anxiety.

Several elements of this sentence make it too informal: the use of first-person ("I") and second-person ("your") pronouns, the contraction "what's" for "what is," and the borderline-slang expressions "Job One" and "get to the bottom of."

A Wordy Piece of Engfish:

Before embarking upon a procedure of psychological treatment, a psychologist will initially at the primary stages of interaction with his or her client seek, with as much accuracy as possible, a kind of ascertainment of the underlying cause or causes residing at the very root of a client's anxiety that has prompted that client to pursue professional diagnosis and resolution in the first place.

That last example is a bit of an exaggeration, but, sadly, student writing sometimes approaches that level of cluttered and confusing sentence structure. How does that happen? Sometimes, a student writer is simply trying too hard to sound smart. Sometimes, a student writer drags out a sentence and packs it full of big words and convoluted phrases in a misguided attempt to lengthen the paper—i.e., to meet a word- or page-count requirement. Don't make that mistake! Your professor is a *reader* first, and if you bog down your sentences with Engfish, your reader (your professor) will become frustrated and irritated. That's not the effect you're after—and you won't be doing your grade any favors.

If you're worried that your paper will be too short or undeveloped, you have better options for lengthening it besides resorting to Engfish:

- Conduct more research that you can include to develop your ideas.
- Provide additional background information and/or historical context that is relevant to your thesis.

- Be sure that you have fully explained your ideas and have provided sufficient examples. Refer to the "General Modes of Writing" section in the "Types of Writing" chapter for ways you can develop your ideas.

- If appropriate to your topic, discuss opposing views that might challenge your ideas—and address them fully.

Be Concise.   One way to achieve a clear and direct style is to be concise. That is, don't use words you don't need. Here are four ways to do just that:

Cut Out the Deadwood (excess words)

Don't write this:	When you can write this:
all of a sudden	suddenly
in spite of the fact that	although
at all times	always
in the event that	if
for the purpose of	for
due to the fact that	because
at that point in time	then
at the present time	currently (or *today* or *now*)
the book that she wrote	the book she wrote

Test *that* to see if you need it or can easily omit it. For example, in which of these sentences can you omit *that* and still have a perfectly fine English sentence?

A. *A policy that addresses homelessness is long overdue.*

B. *A policy that he proposed will address homelessness.*

If you chose "B," you are correct. It would be perfectly fine—and a bit more concise—to write, "A policy he proposed will address homelessness." (In case you're a curious soul who doesn't mind a bit of "grammar talk," here's the explanation for why sentences work that way: When a relative clause begins with *that*, sometimes *that* is the subject for the verb in the clause—as it is with the verb *addresses* in A above—and therefore the *that* is grammatically necessary.)

Sometimes *that* merely introduces a relative clause that already includes its own subject for the verb—as with *he* and *proposed* in B above—in which case, the *that* can be omitted, making the sentence a bit more concise. If that explanation is just a bunch of grammatical gobbledygook to you, you can simply ignore it and rely on your ear to decide if a sentence sounds right when you take out *that*.

Avoid redundancy (needless repetition—a specific form of deadwood)

Don't write this:	When you can write this:
blue in color	blue
large in size	large
round in shape	round
heavy in weight	heavy
each and every	each (or *every*—pick one)
new innovations	innovations
repeat again	repeat
a period of one week	one week
revert back	revert
12 noon	noon
reason why	reason

Limit nominalizations (using wordy noun forms when a strong verb will suffice)

Don't write this:	When you can write this:
provide an education for	educate
complete the registration for	register
give an analysis of	analyze
issue an announcement of	announce
make a decision	decide
pass judgment on	judge
passed judgment on	judged

(i.e., the suggestion applies to both present and past tense verbs.)

In English, we often create nouns from verbs by adding -ion and -ment. *Educate* becomes *education; announce* becomes *announcement.* Look out for those noun forms as you edit for style to see if you can be more concise by using one strong verb instead of a more wordy noun phrase:

Schools must work for the equal education of all students.

Schools must educate all students equally.

Reduce Passive Voice.   Passive voice isn't always wrong—but it can be wordy and unnecessary. Consider this example:

Passive: *Clients <u>were instructed</u> by the counselor to keep a journal.*

Active: *The counselor <u>instructed</u> clients to keep a journal.*

You can see that the sentence written in passive voice takes more space to convey the same message—and aside from that fact, it sounds rather clunky. In passive voice, the verb consists of a being verb (like *be, am, is, are, was,* or *were*) plus a past participle (the verb form you would use with *have, has,* or *had*—like *have written* or *had instructed*). In "Clients were instructed by the counselor to keep a journal," the being verb is *were*, and the past participle form is *instructed*. Note that the subject (Clients) is passively receiving the action of the verb (were instructed). That's why it's called "passive voice"—because the subject is the passive receiver of the action—the clients are being instructed by someone else.

In active voice, the subject is the agent and performs the action of the verb. In "The counselor instructed clients to keep a journal," the subject (counselor) is the agent performing the action of the verb (instructed)—the counselor is doing the instructing.

Again, passive voice isn't always wrong—it just tends to be wordy, limp, and unnecessary much of the time.

> For example,
>   *"Freud is found by some critics to be narrow."*
>
> has more punch as
>   *"Some critics find Freud to be narrow."*

Generally, it's just good stylistic practice to have the subject DOING the action of the verb—and to keep the verbs strong (i.e., action verbs, not being verbs). Sometimes you have to ask WHO is doing WHAT in order to write in crisp active voice:

> Passive: *Many studies were conducted on the effects of spanking.*
>
> (Who or what is doing the conducting?)
> Active: *Researchers conducted many studies on the effects of spanking.*
>
> Passive: *Many statistical analyses are encountered in Young's work.*
> Active: *Readers encounter many statistical analyses in Young's work.*
> *or Young makes extensive use of statistical analysis.*

Important Exception in Writing for Psychology

One instance, however, when the passive voice is actually the standard that is preferred over active voice is when you're writing the "Method" section of a research report. Rather than overuse first-person pronouns like "I" or "we," you'll most likely use passive voice.

Not: *I grouped the participants by age.* (active voice)
Preferred: *The participants were grouped by age.* (passive voice)

Parallel Structure.   Notice how the second sentence reads a bit more smoothly than the first one:

A. Participants learn to make eye contact, use "I" statements, and active listening is encouraged.

B. Participants learn to make eye contact, use "I" statements, and listen actively.

Sentence B is smoother because it is parallel: All three things that participants learn are written in the same format. Each one begins with a verb: *make, use,* and *listen.* In Sentence A, that third item in the list is not parallel with the first two, which begin with verbs. Watch out for nonparallel structure whenever you have coordinate elements in a sentence (i.e., elements joined with a coordinating conjunction like *and, but, so, or, for, nor,* and *yet*) or whenever you have items in a list (like the list of three items in example sentences A and B above).

Nonparallel: Does anyone have the time to be a perfect student, supportive friend, and holding down a job?
Parallel: Does anyone have the time to be a perfect student, supportive friend, and reliable employee? Or Does anyone have the time to study, maintain friendships, and hold down a job?

Nonparallel: Viewers could be very well educated or only a high school diploma.
Parallel: Viewers could have a graduate degree or only a high school diploma.

Nonhuman Entities Performing Human Activities (Anthropomorphism).   In short, most psychology professors will prefer that you *not* write as if a study, article, theory, etc. can perform a human activity like assuming, drawing conclusions, pointing out, arguing, etc. Although we do this frequently in casual speaking, it's best to avoid the practice when writing for psychology. Consider these examples:

Not this: Becker's study concludes that. . . .
But this: Becker concludes that. . . .

Not this: These results argue that. . . .
But this: Theorists use these results to argue that. . . .

Not this: The article suggests counselors should. . . .
But this: In their article, Smith and Jones suggest counselors should. . . .

Positive Language.   As a general rule for clear, direct language, write in the positive style instead of the negative. Positive language is a strategic way to move an audience, especially if you are trying get them to act in a certain way. Note the subtle difference:

Negative: Students should not study their most difficult subject when they are not alert.
Positive: Students should study their most difficult subject when they are most alert.

Negative: Counselors must not neglect to keep thorough yet concise case notes.
Positive: Counselors must strive to keep thorough yet concise case notes.

Negative: Participants did not receive the instructions until midday.
Positive: Participants received the instructions at midday.

A key word to be on the lookout for is *not*. Often—but not always, of course—it is a signal that a sentence could be rewritten more positively.

Nuts and Bolts: Editing for Correctness

Beyond writing sentences that reflect a clear, direct, and professional style, you will also need to allow time toward the end of any writing project to edit for grammar and mechanics. Wait until you're satisfied with the content and organization of your writing before you worry about editing for correctness. After all, if you end up replacing or rewriting a paragraph during the drafting stage, it won't matter how well you had punctuated the sentences in that original paragraph. Plus, sometimes if you worry about correctness too much during the drafting stage, you run into writer's block or—at the very least—you distract yourself from the challenging mental work of developing and organizing your ideas. Just be sure that you *do* allow enough time before your deadline to do that final copyediting. Otherwise, that would be like baking a chocolate fudge cake from scratch and then frosting it with mud. Editing is the icing on the cake of your writing! Give it the time and energy that your strong content deserves.

What careful editing does:

- Provides clarity—ensures better understanding of your meaning
- Allows readers to focus on *what* you're saying rather than on *how* you're saying it

- Creates a persona (you, the writer) that is intelligent and attentive (One of the persuasive appeals, you'll remember, is "ethos," which is essentially the persuasive power of being the voice of someone worth listening to and believing. Editing well helps you to create that kind of voice.)

What neglectful editing does:

- Obscures meaning (sometimes)
- Distracts the reader away from the content/ideas
- Hurts the credibility of your writing (Almost every list of what to look for when determining a source's credibility includes "careful editing." Having editing errors in your paper will automatically bias your reader against what you're saying.)
- Creates a persona that might be perceived as someone who is either unintelligent or inattentive—or who simply does not care much about the subject or the document being written

Now that you know why it's important to edit your writing, where do you begin? Composition researcher Andrea Lunsford (with varied coresearchers) has conducted studies to discover the surface errors that show up most frequently in student writing (e.g., A. Lunsford & K. Lunsford, 2008). The section that follows provides an overview of those surface errors so that you can begin tackling the editing concerns most likely to show up in your writing. If a particular surface error is especially frequent or confusing for you, this brief overview might not be sufficient. In that case, track down a handbook or do an internet search to learn more about that subject.

Choosing the Right Word. Sometimes writers end up with the wrong word because they confuse two or more similar-sounding words (like *affect* and *effect*). Sometimes it's a matter of spelling and technology gone awry: You might misspell a word, and then the spell-check feature on your device makes a wrong guess about which word you were trying to spell. (You might mean *prescience*, but you misspell it as *prescious*, and your spell-checker corrects it to *precious*.) Sometimes you might simply have never encountered an irregular plural form that you need to use (like *crises* as the plural for *crisis*).

Commonly Confused Words. English handbooks often include whole chapters on this problem. Because of space constraints, we won't go into that much depth here, but we will cover just a few of the most common sources of confusion. Beyond those few, try googling "commonly confused words" if you'd like to delve deeper into similar-sounding words that cause even experienced writers to falter.

Affect versus effect. *Affect* is usually a verb meaning "to influence":

- How did the variables *affect* the outcome?
- Divorce *affected* the siblings in different ways.

Affect can, however, sometimes be used as a noun, especially in the fields of psychology and psychiatry. In such cases, it means "feeling" or "emotion"—or "an observed emotional response"—and is pronounced with the accent on the first syllable (AFF-ect):

- People with schizophrenia often display a flat or blunted *affect*.

Effect is usually a noun meaning "result":

- The *effect* was instantaneous.
- Alcohol use has many *effects* on one's behavior.

Effect can, however, sometimes be used as a verb meaning "to bring about as an effect": Researchers developed the treatment to *effect* cognitive change.

its versus it's.   Its without the apostrophe is a possessive pronoun (like *his*):

- The treatment lost *its* effect over time.

It's with the apostrophe is a contraction meaning either "It is" or "It has":

- *It's* time to learn this simple rule. (*It is* time to learn this simple rule.)
- *It's* been proven conclusively. (*It has* been proven conclusively.)

(For formal writing, you will typically avoid contractions like *it's*.)

There, their, they're.   Think of *there* as being similar to *here*—and note how much they look alike:

- Odd numbers go *here*, but the even numbers go *there*.
- *There* is a solution. (*Here* is a solution.)

Think of *their* along with the other possessive pronouns like *her, his, our, your,* and *its*:

- They lost *their* funding. (She lost *her* funding. He lost *his* funding. We lost *our* funding. You lost *your* funding. The clinic lost *its* funding.)

Think of *they're* (the contraction for "they are") along with similar contractions like *we're* or *you're*:

- Hooper believes *they're* wrong. (Hooper believes they are wrong.)
- Hooper believes *we're* wrong. (Hooper believes we are wrong.)
- Hooper believes *you're* wrong. (Hooper believes you are wrong.)

To versus too.   *To* can be either a preposition used with a noun (*to* the house) or an infinitive used with a verb (*to* write):

- Men came *to* the field willingly. (*to* as a preposition with the noun *field*)
- They began *to* dance to the music. (*to* as an infinitive with the verb *dance*)

Too can mean either "also" or "excessively; more than should be; or very":

- Women, *too*, worked on the project. (Women also worked on the project.)
- The intervention was *too* late. (The intervention was later than it should have been.)

Irregular Plurals.   Usually we indicate plural (i.e., more than one) by adding "s" or "es"—one paper, two papers; one box, two boxes. As you know, English contains many irregular plurals as well. You're no doubt familiar with most of those—children, mice, geese, etc.—but below is a list of additional irregular plurals that might not be as familiar to you. The plural options given in parentheses are becoming more common and accepted, but to be safe, you might want to stick with the more traditional irregular forms, especially for formal academic writing. For now, at least, opt for *appendices* over *appendixes*—or check with your instructor or editor.

curriculum	curricula (or curriculums)
datum	data
medium	media (or mediums)
memorandum	memoranda (or memorandums)
criterion	criteria (or criterions)
phenomenon	phenomena
alumna—feminine	alumnae—if all are women
alumnus—masculine	alumni—if all are men, or if including men *and* women
bacillus	bacilli
stimulus	stimuli
antithesis	antitheses
basis	bases
crisis	crises
ellipsis	ellipses
hypothesis	hypotheses
parenthesis	parentheses
prognosis	prognoses
thesis	theses
appendix	appendices (or appendixes)
index	indices (or indexes)
matrix	matrices (or matrixes)

Commas.   If you've been going by "When in doubt, leave it out" or "Put a comma wherever you pause," it's time for you to learn some actual rules! Part of the challenge with commas is the fact that formal English has so many rules governing their use. We won't cover them all here—just the most common rules you will encounter in your writing. And no, you will probably not master the grammatical terminology included here (like *coordinating conjunction* or *nonrestrictive clause*). Having those terms provided, however, will help you if you decide to do any further research on a rule: You'll know which keywords to use in your search.

Rule 1. Use a comma before a coordinating conjunction in a compound sentence (i.e., two sentences written as one). The coordinating conjunctions (called "the fanboys") are:

for	but	so
and	or	
nor	yet	

The clinic expanded its services, and soon the number of clients grew as well.
The results are invalid, for the sample size was too small.

Don't assume that you need a comma every time you see *and*. If the conjunction is joining two words or structures but is not joining two complete sentences, you do not need the comma:

The clinic expanded its services and doubled the number of clients seen each month. (*expanded* and *doubled*)

Rule 2. Use a comma when you use a semicolon (;) and a conjunctive adverb (like *however*) to join two complete sentences (also called *independent clauses*). (This is like rule #1, but instead of a comma and a coordinating conjunction, we're using a semicolon, a conjunctive adverb, and a comma to join two sentences.) Here's a long but partial list of conjunctive adverbs you can use to join sentences with a semicolon before and a comma after:

also	however	namely
anyway	incidentally	nevertheless
besides	indeed	next
certainly	in fact	now
finally	instead	otherwise
for example	likewise	similarly
for instance	meanwhile	still
furthermore	moreover	then
therefore	thus	undoubtedly

The clinic expanded its services.
+ *The number of clients doubled.*
= *The clinic expanded its services; therefore, the number of clients doubled.*

Note: Use commas only (no semicolon) when the adverb is not joining two sentences:
The number of counselors, however, did not double.

Rule 3. Use a comma after an introductory adverb clause. "Introductory" means it begins the sentence (or independent clause). Don't use a comma with an adverb clause that is not introductory. Adverb clauses begin with subordinating conjunctions like these:

After	If	Until
Although	In order that	When
As	Once	Where
As if	Since	Whether
Because	So that	While
Before	Though	
Even though	Unless	

> *If the clinic expands its services, it can expect an increase in the number of clients served.*

No comma below (because the adverb clause comes at the end of the sentence, not at the beginning):

> *The clinic can expect an increase in the number of clients served if the clinic expands its services.*
>
> *Because the stimulus was removed, the behavior ceased.*

No Comma: *The behavior ceased because the stimulus was removed.*

NOTE: There are a few exceptions when it's acceptable to add the comma even when the adverb clause does not begin a sentence. Those exceptions include clauses that begin with *although*, *even though*, and *as* (when it means "because"):

> Exceptions: *The behavior ceased, as the stimulus had been removed.*
>   *The behavior continued, even though the stimulus had been removed.*

Rule 4. Adverb clauses (rule #3) aren't the only kinds of introductory elements that call for a comma. Typically, you'll use a comma whenever you begin a sentence with an introductory word or transition, prepositional phrase, infinitive phrase, or participial phrase. Note these examples:

> Introductory Word
> *Yes, the problem escalated over time.*
> *Granted, most of the participants knew the risks beforehand.*

Introductory Transition
(most of the conjunctive adverbs from rule #2, as well as most –ly adverbs)
For example, addicts in recovery often take up smoking.
Unfortunately, researchers were unable to replicate the results.

Prepositional Phrase
Under the most trying circumstances, participants remained calm.

Infinitive Phrase (to + a verb)
To increase validity, researchers increased the sample size.
To increase validity requires careful planning. (No comma is needed.)
*Note that an infinitive phrase needs the comma only when the phrase is introductory and when a complete sentence remains after the comma. In the above example, the infinitive phrase is not merely introductory. It is actually the subject of the sentence and, therefore, does not require a comma. If you removed the infinitive phrase, you would not be left with a complete sentence.

Participial Phrase (an –ing phrase or an –ed/-en phrase)
Seeking confirmation, Jones repeated the study in a variety of venues.
Convinced of the study's validity, they published the results.

Rule 5. Use commas when you have items in a series (three or more items in a list). Academic style calls for using the "Oxford comma"—i.e., the comma before the conjunction in a series. AP (journalistic) style does not use the Oxford comma. Your writing for psychology calls for the academic style:

Counselors represented schools, hospitals, and private clinics.
Participants set the agenda, brainstormed in groups, and made recommendations.

Note that you must have three or more items in your list before you need commas. If you have just two, you do not need commas:

Participants set the agenda and made recommendations.

Rule 6. Use commas with a nonrestrictive clause. (Sometimes called a "which clause"— but you can also form such a clause with *who* or *whom* or *where*—but never *that.*) Note that you need a comma *before* and a comma *after* a nonrestrictive relative clause:

> *Kansas School for the Deaf, <u>which</u> receives state funds, suffers when those funds shrink.*
>
> *Mary Whiton Calkins, <u>who</u> studied at Harvard, became the first woman to serve as president of the American Psychological Association.*
>
> *Harvard University, <u>where</u> Calkins studied, refused to grant her a degree because she was a woman.*

Note that you do not need commas when the clause is a restrictive clause—sometimes called "essential"). A restrictive clause is necessary to identify *which school* or *which woman* the writer intended in the following examples. Note also that the restrictive clause technically calls for *that* instead of *which*:

> *A school that receives state funds will suffer when those funds shrink.*
>
> *Any woman who studied at Harvard in 1890 was not officially admitted.*

Rule 7. Use commas with nonrestrictive (nonessential) appositives. Appositives are simply nouns that rename other nouns, as in these examples:

> *Maccoby's 1974 book,* The Psychology of Sex Differences, *is a frequently cited classic.*
>
> *Eleanor Maccoby, a renowned researcher, also studied the effects of divorce on children.*

If the appositive is restrictive—that is, it's essential to the sentence in order for readers to get your meaning—then you do not need commas:

J.K. *Rowling's book* Harry Potter and the Sorcerer's Stone *was the first in a series.*

No commas are needed here because *Harry Potter and the Sorcerer's Stone* is a restrictive appositive. Without it, readers would not know *which* of Rowling's books was the first in a series.

Rule 8. Use commas with dates and addresses. Note that you need a comma between the elements in a date or address—and also *after* the final element if the sentence continues:

> <u>*September 11, 2001,*</u> *has become a day etched in individual, national, and global memory.*
>
> <u>*Olathe, Kansas,*</u> *is home to the Kansas School for the Deaf.*

> ***Rule 9.*** Use a comma after *i.e.* (meaning "that is") and after *e.g.* (meaning "for example"):

> *The most common acronym related to gender identity—i.e., LGBTQ—is not the only acronym in use.*
> *Some career options (e.g., school psychologist) come with varying state licensure requirements.*

Comma Splice/Fused Sentence.   A comma splice is two sentences spliced together with just a comma. A fused sentence is two sentences fused together without even a comma.

> Comma Splice:
> *Calkins attended Harvard, she did not receive a degree.*
>
> Fused Sentence:
> *Calkins attended Harvard she did not receive a degree.*

The same fixes will work for either of these surface errors.

1. comma + fanboy The coordinating-conjunction* (compound sentence) fix:
(*the fanboys: for, and, nor, but, or, yet, so) (See comma rule #1 above.)

> *Calkins attended Harvard, but she did not receive a degree.*

2. ; conjunctive adverb, The conjunctive-adverb*-and-semicolon fix:
(*however, therefore, in fact, for example, consequently, thus, moreover, etc.)
(Note the comma after the conjunctive adverb.) (See comma rule #2 above.)

> *Calkins attended Harvard; however, she did not receive a degree.*

3. Subordinate conjunction_____, The subordinate-conjunction* fix (adverb clause):
(*while, when, although, because, if, though, etc.) (See comma rule #3 above.)
Essentially, you're making one independent clause into a dependent clause.

> *Although Calkins attended Harvard, she did not receive a degree.*

4. ; The semicolon fix:

> *Calkins attended Harvard; she did not receive a degree.*

5. : Sometimes it's best to use a colon when the second sentence explains or illustrates the first.

The lack of official credentials did not hold Calkins back: She went on to become the first woman to head the American Psychological Association.

6. period + capital The make-it-two-separate-sentences fix:

> *Calkins attended Harvard. She did not receive a degree.*

Fragment.   A fragment is a group of words posing as a complete sentence, but it's not. Sure, it might have started with a capital letter and ended with a period—but to be a complete sentence, it must meet these criteria:

- It has a subject.
- It has a main verb.
- It makes sense on its own—i.e., it states a complete thought.

Let's look at two common types of fragments to avoid.

Subordinate clause fragment. Look at comma rules #3 and #6 above, which include subordinate clauses attached to the main sentence. If you don't attach the subordinate clause to the main sentence, you're going to end up with a fragment.

> Fragment: *She never actually earned her degree from Harvard. <u>Because, at the time, Harvard was not admitting women</u>.*
> (The underlined portion is an adverb clause that cannot stand alone as a sentence.)
> Corrected: *She never actually earned her degree from Harvard because, at the time, Harvard was not admitting women.*
>
> Fragment: *Participants never signed a release form. <u>Which would have provided some legal protection for the researcher</u>.*
> (The underlined portion is a relative clause that cannot stand alone as a sentence.)
> Corrected: *Participants never signed a release form, which would have provided some legal protection for the researcher.*

Participial Phrase Fragment. You might remember from comma rule #4 above that a participial phrase starts with an –ing verb form or an –ed/–en verb form. These phrases work fine when they are attached to a main sentence, but on their own, they become sentence fragments.

> Fragment: *The results of this otherwise carefully conducted study are invalid. <u>The problem being a sample size that is too small</u>.*
> (The underlined portion is a present participial phrase that cannot stand alone as a sentence.)
> Corrected: *The results of this otherwise carefully conducted study are invalid, the problem being a sample size that is too small.*

Fragment: _Concerned about the safety of the participants in the study._ The IRB would not grant its approval.

(The underlined portion is a past participial phrase that cannot stand alone as a sentence.)

Corrected: _Concerned about the safety of the participants in the study, the IRB would not grant its approval._

Verb Tense.   The basic verb tenses are past, present, and future. A problem arises with verb tense when a writer starts out in one tense and then shifts to another:

Shifting Verb Tense: _Participants completed a survey during the first week of the study.... Toward the end of the project, participants are more willing to engage in conversation._

Corrected: _Participants completed a survey during the first week of the study....Toward the end of the project, participants were more willing to engage in conversation._

The APA manual (American Psychological Association [APA], 2010) makes the following recommendations regarding verb tense:

- Use past tense for the literature review. (Smith and Jones _found_. . . .)
- OR use present perfect tense (_have_ or _has_ plus the verb) for a literature review. (Smith and Jones _have found_. . . .)
- Use past tense for the methodology section if the study has already been completed. (Participants _wrote_ in their journals every day.)
- Use past tense to report results. (Twelve of the fourteen children _slept_ for eight or more hours after reading from print materials at bedtime.)
- Use present tense to discuss implications/conclusions. (The results _indicate_. . . .)

Pronouns.   Two common pronoun issues can be especially tricky: pronoun-antecedent disagreement and vague pronoun reference.

Pronoun-antecedent disagreement—and the "singular they".   For years, handbooks have cautioned writers against sentences like these:

A _counselor_ should write up _their_ case notes soon after each session.
Everyone has _their_ own reasons for how _they_ vote.

The problem is an issue of grammatical agreement. Technically, *counselor* and *everyone* are singular—but the pronouns *their* and *they* are plural. (Yes, *everyone* is grammatically singular. We write, "Everyone is here," not "Everyone are here." And the word is formed from *every one*. The same is true for pronouns like *nobody* and *everybody*.)

In most cases, it's easy enough to avoid this pronoun-agreement issue.

- Make the antecedent—i.e., the word the pronoun is referring back to—plural:
  Counselors should write up their case notes soon after each session.
  Voters have their own reasons for how they vote.

- Occasionally, it's fine to use "he or she," "his or her," or "him or her."
  A counselor should write up his or her case notes soon after each session.

- Rewrite the sentence to avoid the pronoun altogether.
  A counselor should write up case notes soon after each session.
  People vote according to individual preference.

Some so-called "solutions" should be avoided.

- Avoid unnatural forms such as *she/he* or *his/her*.

- Avoid noninclusive options such as using all masculine pronouns (*he, him, his*) or all feminine pronouns (*she, her, hers*).

- Avoid alternating from sentence to sentence, using masculine pronouns in one sentence and then feminine pronouns in the next sentence.

All that being said, the use of *they, their,* and *theirs* to refer to a singular antecedent has been going on for centuries and is gaining acceptance. It is gaining acceptance in part because of sensitivity to individuals whose gender identity is not binary—i.e., not strictly masculine or feminine. It is also gaining acceptance because sometimes it's just plain awkward trying to avoid perfectly natural constructions like "Everyone has their own opinion." The *AP Stylebook* governing journalistic style now accepts the "singular *they*" when a simple solution is not available. In other words, we are in the midst of a language shift similar to the one that occurred when the pronoun *you*, which once was strictly plural, started replacing the singular form *thou*. The shift of *they* from strictly plural to sometimes singular, however, is still in process. Be aware that academic and professional editors (and readers) will likely be the last to accept this shift. For the time being, then, we recommend you follow the suggestions above for avoiding this pronoun-agreement issue in your scholarly writing.

Vague Pronoun Reference.   Two pronouns that novice writers often misuse are *which* and *this*.

Vague which. As you saw in comma rule #6, *which* is a relative pronoun that begins a relative clause. When it does that, the word *which* should refer back to a clear antecedent, as in this example:

> *She attended Harvard, which did not admit women at the time.*

Here the pronoun *which* clearly refers to *Harvard*. It's Harvard that did not admit women at the time. (*Harvard* is the antecedent for *which*.)

In the following sentence, however, the pronoun *which* does not appear to have a specific antecedent:

> *Harvard did not admit women, which was a common form of gender-based discrimination.*

Technically, there is no antecedent. It's a case of vague pronoun reference.
Better:

> *Harvard did not admit women—a practice that was a common form of gender-based discrimination.*

Now the pronoun *that* refers to the antecedent *practice*.

Vague this. The pronoun *this* is a demonstrative pronoun, and careful writers will be sure to have the pronoun demonstrate "this *what*" when they write. Consider this example, which has a vague *this*:

> *Harvard did not admit women at the time. This was a common form of gender-based discrimination.*

This *what* was a common form of gender-based discrimination?
Better:

> *Harvard did not admit women at the time. This practice was a common form of gender-based discrimination.*

Ah-ha! This *practice* was a common form of gender-based discrimination. A couple of further examples might help to illustrate this issue—and might help you see how specifying "this *what*?" can make your meaning more precise.

> *Only six children participated in the study. This rendered the results invalid.*
>
> Better:
>
> *Only six children participated in the study. This small sample size rendered the results invalid.*
>
> *The teacher kept the student in from recess. This made him even more restless and disruptive later in the afternoon.*
>
> Better:
>
> *The teacher kept the student in from recess. This punitive discipline made him even more restless and disruptive later in the afternoon.*

Apostrophes.   The trouble with apostrophes is that we have no verbal cues for this punctuation. At least with commas, you sometimes can hear a pause or a change in intonation (like when your voice drops while you say a nonrestrictive clause, as in comma rule #6)—but *clients*, *client's*, and *clients'* all sound the same, so it's no wonder that apostrophes plague novice writers (and even some not-so-novice writers).

Possessive apostrophes.   To form a possessive in English, you'll need two things: an apostrophe and an *s*. It is the order of those—should it be *'s* or *s'* ?—that can be confusing. Study these examples:

For singular nouns—<u>even ones that end in *s*</u>—add an apostrophe + *s*.

- *this client's profile*
- *William James's pragmatism*
- *a day's pay*
- *the hypothesis's flaw*

For plural nouns that end in *s*, simply add an apostrophe after the *s*.

- *these clients' profiles*
- *the four researchers' credentials*
- *two weeks' work*
- *these hypotheses' flaws*

For irregular plural nouns that do not end in *s*, add an apostrophe + *s*.

- *women's studies*
- *children's behavior*

NOTE:

- Don't be tempted to add an apostrophe to these possessive pronouns, none of which should ever have an apostrophe:
  hers   its   ours   theirs   yours
- Don't be tempted to add an apostrophe when you are forming a simple plural:
  five clients in the study
  after two weeks had passed

Contraction apostrophes. Contractions are common in informal writing—but not in the more formal (i.e., academic and professional) writing you'll do in psychology. When you do form contractions, however, you'll use an apostrophe to stand in for any letter(s) you omit:

it is	=	*it's*	*It's late.*
it has	=	*it's*	*It think it's been great.*
do not	=	*don't*	*I don't mind.*

The contraction apostrophe also applies to years when you're omitting some of the numbers:
The '60s were a turbulent time.

The apostrophe replaces the "19" in "1960s." Note the way the apostrophe faces; you might have to copy and paste an apostrophe to make it face the correct way when you type it. Also, note that you should not add an apostrophe before the *s*. (See the "No Apostrophe" section below.)

Proper noun apostrophes. Sometimes you'll need to check *Merriam-Webster's Collegiate Dictionary* or a business's official website (or the phonebook) to determine whether an apostrophe is needed, as in these examples:

Crohn's disease
Alzheimer's disease
McDonald's (restaurant)
Dillons (grocery store) (no apostrophe)

No apostrophe. APA format dictates that you *not* use apostrophes to form plurals of numbers, letters, or acronyms:

Years: *1800s*
Ages: *men in their 30s*
Acronyms: *DVDs*
Numbers: *more 1s than 2s*
Letters: *ps, ns, Cs*

Hyphens.   Use hyphens to form compound adjectives that appear before the noun they are modifying:

> *a well-written article*
> *a not-so-novice writer*
> *a six-inch blade*
> *a 4-year-old child*

Note that you don't need hyphens when it's not a compound adjective *before* the noun:

> *The article was well written.*
> *The writer was not a novice.*
> *The blade was six inches long.*
> *The child is 4 years old.*

You also will never use a hyphen with an –ly adverb:

> *a badly written article*
> *a heavily edited version*
> *a newly certified clinician*

Keep in mind that some words are always hyphenated as their form of spelling. Check *Merriam-Webster's Collegiate Dictionary* when in doubt.

> *drop-off*   *The drop-off was not visible at night.*
> *build-up*   *The build-up to the election caused stress.*
> *twenty-one*   *Twenty-one is the first of the hyphenated numbers up to ninety-nine.*
> *1-year-old*   *Most 1-year-olds are beginning to walk.*

You won't find this one (above) in the dictionary, but if a construction like this is used as a noun or as an adjective before a noun, it is hyphenated:

> *A 3-year-old is a handful.* (noun)
> *My 3-year-old niece is a handful.* (adjective)
> *Emma is 3 years old.* (no hyphen)

Capitalization.   You know to capitalize the first word of a sentence, and you probably know to capitalize proper nouns that refer to a specific person, place, or thing:

Regular noun	Proper noun
river	Yellow River
ship	Enterprise
aunt	Aunt Neita
restaurant	Olive Garden
bandage	Band-Aid
soda	Pepsi

Below are two additional capitalization rules to keep in mind.

Titles.   When you refer to the title of an article or book <u>in the body of your paper</u>, you should capitalize the first word of the title (and the subtitle after the colon if there is one), the last word of the title, and all other words in between <u>except for</u> articles (*a, an, the*), coordinating conjunctions (*and, but, so, or, for, nor, yet*), and prepositions of three letters or fewer (such as *in, of, on, for, to*). Please note that, even though they can be short words, you should capitalize all verbs (including *be, am, is, are, was*) and all pronouns (including *she, her, hers, he, him, his, it, me, my, us, we, our, you*).

Example of a title as it would appear in the text of your paper:

In her recent article, "How We Respond to Alzheimer's Disease: A Call to Action," Luhman outlines her strategy.

When that same title appears in your reference list, however, you will capitalize only the following words:

- The first word of the title
- The first word of the subtitle after the colon (if there is one)
- Any proper nouns or acronyms (like NASP)

Example of that same title as it would appear in your reference list:

How we respond to Alzheimer's disease: A call to action

Partially Proper Nouns.   What we're calling "partially proper nouns" are simply nouns where part is proper (capitalized) and part is not. Be careful not to mistakenly capitalize the non-proper-noun part. Here are a few examples to illustrate:

Alzheimer's disease
Kepler's laws
German shepherd
Kung Pao chicken

Proofreading: The Last Critical Step in Your Writing Process

The last step before submitting your writing is the proofreading step. Make no mistake: *Proofreading* is not the same as merely *rereading* your paper. And ignoring the proofreading stage in your writing process could cost you points and credibility that you have worked so hard to earn. Follow these suggestions to get the most out of this critical process.

- Most writers find it easier to proofread a printout rather than a computer screen, so print out the draft you're trying to proofread.

- If you have an especially long paper, proofread one section at a time rather than trying to proofread the whole paper at once.
- Read slowly. This is not a job done by skimming. Look at every word. Read aloud what you've written.
- So that you don't get caught up in reading the content (and overlooking the sentence-level concerns), try starting with the last sentence and proofreading that. Then move on to the second-to-the-last sentence, and so on. It's slow—but proofreading should be slow.
- Or use a ruler or a blank sheet of paper below each line as you move through your paper. This will help you avoid reading too swiftly. The fewer words you examine at a time the easier it is to find errors.
- Try pointing to each word as you pronounce it to see if it's correct.
- Be aware of your usual errors. Check your last paper to see what corrections your instructor pointed out. For example, if you had a few comma splices on your last paper, look specifically for comma splices when you proofread.
- Be sure you go over your marked, returned papers carefully, noting your instructor's marks and making corrections. For example, if your instructor comments that your tone is "too informal," review the differences between formal and informal tone—and then edit that paper for informal tone. Then you'll be in a much better position to edit your *next* paper.
- Proofread at least twice—once before you revise your final draft copy and once after you revise (just before you submit it). Maybe even proofread multiple times for different concerns: Edit once for punctuation. Edit another time for word choice and formal/informal tone. Edit again for grammar and sentence structure. Edit yet again for APA format and use of sources.

Final Suggestion: Use the Resources Available to You

This one chapter will not answer every question you might have as you strive to write well. For that reason, we're ending this chapter by pointing you toward other resources you should consider if you truly desire to write like a careful, professional psychologist.

Writing Center.   Chances are good that your campus has a writing center—use it! What a Writing Center Is:

- A writing center is a place, quite simply, to talk about your writing with someone trained for that very purpose.
- The writing consultant you work with might be a peer tutor—a student just like you who will understand where you're coming from, but who also is a strong writer. Or your writing consultant might be a graduate student, an instructor, or simply a staff member hired to help students with their writing.

- The writing center is typically a free service provided for enrolled students, and each session will probably last anywhere from 20 minutes to an hour. You'll be able to leave whenever you want in order to get to class or to work or whatever.
- Some writing centers operate on a drop-in basis, but for some, you'll need to make an appointment.
- You can come to the writing center at *any* stage of the process: as soon as you get the assignment, before you've chosen a topic, once you're ready to organize or outline your ideas, after you've written a first draft, once you have a final draft you're ready to edit—whenever.

What a Writing Center Is Not:

- The writing center is not a proofreading service, so don't expect to drop your paper off and come back later! And don't expect to just sit there while the writing consultant makes changes to your paper. The goal of every writing center is to make better writers, *not* simply to make a better piece of writing.
- You might think the writing center is just for "poor writers," but that simply is not true. It's for *any* student. It's for B writers who want to be A writers, and for A writers who want to be sure they're submitting their best possible work. And yes, it's also for poor writers just hoping to submit a passing paper.
- Going to the writing center does not ensure a good grade on your paper—but it does improve your chances, especially if you follow the tips below.

Tips for Getting the Most Out of Your Writing Center Experience:

- Go early in your writing process—don't wait until the last minute!
- Yes, the first visit might seem a little intimidating. But be bold! By taking this small risk, you're likely to see great gains in your writing confidence and your writing abilities.
- Consider going more than once—maybe early in the process, then again in the middle of the drafting stage when you have just a partial draft, and again when you're close to having a final draft.
- Bring everything you might need:
  - The assignment
  - Your notes
  - Your draft so far
  - Your laptop AND your charger
  - Your textbook
  - Your outside sources
  - Paper and pencil/pen for jotting notes

- Be an active participant in the session. Jot notes. Ask questions. Listen attentively. Smile and say thank you.

- It might be difficult to get in to see a consultant during crunch times like midterm and the end of the semester. Your best bet will be to make an appointment well in advance of when you might actually need it near midterms and finals week. (Some writing centers are not open during finals week—so, again, plan ahead.)

- If you have the option of having your professor notified of your visit, do so. Your professor will likely be impressed by your diligence and initiative.

Even if you're an off-campus student taking classes online, your campus writing center might offer online consulting sessions. If not, your school might offer its online students access to an online-only support program for student writers—Smartthinking.com or something similar.

APA Style Blog.   This resource includes dozens of short blogposts about everything from "Abbreviations" to "YouTube." Find it online at https://blog.apastyle.org/. If you have a question not answered in this chapter, you'll likely find the answer somewhere within the APA Style Blog.

Purdue OWL (Online writing lab).   This free online service includes handouts, videos, and a wealth of material related to all aspects of writing. You might find the "APA Guide" to be especially helpful. Find the Purdue OWL online at https://owl.purdue.edu.

References

American Psychological Association (APA). (2010). *Publication manual of the American Psychological Association* (6th ed.). Washington, DC: American Psychological Association.

Lunsford, A. A., & Lunsford, K. J. (2008). "Mistakes are a fact of life": A national comparative study. *College Composition and Communication, 59,* 781–806. Retrieved from http://stabler3010.pbworks.com/w/file/fetch/58546609/lunsford%20mistakes.pdf

Nordquist, R. (2019). Engfish (Antiwriting). Retrieved from https://www.thoughtco.com/engfish-antiwriting-term-1690596

Scientific Writing and APA Style Guide

by Janett M. Naylor-Tincknell, PhD

Psychologists use the *Publication Manual of the American Psychological Association (6th Edition)* to properly report and credit information in the field (APA, 2010). Scientific writing in psychology differs from writing available in popular press books found in bookstores. Psychologists use scientific writing to disseminate information to other psychologists or psychologists-in-training. The intended audience for scientific writing reads with more attention to detail and different levels of expertise, which requires the prose to take a more formal and objective tone. Scientific prose must be technical to convey complex details of theories, experiments, and statistical analyses.

Often scientific writing is not a place for your opinions. Arguments must be supported by empirical evidence discussed in the work of others. Describing the work of others is not like writing a fictional story that weaves together storylines of characters. Scientific writing is exact and straightforward content that presents support for your thesis statement. When we discuss empirical evidence, remember that science does not "prove" anything. We really can only provide evidence for or against a claim in the form of research studies conducted by others.

The empirical research we chose to support our ideas should be focused on the topics of research or the findings not the authors. For example, rather than writing "Smith and Jones (2017) found that children liked sweet foods better than salty foods.", you should start with "Children prefer sweet foods rather than salty foods." The second sentence focuses the reader's attention on the important findings rather than the authors. So by shifting the noun of the sentence from the authors to the findings, the focus of the sentence changes, making the sentence clearer and more concise.

Also when discussing the work of others, you want to paraphrase or summarize their work rather than use direct quotes. This will allow you to integrate various empirical findings into one argument rather than writing a more annotated bibliography style paper where you discuss topics one research study at a time. Focusing on your arguments on the findings and highlights of the research study makes your writing more concise and impactful.

Scientific writing is direct and active. Paragraphs and sentences should contain only one topic at a time. Do not combine ideas into one paragraph to create a "sentence salad," meaning each sentence stands alone by are not held together by a unifying idea. You also want to avoid "paragraph salad" in which the paper has disjointed paragraphs with no binding transitions. Don't forget your salad dressing!

Scientific writing can be frustrating because it differs from our natural conversation and writing patterns. We must learn the skills of scientific writing with practice, criticism, and editing. Keep in mind that everyone struggles at first with scientific writing and everyone receives criticism (even your professors and other psychologists get editorial criticisms from reviewers). Take that criticism and feedback and learn from your mistakes. This will make for stronger papers and better grades.

Plagiarism

According to Merriam-Webster, plagiarism is "to steal and pass off (the ideas or words of another) as one's own or to use (another's production) without crediting the source" (Merriam-Webster, n.d., para. 2). Plagiarism is from the Latin work "plagiarius" which means kidnapper (Maurer, Kappe, & Zaka, 2006). To avoid kidnapping the work of others, you are required to give proper credit to the original source. Plagiarism comes in many forms including:

- Accidental plagiarism is due to lack of knowledge about plagiarism and proper citation in the field.
- Unintentional plagiarism can occur when you have read and discussed a topic so thoroughly that the ideas and works of others become so ingrained they are like your own.
- Intentional plagiarism is when people purposefully use the work of others without properly citing the original source, whether quoted or paraphrased.
- Self-plagiarism involves using your own work (from other classes or assignments) without citing the original source.

No matter the intent or the source, plagiarism is more than not properly citing and references the words of others. More broadly defined, plagiarism is also improperly interpreting the words and taking the artistic expressions, ideas, or coding of others, as well as inaccurately translating, incorrectly referencing, and falsely quoting the work of others.

Unfortunately, the issue of plagiarism is rather common among students at colleges and universities. In fact, 12 to 40% of students reported having plagiarized at some point in their academic careers (Fish & Hura, 2013; Walker, 2010). Plagiarism is commonly unintentional (Brown & Murphy, 1989) but can still result in severe consequences for students ranging from failing an assignment to dismissal from a university or program (Maurer et al., 2006).

Although unintentional plagiarism may be prevented with knowledge of citation and sources, there are several other preventable reasons students may not properly cite information (Insley, 2011). So ignorance is not an excuse to cut corners or take risks. The preventable reasons students plagiarize are:

- Confusion about proper paraphrasing and citations.
- Procrastination on assignments limits time.
- Belief that plagiarism is quick-and-easy.
- Did it before and did not get caught.
- Lack of interest or desire to complete the assignment.

Once students know the types of plagiarism, the proper way to cite works, and the consequences for cutting corners, plagiarism is preventable and can have long-lasting impacts on your education and future careers.

Do's and Don'ts of Effective Scientific Writing in Psychology

- Do tell a story to address your thesis statement; do not write an annotated bibliography.
- Do have a clear, concise thesis statement; do not have a vague thesis statement.
- Do provide empirical support for your ideas; do not editorialize or use opinions.
- Do use high quality, research-based sources; do not use unreliable sources.
- Do read all the work you cite; do not rely on secondary sources.
- Do define key terms; do not use excessive jargon.
- Do rephrase or summarize other writers' work; do not use direct quotes.
- Do write in third-person; do not write in first-person.
- Do use obvious referents; do not use nondescript pronouns.
- Do use past or present perfect tense; do not overuse present tense.
- Do use active voice; do not use passive voice.
- Do keep paragraphs and sentences short and focused on one topic; do not have paragraphs and sentences with multiple ideas.
- Do use precise, clear, exacting language; do not use colloquialisms.
- Do allow time to edit and revise; do not rely on a single draft.
- Do credit the work of others; do not plagiarize.

APA Style Guidelines

General Formatting

When writing any paper in APA style, students should follow a common set of guidelines. Although each instructor or journal may have additional requirements, these general formatting instructions should apply.

- Use one-inch margins throughout the entire paper.
- Double space the entire paper, including references.
- Left-justify all text with new paragraphs indented.
- Use 12-point font (recommended: Times New Roman).
- Always include a title page and abstract.
- Use one space after the period.
- In Word, use the no spacing style or remove the extra spacing between paragraphs.

Title Page Formatting

Title pages should be the first page of all APA style papers. The title of your paper should highlight the main idea of the paper concisely (APA, 2010). Titles should provide enough detail about the content of the paper that readers understand the objective of the paper and theoretical areas of study. Avoid unnecessary words to keep the title brief (recommended: less than 12 words).

- Running head: SHORT ALL CAPS TITLE
  - Left justified with page number right-justified.
- Center title, author name, and other identifiers (class, university, etc.) right/left and near the upper half of the page.

Abstract

Starting on a new page, an abstract should briefly (150 to 250 words), yet completely, summarize the contents of the paper (APA, 2010). The abstract should provide enough information to stand alone, allowing readers to get a general sense of the paper details to know what the paper is about. The abstract is often dense with information and is the first paragraph readers see. It may also determine whether they continue on to read the article. Therefore, the abstract is very important.

- Begin abstract on new page.
- The SHORT ALL CAPS TITLE and page number should be in header.
- "Abstract" should be centered, and not bold, on the top of the page.
- Abstract should be one paragraph with no indentation.

In-Text Citations

Because scientific inquiry relies on replication and extension of the work of others, writers need to always give credit to the work and ideas of others with in-text citations of author(s) and year of publication (See Table 1). When using works from multiple sources in one sentence, students can cite all the sources in one location by listing the citations alphabetically by first author's last name with each source separated by a semicolon. For example, writing tips for this chapter have been adapted and combined from several reputable sources (APA, 2010; Carson, Fama, Clancy, Ebert, & Tierney, 2012; J. Scott, G. Scott, & Garrison, 2019).

Table 1 In-Text Citation Guide and Examples

	In Text	Parenthetical
One Author		
First Use	Smith (2018)	(Smith, 2018)
Later Uses	Smith (2018)	(Smith, 2018)
Two Authors		
First Use	Smith and Jones (2019)	(Smith & Jones, 2019)
Later Uses	Smith and Jones (2019)	(Smith & Jones, 2019)
Three, Four, & Five Authors		
First Use	Smith, Jones, Johnson, Williams, and Brown (2017)	(Smith, Jones, Johnson, Williams, & Brown, 2017)
Later Uses	Smith et al. (2017)	Smith et al. (2017)
Six or More Authors		
Frist Use	Smith et al. (2016)	(Smith et al., 2016)
Later Uses	Smith et al. (2016)	(Smith et al., 2016)

Direct quotes should be used only on the rare occasion that the source cannot be paraphrased without losing the quality or integrity of the original work. Direct quotes will also cite the author(s) and year of publication, as well as the page number or location of the quoted material. For direct quotes that are less than 40 words, put quoted text in quotation marks followed by citation such as "quoted text from source" for example: (Miller, 2015, p. 3). For quotes that are more than 40 words, the quoted text should not be in quotation marks, but instead in a block quote format with the same citation style after the period.

Reference Section

Every paper needs a reference section. Be sure to have a reference listed for every citation used in the text and that all references cited in the text. The reference section should start on a new page at the end of the text (APA, 2010). The word "References" should be centered and not bolded on the top of the page. Each reference should be double spaced and use the hanging indent format. All references should be alphabetized by first author's last name. In the case of multiple sources by the same author, alphabetize overall by first author's last name then by second author's last name. If only one author, place in order by publication year.

The most commonly used sources are journal articles, books, and book chapters. Reference styles for those are explained below. For other types of sources, (e.g., theses, newspaper articles, etc.), please refer to the APA Publication Manual, 6th Edition (APA, 2010).

Journal Articles:

- Author(s): Smith, J. A., Jones, B. C., & Johnson, D. W.
- Publication Date: (2019).
- Title of Work: Psychology student writing: A guide for undergraduates.
- Name of Journal: *Journal of Student Writing,*
- Volume Number(Issue Number): *24*(2),
- Page Numbers: 15–23.
- Digital Object Identifier (doi) or Permalink: doi:10.1385.jsw.24.2.15

Example Journal Article Reference

Smith, J. A., Jones, B. C., & Johnson, D. W. (2019). Psychology student writing: A guide for undergraduates. *Journal of Student Writing, 24*(2), 15–23. doi:10.1385.jsw.24.2.15

Books:

- Author(s): Williams, A., Brown, J. T., & Miller, S. R.
- Publication Date: (2015).
- Title of Book: *Understanding the importance of scientific writing.*
- City and State of Publication: Austin, TX:
- Publisher: Smiling Texans Publishers.

Example Book Reference

Williams, A., Brown, J. T., & Miller, S. R. (2015). *Understanding the importance of scientific writing.* Austin, TX: Smiling Texans Publishers.

<u>**Chapters in an Edited Book:**</u>

- Author(s): Davis, J., & Moore, B. R.
- Publication Date: (2014).
- Name of Book Chapter: Basics of writing.
- Name of Editors: In S. Wilson (Ed.),
- Title of Book: *Writing Made Simple.*
- City and State of Publication: Philadelphia, PA:
- Publisher: Liberty Bell Publishers.

Example Chapter in an Edited Book Reference

Davis, J., & Moore, B. R. (2014). Basics of writing. In S. Wilson (Ed.), *Writing Made Simple* (pp. 15–47). Philadelphia, PA: Liberty Bell Publishers.

Headings

Headings can be very helpful in scientific writing. Having a clear, organized structure to your paper makes the paper precise and logical (APA, 2010). The levels of headings form a hierarchy much like an outline with major points and subpoints. Just like an outline, you should avoid having only one heading and one subheading. You should ideally have at least two subheadings under each main heading. Make sure the headings are truly needed to help organize ideas into overall ideas and subideas. APA formatting of heading depends on the number of levels of subordination (See Table 2).

Table 2 APA Heading Formatting by Levels

Level	Format
1	**Centered, Bolded, Upper and Lowercase Heading** Paragraph begins on next line, indented like regular paragraph
2	**Left-aligned, Bolded, Upper and Lowercase Heading** Paragraph begins on next line, indented like regular paragraph
3	**Indented, Bolded, lowercase heading ending with a period.** Paragraph begins right after period on same line as heading.
4	***Indented, Bolded, Italicized, lowercase heading ending with a period.*** Paragraph begins right after period on same line as heading.
5	*Indented, Italicized, lowercase heading ending with a period.* Paragraph begins right after period on same line as heading.

Below is an example of headings for a pro/con persuasive style paper about whether violent video games are harmful to children and adolescents.

Introduction

Violent Video Games Are Harmful

Text begins here with an indented paragraph.

Decreases school performance. Text begins here after the period.

Changes to brain structures. Text begins here after the period.

Changes to frontal lobe. Text begins here after the period.

Changes in executive control. Text begins here after the period.

Desensitization to violence. Text begins here after the period.

Violent Video Games Are Not Harmful

Text begins here with an indented paragraph.

Methodological flaws. Text begins here after the period.

Correlation based studies. Text begins here after the period.

Small sample sizes. Text begins here after the period.

Other influences. Text begins here after the period.

Research showing no harm or benefits. Text begins here after the period.

Word Usage and Unbiased Language

Psychologists are committed to equal treatment and reducing stigma toward persons based on gender, sexual orientation, racial or ethnic group, disability, or age. The APA Publication Manual (APA, 2010) has a series of suggestions to help reduce bias in writing and language. These are not strict guidelines but are best practices for inclusive writing yet still provide the appropriate level of detail, sensitivity, and respect (See Table 3).

Grammar and Word Usage

In scientific writing, precision and accuracy of language is extremely important. Therefore, word economy and clarity are essential components of papers with good flow and continuity of ideas (APA, 2010). Readers will better understand your paper if your ideas are presented in a logical order with transitions that highlight the relationship between ideas. You should not make the reader work to understand or follow your arguments. Your arguments and supporting empirical findings should lead the reader to your conclusions in a natural and an obvious manner.

Additionally, be economical with your word choices. Scientific writing is not flowery and creative. Do not use words that are excessive or redundant. This includes the overuse of jargon, colloquialisms, pronouns, faulty comparisons, and illogical attributions, such as attributing human qualities to inanimate objects or animals, essive, or redundant.

Table 3 Reducing Bias in Language

Biased Language	Unbiased Language	Note
Gender		
Husband/wife	Spouse	Use gender neutral
Mailman	Mail Carrier	language when
Mankind	People, Humans	possible
Sexual Orientation		
Homosexuals	Gay Men	Use these terms to
	Lesbian Women	people who identify
	Bisexual Men/Women	this way.
Racial or Ethnic Identity		
Negro	Black/African-American	Use specific race or
Oriental	Asian-American, Asian	nation when possible
Disability		
Autistics	People with Autism	Use people-first
Physically Challenged	Person with Disability	language to describe
Mentally Ill	Person with Depression	groups
Age		
Under 18	Girls/Boys (under 12 years)	Avoid open-ended
	Adolescents (13–17 years)	definitions and
Elderly	Older Adults	generational labels

Numbers

When using numbers in text (APA, 2010), numbers below 10 should be spelled out (e.g., one, two) and numbers 10 and greater should be expressed with numerals (e.g., 10, 11). Also, express in words any numbers that (a) start a sentence, title, or heading; (b) are common fractions; (c) are universally accepted usage, like Seven Wonders of the World; or (d) words to estimate time (about two years ago). Various exceptions do apply when writing the Methods and Results sections of a research report (see sections 4.31 through 4.49 of the APA Publication Manual 6th Edition).

Numbers with decimal places should be round to two decimal places. When typing decimal numbers in text, place a zero in front of the period, such as 0.25. However, when using decimals in statistical statements do not place a zero in front of the period, for example, $t(124) = -.57, p>.05$.

References

American Psychological Association (APA). (2010). *Publication manual of the American Psychological Association* (6th Ed.). Washington, DC: American Psychological Association.

Brown, A. S., & Murphy, D. R. (1989). Cyrptomnesia: Delineating inadvertent plagiarism. *Journal of Experimental Psychology: Learning, Memory, and Cognition, 15,* 432–442. doi:10.1037/0278-7393.15.3.432

Carson, S. H., Fama, J., Clancy, K., Ebert, J., & Tierney, A. (2012). *Writing for psychology: A guide for psychology concentrators.* Retrieved from https://writingproject.fas.harvard.edu /files/hwp/files/writing_for_psych_final_from_printer.pdf

Fish, R., & Hura, G. (2013). Students' perceptions of plagiarism. *Journal of the Scholarship of Teaching and Learning, 13*(5), 33–45. Retrieved from https://files.eric.ed.gov/fulltext/ EJ1017029.pdf

Insley, R. (2011). Managing plagiarism: A preventative approach. *Business Communication Quarterly, 74*(2), 183–187. doi:10.117/1080569911404058

Maurer, H., Kappe, F., & Zaka, B. (2006). Plagiarism-A survey. *Journal of Universal Computer Science, 12,* 1050–1084. Retrieved from http://jucs.org/jucs_12_8/plagiarism_a_ survey/jucs_12_08_1050_1084_maurer.pdf

Merriam-Webster. (n.d.). Retrieved from https://www.merriam-webster.com/dictionary/ plagiarize

Scott, J. M., Scott, G. M., & Garrison, S. M. (2019). *The psychology student writer's manual and reader's guide* (3rd ed.). Lanham, MD: Rowman & Littlefield Publishing Group.

Walker, J. (2010). Measuring plagiarism: Researching what students do, not what they say they do. *Studies in Higher Education, 35,* 41–59. doi:10.1080/03075070902912994

How to Read a Scientific Journal Article

by Kaira Hayes, PhD

As a psychology student, you will undoubtedly be required to write a research paper or a literature review, probably in multiple courses. Although you likely have written papers, including research papers, in the past, use of scientific journal articles as your primary or only references may not have been a requirement. Reading and comprehending scientific articles can be difficult for undergraduate psychology students just beginning their education. These articles are essentially technical reports of original research conducted by individuals who are often experts in their field. If the technical jargon and vocabulary is not familiar to you, the articles can be difficult and frustrating to comprehend. However, be patient with yourself. With knowledge of the basic structure of a scientific article as well as some of the technical language, you will be on your way to becoming an expert yourself! As you progress through your program, you will find that reading scientific articles becomes easier and perhaps even enjoyable!

Structure of a Scientific Article

In addition to the title and author names, scientific articles always contain the following sections: Abstract, Introduction, Methods, Results, and Discussion. Each of those sections may also contain subsections although subsections and their headings will sometime vary depending upon the article.

Title.   The title of the article is your first clue regarding the topic and research method used. The general purpose of the study and the variables investigated may be evident in the title. In addition, in some instances, you may be able to discern the research design of the study.

If the title includes the terms...

- *"Effect of"* or *"impact on"* or *"influence"* → the impact, effect, or influence of one or more variables on another variable or set of variables was investigated. This often denotes an experimental or quasiexperimental design, although this would always need to be confirmed by reading the article. In an experimental design, researchers manipulate a variable and then measure the effect on another variable. In a quasi-experimental design, researchers investigate the difference between two or more groups who already differ in one variable. For example, if we are interested in investigating the difference in personality traits of psychology majors and business majors, we would use a quasi-experimental design. The groups differ in a way that is of interest to the researchers. Later in this chapter, in the section devoted to the Methods section of an article, you will learn more about how variables are manipulated or measured. If you are asked by your instructor to identify the independent and dependent variables, and the title has these terms, you may be able to determine the variables from the title alone. Here's how: The variable name that appears immediately after the terms *effect of/impact on/influence* is the independent variable; the variable at the end of the title is the dependent variable. Consider the following fictitious title: "The Effect of Classroom Lighting on Quality of Note-taking." Classroom lighting is the independent variable and the quality of notes taken is the dependent variable.

- "Relationship between" or "association with" → These terms suggest a correlational study. You may have learned that "correlation does not equal causation." Results of correlational studies tell us whether two variables are associated or vary together, but we cannot assume that the association is a causal (i.e., that a change in one variable causes the other variable to also change). For example, researchers have discovered a positive relationship between internet use and depression among adolescents and adults (Morrison & Gore, 2010). As internet use increases, depression scores also increase. However, because this is a correlational study, we cannot conclude that internet use causes depression. In fact, it is possible that a third variable, such as loneliness, leads to greater internet use and depression. Additional research would need to be conducted to learn more about why depression and internet use are correlated.

- "Predictors" → Suggests that the researcher investigated how well one set of variables predicted another set of variables or outcomes. This is a variation of a correlational research design.

- "Meta-analysis" → This means that the researchers found all published research studies on a specific topic and meeting specific criteria and analyzed the results together as one big research study. This is often useful when there have been many small studies completed. Analyzing the results of many smaller studies together may allow researchers be more definitive in their conclusions.

- "Validity" or "Reliability" → The primary purpose of the research was to investigate and determine the validity or reliability of a specific test, survey, scale, or other measurement tool.

- "Development and Validation" → Similar to the terms "validity" and "reliability," these terms suggest that the primary purpose of the research was to further develop and determine the validity of a specific measurement tool.

- "Ratings of" (or "perceptions of") → Suggests that the researchers' primary goal was to investigate attitudes, opinions, or perceptions of a group of people. This often suggests a descriptive research method, depending upon the statistical analysis conducted.

Activity: Using your favorite search engine, find the webpage for the Psi Chi Journal of Psychological Research. Psi Chi is a national honor society in psychology. Psychology students, as well as faculty, who meet membership criteria can become members. Many universities have a Psi Chi Chapter and, if not already, you may wish to apply for membership. Psi Chi publishes student-authored scientific research articles. You can download current and past issues from their website. After opening one issue, read the titles. Can you identify the purpose of the study, the variables investigated, and the research design used?

Abstract.   The abstract is a short paragraph, printed at the top of the first page of the article. The abstract provides a summary of the research conducted, with a focus on the general research question and the results. When your instructor has required you have at least 10 scientific journal articles as references for your paper and you have found 100 that may seem relevant, reading the abstract can be very useful in weeding out those less relevant without having to read the entire article. As you are reading the abstract, ask yourself the following questions: Does the article report results of a study investigating variables in which you are interested? Did they investigate a population (e.g., children, college students, rural dwellers) in which you are interested? Are the results of the study, as summarized in the abstract, relevant to the topic of your paper? If the answers to any of these questions are yes, then you likely want to keep that article as a potential reference. If the answers are no, strike it from your list and read the next abstract.

Activity: Read the abstracts of the articles published in the issue of the Psi Chi Journal of Psychological Research that you found online. Answer the following questions in one or two complete sentences. Try to paraphrase your responses; if you do quote from the abstract, be sure to use quotation marks. Using quotation marks when you quote information in your notes is good practice and prevents you from unintentionally plagiarizing later. You may think that you will remember which notes you quoted and which you paraphrased, but anyone can easily forget.

- *What is the general purpose of the study?*
- *Were additional variables, not mentioned in above, are included in the abstract?*
- *What population was studied?*
- *What were the results?*

Introduction.   Prior to conducting a scientific study, researchers will *review the literature*, which means they will read all the relevant published scientific articles. They will then write a paper, using these articles as their references, not unlike what you are required to do as a psychology student. Researchers will then use the information they gathered to design their own research study. Once they have conducted the study, they may then write a scientific article that they submit for publication. The paper they started with will be the *Introduction* section of the scientific article. The Introduction section is the first section after the Abstract; it is often not labeled "Introduction" so do not despair if that heading does not appear in the article.

Initially you should peruse the Introduction section quickly, looking for the following information: the purpose or goal of the study (if not already described in the Abstract) and the specific research question(s). The hypothesis of the study may also be included in this section. Write this information in your notes, as this will be most relevant to the paper you are writing.

You may be tempted to spend a lot of time reading and rereading the additional background information included in this section, taking careful and meticulous notes. However, this is likely not an efficient use of your time and so you should resist this urge. Keep in mind that this section of the article is essentially a research paper written by the researchers to provide background and context for their own original research. If you are required to use scientific articles as references for your research paper, you should not be relying on the information provided in the Introduction sections of your references. However, if you find information in this section that you would like to use in your own paper (and you probably will!), you will need to find the reference for that information, and then read it before using the information in your own paper.

For example, imagine that you are interested in writing a paper on the association between mental health and academic performance among college students. You find an article published in the Spring 2019 *Psi Chi Journal*, written by Dominique Giroux and Elisa Geiss of Olivet College, relevant to this topic. You read the following sentence in the Introduction section "Further, distressed students have worse academic performance and exhibit high drop-out rates (Kitzrow, 2003)" (in Giroux & Geiss, 2019, p. 61). This seems quite relevant to your own paper and you would like to include this information. To do that, you need to find the paper written by Kitzrow, published in 2003, and read it. If you are unable to find the original reference, your instructor may still allow you to use the information but you will need to cite it as a secondary source. You should ask your instructor if this is acceptable and, if so, how to cite the information properly. You may be wondering, is this an acceptable way to find additional references to use when writing a paper? The answer is a resounding, "Yes!" All researchers do this as it ensures that we are accessing all relevant research but not relying upon another author's interpretation of a study.

Activity: Find the article by Giroux and Geiss in the Spring 2019 issue of the Psi Chi Journal. Read the introduction section and write one to two sentences summarizing the general purpose of the study. Select one reference cited in the Introduction section and find its full reference printed at the end of the paper. Search the web and your university library to see if you could obtain a copy of this article.

Method.   This section is usually labeled and often includes subsections, also labeled. As its name implies, this section provides an overview of the methods used by the researchers. Ideally, the method is described in enough detail to allow other researchers to replicate the study exactly. When reading the method section of a scientific article, first peruse the section quickly, looking for subheadings. The subheadings likely tell you where to find information about the participants used in the study, the materials or measurement tools used, and the general methodology and research design.

The participant group used by the researchers is referred to as the *sample*. The sample consists of a specific number of individuals that come from a larger *population*. For example, a study conducted on college students at your university is considered a *sample* of the larger *population* of all college students in the region. Researchers will generally describe how the sample was recruited to be in the study. In addition, they will describe the sample by reporting the number of males and females, the average age and range of ages, and other basic demographic information. This descriptive information is often included in the Method section although it may, instead, appear in the *Results* section, which is discussed later in this chapter. The description of the sample is often summarized in a table.

Information about the participants and how they were recruited can help us decide how well the results might generalize to the population from which the sample was drawn, or to other populations. For example, if the participants were all college students, the results may not generalize well to children or senior citizens but may generalize to college students in other regions of the country, perhaps depending on other characteristics of the sample such as age, socioeconomic status, or race. If the sample was recruited by paying individuals $50 for their participation, we might wonder if similar results would be obtained if participants were not paid. We may decide payment likely did not impact the results or how well they generalize, but we need to at least consider this possibility. If the sample size is small, we are less certain of the results than if the sample size is very large. Generally, studies with small sample sizes need to be repeated or replicated before we can be confident that results were not simply a fluke.

In addition to a description of the participants, this section will also include information about the general procedures and materials used by the researchers. Before reading about the procedures and materials, review what you know about the variables that were studied by the researchers. As you are reading the Methods section, you will want to find out how each of those variables was *measured* or *manipulated*. When a variable is *manipulated* by researchers, they create a condition or specific circumstance to which the participants are exposed. For example, consider a fictitious research study investigating the effects of classroom lighting on note-taking. In such a study, researchers will manipulate classroom lighting. In other words, they will create several lighting conditions (i.e., low, medium, and bright lighting) and expose students to those conditions while they are taking notes. How they did that will be described in this section of an article. In addition, the researchers will include detailed information on how the note-taking quality was measured. Alternatively, in some research, rather than manipulating a condition or circumstance to which some participants are exposed, researchers will implement an intervention, program, or treatment and then measure its impact. The program or treatment will be described in this section, as well as the method used to determine its impact.

Learning how variables were manipulated can also help you decide how well results of the study might generalize to other circumstances or situations. For example, imagine that our fictitious study on the effects of lighting on note-taking finds no difference between lighting conditions. We might wonder if the different lighting conditions differed so minutely that differences were undetectable by the human eye, or if the lighting levels are similar to those found in a college classroom.

Information on how variables were measured can be very useful if you are required to write a research proposal outlining how you would conduct a research study of your own. You may wish to use the same measures that were used by other researchers. If a survey or questionnaire was used, the researchers might include a copy in the article, which can be very useful!

Activity: Read the Methods section of the article by Giroux and Geiss and answer the following questions: (1) What information about the sample is included in this section (look for information on the size of the sample, description of the sample, and how the sample was recruited)? (2) List each variable and how it was measured or manipulated. If a treatment or program was introduced to the participants, briefly describe it. Remember, when taking notes on an article you are reading, be sure to paraphrase or use quotation marks when quoting.

Results.   This section will include the statistical analyses conducted by the researchers. This is can be difficult to read and understand without having first completed an applied statistics course, which is typically required of psychology majors. However, if you have not yet taken such a course, you can still gain information that will be useful when writing your paper.

If the description of the sample was not included in the Methods section, it will be included here. This section will also always include the results of the statistical analyses. Prior to reading this section, review the purpose or goal of the study as well as the research questions and hypotheses. The authors will generally address the goal(s) and each of the questions and hypotheses one by one. When reporting the statistical analysis, the statistical probability or p-level will be provided. Generally, a statistical result with a p-level of less than .05 or .01 (which may be written in the article like this: $p < .05$ or $p < .01$) is considered statistically significant. This means the results mostly likely did not occur by chance, but rather, reflect that the treatment had an impact, or that the variables studies are related or correlated, or that the manipulation of one variable caused a change in another variable.

When reading a scientific article, look for each goal, question, or hypothesis and note the results pertaining to each.

Activity: Review your notes over the Introduction section of the article by Giroux and Geiss. For each goal, research question, or hypothesis, look for the result and summarize it. Summarize any additional information about the sample included in this section.

Discussion.   This section will contain a discussion of the results. If you had difficulty understanding the statistical information in the last section, this section will be especially helpful. In addition to explaining the results of the study, the researchers will attempt to relate the results to other relevant research reviewed in the Introduction section. For example, they may indicate that their results were consistent or inconsistent with results of other similar studies. If results were inconsistent, they will provide some possible explanations. The *implications* of the results will also be discussed. For example, if the study investigated the impact of a treatment or program, the researchers will likely discuss how this program might be useful to others. They may also discuss the importance of the results and other similar research. *Limitations* of the study and its results are also often outlined in this section. Limitations generally include a critique of specific aspects of the study. For example, if the sample size was small or unusual in some way, or if the procedure was found to be imperfectly implemented, the researchers will discuss this and how these factors limit the generalizability or usefulness of the results. Finally, the researchers will typically discuss their *recommendations for future research*, based upon their experience and the results of their own study. If you have not had much experience reading scientific articles, you may be surprised with how critical scientists are of their own research!

When you read the discussion section of a scientific article, look for an explanation of each result previously discussed in the Results section, the implications of each result or the study as a whole, and the limitations discussed. Are there any additional implications or limitations that the authors did not include? If you plan to use the scientific article as a reference for a research paper or proposal, information from the Results and Discussion sections of the article is typically the information you include in your paper.

Activity: Read the Discussion section of the article by Giroux and Geiss. Summarize each result discussed in this section. Remember to paraphrase or use quotation marks. Summarize the implications of the study and this area of research, as discussed by the authors. Finally, summarize the limitations discussed. Can you think of any other implications or limitations? What future research might be interesting or useful?

References.   The last section of a scientific article is the Reference section. You will find all the articles and resources cited elsewhere in the article here. As mentioned earlier in this chapter, the reference section can provide you with additional sources to use in your own research paper.

Scientific Article Summary Worksheet

Use this worksheet to take notes while reading a scientific article. Remember to paraphrase or use quotation marks when quoting information taken directly from the article.

1) What is the article title?

2) What does the title tell you about the study? *Can you identify the purpose of the study, the variables investigated, and the research design used?*

3) Abstract. Use the abstract to answer the following questions:
   - What is the general purpose of the study?
   - Were additional variables, not mentioned above, also studied?
   - What population was studied?
   - What were the results?
       Remember, you might decide, after reading the abstract, that you do not want to use this article for your paper.

4) Introduction: Find the following information:
   - The purpose or goal of the study (if not already described in the Abstract). There may be more than one. List all of them.
   - Specific research question(s) (if provided).
   - Hypotheses (if provided)

5) Method: Find the following information:
   - Describe the sample (size, description, and how it was recruited)
   - List each variable and how it was measured or manipulated. If a treatment or program was introduced to the participants, briefly describe it.

6) Results: Find the following information:
   - List each goal, question, or hypothesis and the result(s) pertaining to each.

7) Discussion: Find the following information:
   - Provide a brief summary of each result previously discussed in the Results section
   - What are the implications of each result and the study as a whole?
   - Limitations discussed in the article
   - Are there any additional implications or limitations that the authors did not include?

References: Are there any references cited in this article that you need to find and read? List them here.

References

Giroux, D. & Geiss, E. (2019). Evaluating a student-led mental health awareness campaign. *Psi Chi Journal of Psychological Research, 24,* 61–66. doi:10.24839/2325-7342. JN24.1.52

Morrison, C. M., & Gore, H. (2010). The relationship between excessive internet use and depression: A questionnaire-based study of 1319 young people and adults. *Psychopathology, 43,* 121–126. doi:10.1159/0002777001

Assessing the Legitimacy of ADHD

Taylor Willits

Abstract

The validity of attention-deficit/hyperactivity disorder (ADHD) as a psychiatric disorder is a controversial and highly debated topic in both scientific literature and public opinion. The empirical research regarding ADHD is important to understand, as well as the multitude of challenges that develop when diagnosing, treating, and living with ADHD. Although there is considerable research in favor of ADHD as a disorder, no etiology has been found, and there continues to be a large amount of conflicting literature about whether it is a true disorder or not. Without established evidence to disprove the legitimacy of ADHD, it will stay a diagnosable disorder, despite the skepticism of those who continue to challenge it. This review examines and compares the most prominent thoughts and relevant literature on both sides of the argument.

ADHD is currently the most prominently diagnosed disorder in pediatric psychiatry, with
a worldwide prevalence rate of 8 to 12% in all children (Faraone, 2005). Subsequently, this
disorder is common in the school system, and produces impairments adverse to the goal of a
child's education. Kovshoff et al. (2012) found that children with ADHD are more likely to be
unsuccessful in school and have higher rates of unemployment, criminal activity, additional
mental health disorders, and other social and interpersonal problems (as cited in Taylor &
Sonuga-Barke, 2008). This disorder has not only a debilitating effect on children, but can also be
a serious burden on families and home life, especially with the estimated cost per diagnosed
child totaling between $12,005 and $17,458 a year (Pelham, Foster, & Robb, 2007).

Although there has been rigorous and continuous research done on ADHD, including
studies in support of both biological and
for the disorder (Loo et al., 2008). This h
is a valid psychiatric disorder, and contr
literature and public opinion. Some of th
complications and complexities of the di
disorder, environmental influences, and
disorder; but are continually being challe
guidelines, a biased perception of ADHE
evidence, and the proven efficacy of stim
to be disputed, and a resolution on the m
costs, medication, and symptoms of this

Pro: ADHD is a real disorder

Currently, one of the strongest and most certain arguments in support of the validity of
ADHD is the fact that there are clinical guidelines that support ADHD as a valid and objectively
diagnosable psychiatric disorder, and are supported by psychologists and psychiatrists. The
DSM-V, the most current diagnostic manual published by the American Psychiatric Association
(APA), has made several revisions in the diagnostic criteria of ADHD for a more sensitive and
reliable diagnosis (APA, 2013). The inattentive and hyperactivity-impulsive symptoms remain
the same, however, the DSM-V now requires only five symptoms, instead of six, from
individuals 17 years of age or older in order to be more sensitive to ADHD in adolescents and
adults (Rabiner, n.d.). Other adjustments in the criteria include: ADHD diagnosis in conjunction
with Autism Spectrum Disorder and severity specifications. Together, these modifications work
to provide a more specific and objective guideline for practitioners to utilize in ADHD diagnosis.

Even though a diagnostic decision is reached using clinical guidelines, public perception
and bias toward the overdiagnosis of ADHD still work to invalidate the practitioners'
assessments. According to Sciutto and Eisenberg (2007), the origins of these perceptions are
most likely based on the information people are exposed to by mass media and personal
experiences, rather than from qualified resources. Mass media plays a large role in availability
bias, meaning that people will easily recall media stories that portray exaggerated and highly
salient cases of ADHD (e.g., a child who experiences negative effects of stimulant medication as
a result of being falsely diagnosed with ADHD) (Sciutto & Eisenberg, 2007). Other biases arise
when people are highly influenced by a catchy article title or when they pay attention to only the
confirmatory evidence of a single hypothesis they support. These perceptions are unfairly biasing
people toward information that only supports the opposing arguments, and implications of the

article should be to inform the public of issues regarding ADHD in a less entertaining, more

objective, and more informative way.

Although there is no official recognized etiology of ADHD, there is an abundance of

literature in support of a biological origin. These articles investigate the heritability, genetic

effects, and brain regions associated with ADHD. A firm support for the heritability and genetics

of ADHD comes largely from family, adoption, and twin studies. One frequently cited study

from Faraone et al. (2005) calculated a mean heritability estimate of 0.76 from a total of 20 twin

studies spanning four different countries, supporting ADHD as a highly heritable disorder. More

specifically, different candidate genes for ADHD are being proposed through family studies, and

a large amount of literature seems to suggest that dopaminergic genes play a large role in the

cognitive performance deficits of ADHD

One such study by Loo et al. (200

ADHD and the dopamine (DA) genes (D

Four different tests were used to measure

251 families, and DNA was gathered fro

that the presence of the DRD4 7-present

on cognitive functioning than those who

observed that maternal ADHD seemed to

genotype and cognitive functioning, so c

genotype" would perform worse than tho

results conflicted with previous literature

genes, but this could be attributed to the

the others.

In addition to possible genetic etiology, neuroimaging studies have found specific brain

regions to be associated with the cognitive deficits and symptomology of ADHD. In a study by

Depue et al. (2010), a Color-Word Stroop task and functional magnetic resonance imaging

(fMRI) were used to locate brain regions linked with inattentive symptoms of ADHD. By

comparing the brain images of a control group to an ADHD group, they found 13 regions (ROIs)

with significant negative correlation to inattentive symptomology, including major structures

such as the prefrontal cortex, dorsal striatum, ventral striatum, posterior cortex, and cerebellum.

Moreover, individuals with ADHD had a larger variability in blood oxygen level--dependent

(BOLD) signals within those ROIs than did the control group. To help further validate study

results, Depue et al. used a discriminant analysis to determine whether variability of BOLD

signals in the 13 ROIs could successfully classify individuals into the ADHD or control group. A

0.95 probability of correctly classifying ADHD within study subjects was found, indicating

variability in the BOLD signal as an effective gauge in characterizing ADHD. Although this was

a noteworthy finding, it is unclear as to whether other psychiatric disorders would display

comparable BOLD signals. Another limitation to this study was the significant age difference

found between ADHD and control groups, although they did limit group differences by matching

groups in academic skills and IQ, as well as excluding comorbid individuals.

As discussed earlier, ADHD is known to be a disorder of cognition, and a vast amount of

literature provides evidence of stimulant efficacy in treating ADHD cognitive deficits, but it is

less known if stimulants can treat all ADHD symptomology including emotional deficits. Using

both an emotional and cognitive Stroop task along with fMRI, one study by Posner et al. (2011)

assessed the effects stimulants have on ADHD emotional deficits. Although the sample size of

30 subjects (15 ADHD, 15 control) was small, the researchers made sure there were no

significant differences among IQ, age, puberty stage, or socioeconomic status. It was found that

off stimulant medication, ADHD participants showed increased activity in the medial prefrontal

cortex (mPFC), the brain region associated with altered emotional processing in ADHD youth.

However, on stimulants, mPFC reactivity was lowered to levels more like those of the controls.

This indicates that stimulants play an important role in attenuating abnormal emotional processes

by altering mPFC performance. One important thing to note about this study is that the ADHD

participants were already taking stimulants before study participation, so the study sample could

possibly be biased to those who were already experiencing beneficial effects from stimulants.

Additionally, there was no control for homogeneity of stimulant medication. Positive responses

to stimulant medication in a wide range of ADHD symptoms provide additional evidence in

support of ADHD as a valid, treatable dis

Another controversial topic conce

cultures, or if ADHD symptoms are only

Canino, 2010). One study reviewed 112 s

from North America and 32 from Europe

ADHD prevalence were found after adju

de Lima, Horta, Biederman, & Rohde, 2(

review of worldwide ADHD prevalence

unique to Western culture.

Con: ADHD is not a real disorder

Even though the DSM-V has esta

an outstanding amount of diagnostic chal

contributing to inaccurate diagnoses of A

total of 50 child pediatricians and psychiatrists from the United Kingdom and Belgium, and

using a semistructured interview technique, participants were able to openly discuss how they

made decisions regarding the assessment and diagnosis of ADHD. In attempt to lessen reporting

bias, clinicians were asked to explain their diagnostic procedures in accordance to their most

recent clinical cases. Results indicated that coming to conclusions regarding ADHD management

is a complex and time-consuming process. In respect to diagnostic guidelines, it was found that

only 14% of clinicians responded saying that they deliberately followed published diagnostic

criteria, and that most managed ADHD diagnosis with a broader focus, relying on personal

clinical experience and evaluation instead of a more systematic approach. These findings imply

that adhering to the diagnostic guidelines of ADHD seems to be the exception rather than the

rule, and this not only introduces bias into the diagnostic procedure, but also challenges the

validity of ADHD itself (Kovshoff et al., 2012).

Even when psychologists and psychiatrists adhere to guidelines, it seems that ADHD

cases are only continuing to increase as the diagnostic criteria evolve. Sciutto and Eisenberg

(2007) found evidence showing an increase in the probability of an ADHD diagnosis after

switching from the DSM-III-R to the DSM-IV criteria (as cited by Cuffe, Moore, & McKeown,

2005). According to Rabiner (n.d.), the DSM-V seems to have less restricting guidelines. For

instance, the requirement of "clinically significant impairment" in the DSM-IV is now changed

to "…clear evidence that the symptoms interfere with, or reduce the quality of, social, academic,

or occupational functioning" (para.1), and these lowered thresholds could lead to an increase in

ADHD diagnosis.

Furthermore, another reason practitioners may be having such a difficult time in the

diagnosis and management of ADHD is the extraordinary prevalence rates of psychiatric comorbidity found among ADHD children and adolescents. One study by Yoshimasu et al.

(2012) examined comorbidity rates of 343 ADHD cases and their matched 712 non-ADHD

controls, spanning from the child's birth until the age of 19, high school graduation, drop-out,

death, or emigration. A key strength in this study's design is the population-based birth cohort, as

all their participants were born in Rochester, Minnesota between the dates of January 1, 1976,

and December 31, 1982. Also, unlike many previous studies that used interviews to determine

the incidence of a comorbid disorder, this study established comorbidities only through clinical

diagnoses, and therefore reduced possible self-report and rater biases. Yoshimasu et al. found

that 63% (213 participants) had at least one comorbid psychiatric disorder before they turned 19,

and that this number was significantly larger than the 19% of non-ADHD controls found with a

comorbid disorder. The most prevalent co

oppositional defiant disorder and conduct

differences in the total number of comorb

more internalizing-only comorbidities (an

significantly higher externalizing-only co

disorders). Moreover, results observed a f

children with ADHD, suggesting that a so

infrequent in clinical samples. These com

whether ADHD, and the symptoms assoc

separate psychiatric disorder, or if ADHD

a child may have or be at risk for.

On the issue of ADHD causation,

variables may significantly influence the

origins of the disorder. Pineda et al. (2007) studied the Paisa community in Colombia, South

America and the effects that some environmental influences may have had on the development

of ADHD in a sample of 200 randomly selected ADHD children. Concerning risk factors, the

study found 11 significant prenatal, neonatal, and early-childhood health variables, of which

prenatal alcohol exposure was the highest risk factor for ADHD. Additionally, moderate brain

injury was discovered to be highly associated with the development of ADHD, as well as

excessive cigarette exposure in the prenatal period, and febrile seizures. A couple of limitations

of this study were that they did not control for comorbidities, and the relatively small sample size

was only capable of identifying the more common risk factors. However, for future studies, the

researchers proposed that exploring environmental variables associated with large family

samples could potentially expose environmental risk factors that are separate from genetic

factors.

As discussed in the pro section, a wide range of ADHD symptomology is being

successfully treated with prescribed stimulant medication. However, some studies examining the

chronic effects of long-term stimulant treatment have found some potentially unhealthy effects

caused by the drugs. One relevant study by Wang et al. (2013) hypothesized that long-term

chronic treatment using the common stimulant methylphenidate (MPH), which blocks the

dopamine transporter (DAT) to boost DA signaling, would cause the upregulation of DAT

leading to a reduction of dopaminergic signaling when an ADHD individual is off medication.

The researchers provided 1 year of MPH for 18 adult ADHD individuals who had never

experienced stimulant treatment previous to this study (6 males, 12 females). They compared

DAT availability of 11 adult controls with the ADHD group both before and after the period of

MPH treatment using a positron emission topography (PET) study, specifically studying the brain region of the striatum (caudate, putamen, and ventral striatum). Results found no difference

between the ADHD and control group in baseline DAT availability, but did discover

significantly greater DAT availability in the putamen and caudate after 1 year of MPH treatment.

This study provides some of the first evidence indicating that long-term use of MPH leads to

DAT neuroplasticity, which may intensify ADHD symptoms when no stimulant medication is

being used and decrease the overall efficacy of MPH, thus requiring elevated doses of the

stimulant. Although results of the study found an increase in DAT availability, other literature

has presented conflicting results, which the researchers propose could be a result of past

treatment history. Also, it would have been more ideal for this study to use a "double-blind,

drug-placebo randomized" design, so that they could have observed and compared any DAT

changes for ADHD subjects not under the

Another problem that ADHD diag

if an individual with ADHD is able to con

produces a negative association. Utilizing

undergraduates, Canu, Newman, Morrow

ADHD by measuring participants' attitud

vague weakness. Participants first read a

desirability appraisal, in which participan

the target individual on a team project, be

friends. Results revealed that ADHD targe

that female dispositions toward women w

higher reluctance to start a social relation

labeled as ADHD, and male ADHD targe

domains, including the probability of a female to favorably rate the likelihood of dating a male

with ADHD. Overall, evidence of participant hesitation to become involved with ADHD targets

was clear across many conditions, but most consistently, in situations that involved professional

or scholastic teamwork. These findings suggest that the stigmatization of ADHD plays an

important role in the social challenges of individuals with ADHD, and the implications of the

psychiatric label should be a factor to consider while in the diagnostic process. Future research

should use a more ethnically diverse sample to examine the consistency of the current results and

also look into measuring prejudiced behavior along with cognitive biases.

Conclusion

Conflicting literature regarding the complications of ADHD as a legitimate disorder is

abundant and only growing larger. The research in favor of ADHD supports objective diagnostic

guidelines, biased perceptions toward the misdiagnosis of the disorder, a biological origin, the

proven efficacy of stimulant treatment, and the disorder's prevalence across changing cultures.

On the other hand, those who argue against ADHD validity feel that an accurate diagnosis of

ADHD is too complicated to make. They believe there is excessive comorbidity within the

disorder, that environmental causation may be dominant factor, and that there are significant

problems associated with stimulant medication and the negative stigma of ADHD. With that

said, there is no official etiology of ADHD, but neither is there enough sound, empirical

evidence to disprove the validity of ADHD as a clinically diagnosable disorder.

ASSESSING THE LEGITIMACY OF ADHD   13

References

American Psychiatric Association (APA). (2013). *Diagnostic and statistical manual of mental*
    disorders: DSM-5. Washington, DC: APA.

Bauermeister, J. J., & Canino, G. (2010). ADHD across cultures: Is there evidence for a
    bidimensional organization of symptoms? *Journal of Clinical Child & Adolescent*
    Psychology, 39(3), 362--372. doi:10.1080/15374411003691743

Canu, W. H., Newman, M. L., Morrow, ͅ
    ADHD: Stigma and influences of
    Attention Disorders, 11, 700--710

Cuffe, S. P., Moore, C. G., & McKeown,
    symptoms in the national health i
    -401.

Depue, B. E., Burgess, G. C., Willcutt, E
    Symptom-correlated brain region
    organization variability, and relat
    Neuroimaging, 182, 96--102. doi

Faraone, S. (2005). The scientific founda
    disorder as a valid psychiatric co
    -10. doi:10.1007/s00787-005-042

Faraone, S. V., Perlis, R. H., Doyle, A. E
    Sklar, P. (2005). Molecular genet
    Biological Psychiatry, 57, 1313--

ASSESSING THE LEGITIMACY OF ADHD   14

Kovshoff, H., Williams, S., Vrijens, M., Danckaerts, M., Thompson, M., Yardley, L., …
    Sonuga-Barke, J. S., E. (2012). The decisions regarding ADHD management (DRAMa)
    study: Uncertainties and complexities in assessment, diagnosis, and treatment, from the
    clinician's point of view. *European Child & Adolescent Psychiatry, 21,* 87--99.
    doi:0.1007/s00787-011-0235-8

Loo, S. K., Rich, E. C., Ishii, J., McGough, J., McCracken, J., Nelson, S., & Smalley, S. L.
    (2008). Cognitive functioning in affected sibling pairs with ADHD: Familial clustering
    and dopamine genes. *Journal of Psychology and Psychiatry, 49*(9), 950--957.
    doi:10.1111/j.1469-7610.2008.01928.x

Pelham, W. E., Foster, E. M., & Robb, J. A. (2007). The economic impact of attention-
    deficit/hyperactivity disorder in children and adolescents. *Journal of Pediatric*
    Psychology, 32(6), 711--727. doi:10.1093/jpepsy/jsm022

Pineda, D. A., Palacio, L. G., Puerta, I. C., Merchán, V., Arango, C. P., Galvis, A. Y., … Arcos-
    Burgos, M. (2007). Environmental influences that affect attention deficit/hyperactivity
    disorder. *European Child and Adolescent Psychiatry, 16,* 337--346. doi:10.1007/s00787-
    007-0605-4

Polanczyk, G., Silva de Lima, M., Horta, B. L., Biederman, J., & Rohde, L. A. (2007). The
    worldwide prevalence of ADHD: A systematic review and metaregression analysis. The
    American Journal of Psychiatry, 164, 942--948. doi:10.1176/appi.ajp.164.6.942

Posner, J., Maia, T. V., Fair, D., Peterson, B. S., Sonuga-Barke, E. J., & Nagel, B. J. (2011). The
    attenuation of dysfunctional emotional processing with stimulant medication: An fMRI
    study of adolescents with ADHD. *Psychiatry Research: Neuroimaging, 193,* 151--160.
    doi:10.1016/j.pscychresns.2011.02.005

ASSESSING THE LEGITIMACY OF ADHD   15

Rabiner, D. (n.d.). *New diagnostic criteria for ADHD*. Retrieved from

    www.add.org/?page=DiagnosticCriteria

Sciutto, M. J., & Eisenberg, M. (2007). Evaluating the evidence for and against the

    overdiagnosis of ADHD. *Journal of Attention Disorders, 11,* 106--113.

    doi:10.1177/1087054707300094

Taylor, E., & Sonuga-Barke, E. (2008). Disorders of attention and activity. In M. Rutter, D.

    Bishop, D. Pine, S. Scott, J. S. Stevenson, & E. A. Taylor (Eds.), *Rutter's Child and*

    Adolescent Psychiatry (5th ed., pp. 521--542). Hoboken, NJ: Wiley Blackwell

    Publishing.

Wang, G-J., Volkow, N. D., Wigal, T., Kollins, S. H., Newcorn, J. H., Telang, F., ... Swanson, J.

    M. (2013). Long-term stimulant treatment affects brain dopamine transporter level in

    patients with attention deficit hyperactive disorder. *PLOS ONE, 8*(5), e63023.

    doi:10.1371/journal.pone.0063023

Yoshimasu, K., Barbaresi, W. J., Colligan, R. C., Voigt, R. G., Killian, J. M., Weaver, A. L., &

    Katusic, S. K. (2012). Child ADHD is strongly associated with a broad range of

    psychiatric disorders during adolescence: A population-based birth cohort study. *Journal*

    of Child Psychiatry and Psychology, *53*(10), 1036--1043. doi:10.1111/j.1469-

    7610.2012.02567.x

Information Literacy

by Robyn Hartman, MA

What is Information Literacy?

Information surrounds us. News, advertisements, social media, research reports, politics, entertainment, and more vie for our attention every day. Fake news and misinformation are popular buzzwords and the focus of investigations, campaigns, and reports. In our lives or careers, when we have a question or need information, how do even begin to look for the answer? How do we determine what "good" information is? How do we present that information to the world?

Information Literacy is the skillset that will help you answer these questions. The Association of College & Research Libraries (ACRL), a division of the American Library Association (ALA), defines Information Literacy as "the set of integrated abilities encompassing the reflective discovery of information, the understanding of how information is produced and valued, and the use of information in creating new knowledge and participating ethically in communities of learning" (ACRL, 2015). ACRL has also established four standards for Information Literacy for psychology students (ACRL, 2010). The information literate psychology student:

- Determines the nature and extent of the information needed.
- Accesses needed information effectively and efficiently.
- Evaluates information and its sources critically and incorporates selected information into her or his knowledge base.
- Individually or as a member of a group, uses information effectively to accomplish a specific purpose.

This chapter's objective is to guide you in achieving these standards by Gathering, Evaluating, and Using Information in your psychology work and day-to-day information needs.

Gathering Information

Finding information in this modern age is easy, right? As stated before, information surrounds us, in books, magazines, television, and social media, accessible in our homes, workplaces, schools, and even our pockets. Stop and think a moment, have you ever:

- Had no idea what to write a research paper on?
- Been told your topic for your research paper was too broad?
- Felt lost about knowing where to start your research for a paper?
- Missed points on an assignment because your sources were not "scholarly"?
- Felt lost after not working on your project for a time?

These are common problems when gathering information and this section will help you determine the information you need by exploring research topics, creating a research question, and helping you access information effectively by creating a research plan with keywords and operators.

Research Topics.   *The scenario: In your psychology class, your assignment is to write a 10 page paper on the topic of your choice.* Although it might seem overwhelming at first, you can narrow down your options for your research topic in many ways.

Find ideas through your class.

- Determine the broad focus of your class.
- Look at your class syllabus for the topics you are learning about in class.
- Look through your textbook and notes for topics, examples, or case studies that catch your interest.
- Make an appointment or visit with your instructor during office hours to discuss possible ideas.

Find ideas through media.

- Look at topics related to your course trending on Facebook, Twitter, Instagram, and other social media
- Get ideas from scenarios in popular videos, TV shows, and movies.
- Find ideas through news and current events
- Connect stories in the news to your course
- Read The New York Times (students may have free access through the Library)
- Watch NBC Learn (students may have free access through the Library)

Find ideas from scholars and professionals.

- Search your library for psychology journals and publications related to your course and browse them for ideas.
- Browse online discussion forums, news, and blogs for professional psychology organizations for hot topics.

Create a mind map.   One way to visualize your options is to make a concept map, also called a mind map.

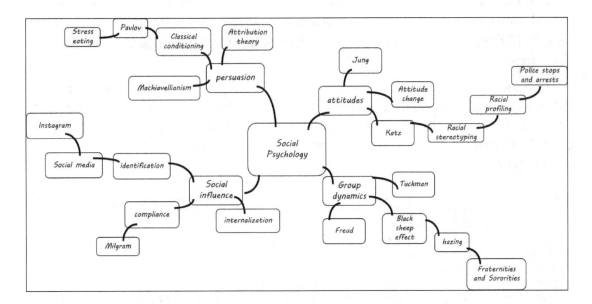

All you need to create a mind map is paper and pencil, but you can also use word processing software or free websites online (See Chapter 13). Start with your main idea in the middle, and branch out ideas and topics from there. Once you have your ideas all in one place, you can focus on the one that interests you the most.

Research Questions.   *The scenario: In your psychology class, your assignment is to write a 10 a page paper on the topic of your choice. You have decided to focus on the idea of social influence and compliance.* Once you have your general topic, you can create your research question. Your research question is NOT your thesis, but it will help you focus your topic even further. Understanding this is key if you often hear that your research topic is too broad. You could write an entire book on the topic of social influence, but by creating a research question, you can narrow down your topic to something that is achievable in 10 pages.

To do this, you can use the Five W's.

- **Who?** Who are the key people involved? What groups are involved? Who are key researchers on this topic?
- **What?** Are there subtopics to this idea? What are some well-known examples or research findings?
- **When?** Is there a time that researchers focused on this topic? Is there a time that interests you?
- **Where?** Is there an area of the world or country that this research explores? Are there businesses, institutions, or other places that are involved in this topic?
- **Why?** What were researchers trying to find out? Why are you curious about this topic?

To answer these questions, you will have to do some preliminary background research. This research will help you have enough information to form your research question. Typically, you will not use this information or cite it in your research paper. You can find background information in encyclopedias, textbooks, class notes, and other resources with general information on a topic.

> **Who?** *Stanley Milgram (original), Robert Shiller and Mel Slater (alternatives), Philip Zimbardo, Kelman & Hamilton, Solomon Asch*
> **What?** *Milgram shock experiment, Asch conformity experiments, variations, alternatives, replications, news and social media, groupthink*
> **When?** *1960s, present*
> **Where?** *Yale Uni (original), military, social groups, sports teams*
> **Why?** *theory of conformism, agentic state theory, belief perseverance (alt theory), engaged followership (alt theory), applicable to genocide? Valid across cultures, groups, genders, ages?*

As you answer the Five W's, you may see connections to your mind map, or think of new ideas and connections inspired by your topic. You will probably not use all the ideas in your research question, but try to use several of the Five W's in your question.

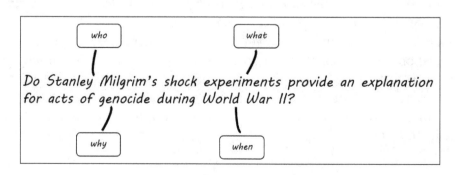

Create several research questions to pick the one you want to use for your research paper.

- *Do Stanley Milgrim's shock experiments provide an explanation for acts of genocide during World War II?*
- *How have replications of obedience experiments shown differences in conformism across cultures?*
- *How does belief perseverance affect an individual's ability to evaluate social media and fake news?*
- *Can the theories developed from compliance experiments be used to prevent hazing in university groups and sports teams?*

Research Plan.   *The scenario: In your psychology class, your assignment is to write a 10 a page paper on the topic of your choice. You focused on the idea of social influence and compliance. You chose the research question: Do Stanley Milgram's shock experiments provide an explanation of acts of genocide during World War II?* You have created your research question, and you may be tempted to jump onto the internet and start searching for resources. However, if you stop to create a research plan before typing and clicking, your search will be much more organized and productive. Create a plan that includes the types of sources you need, where you can find them and the keywords and operators you can use in your searches.

Types of Sources.   Review your assignment and note if it says that you must use scholarly sources or forbids the use of websites. Look to see if you must use peer-reviewed journal articles, qualitative or quantitative data, or primary or secondary sources. These rules will guide where you search for information and what you choose to include in your paper. If it does not specify, using scholarly articles is the standard for academic and professional papers.

- **Scholarly/journal article:** a paper researched and written by an expert(s) in their field meant to inform and educate other professionals in that field.
- **Peer-review:** the process in which professional journals have other experts in a field read, review, and approve a scholarly article before publishing it.
- **Qualitative data:** research where the results are not in numbers or statistics. These can be from research such as unstructured interviews and use a descriptive, narrative style to explain how or why.
- **Quantitative data:** research where the results are in numbers or statistics, from research such as controlled observations and experiments. These can be interpreted with statistical analysis and used to measure things.
- **Primary source**: sources that are firsthand accounts or as close to the original event or source as possible. These also include data sets and original research. For example, an autobiography is a primary source because the person that it is about wrote it.

- **Secondary source**: sources that interpret and analyze primary sources. For example, a biography is a secondary source because someone else wrote it about another person.

Where to Search.   You may often hear your instructors say "No websites!" They say this because:

- Publishing web content is often not controlled (as journal articles are). Pseudoscience, medical myths, advertisements, and clickbait often masquerade as scholarly research.
- It can be difficult to tell the purpose behind the information.
- Web content, even from the news or other more trusted sources, is often too general for an in-depth analysis.

Finding scholarly sources, written by people in your field, for people in your field, will give you the specific information you need for your paper. The best place to find scholarly, academic sources is to use academic library catalogs and research databases.

- **Database:** a collection of information, can cover a wide range of topics, or specialize in the professional field of study or subjects. Academic research databases help you find and access scholarly information, such as peer-reviewed journals, conference papers, dissertations, and primary sources.
- **Catalog:** an organized list of items. A library catalog is a list of a library's physical and digital material. In academic libraries, this can include books, journals, newspapers, historical items, and archives, plus the material in the academic research databases that the library subscribes to for students and faculty to use.

Before you start searching, explore what library catalogs and academic databases are available to you (See Chapter 12). This list will give you a checklist of places to search for scholarly sources for your research paper.

Sources Needed:
- *At least 20 sources*
- *Scholarly articles*
  - *Peer-reviewed*

Where to Search:
- *Fort Hays State University Forsyth Library*
  - *Catalog https://www·fhsu·edu/library/*
  - *Research Databases*
    - *EBSCO Psychology & Behavioral Sciences Collection*
    - *EBSCO PsycARTICLES*
    - *Gale Psychology Collection*
    - *Sage Premier*

How to Search.   You may think that using a popular search engine to find information is easy because you can simply type in your question "Do Stanley Milgram's shock experiments provide an explanation of acts of genocide during World War II?" and get thousands of answers. This question is a natural language type of search, typing your question as you would speak it. However, you cannot use natural language searching to narrow your results, find all of the results, or even find the best results.

Because library catalogs and academic databases are specialized collections of information, they often use a programmed logic type of search called Boolean searching instead of natural language searching. This logic allows your search results to be much more specific and easily narrowed down to exactly what you want. Instead of typing your question, as you would say it aloud, instead, you will search using keywords, connecting them with operators.

- **Keywords:** words or phrases that are important to your search

Start by picking out the most important ideas from your research question. Consider using your answers to the Five W's: Who, What, When, Where, and Why. Then, brainstorm alternative words and phrases, synonyms, and related words for each of your keywords. Using keywords gives you an alternate list, as not everyone will use the same terms, even when you are talking about the same thing.

Create a chart with your main ideas across the top, with columns underneath for your alternates. You might need to do some more background research for this, or you might find more terms to add to your chart later in your search.

If there are any of your keywords that are phrases, where you want to see results with those exact words in that exact order, put quotation marks around them. Using phrases will make sure you do not get a result with "world" in the first paragraph and "war" in the last paragraph.

"Stanley Milgram" (psychologist)	"Shock experiments"	Genocide	"World War II"
"Robert Shiller"	obedience	Holocaust	"World War Two"
"Mel Slater"	"authority figures"	Shoah	"Second World War"
"Phillip Zimbardo"	conformism	murder	WWII
	"Following orders"	"War crimes"	WW2
	"Milgram experiments"	"Ethnic cleansing"	(where) Europe, "Nazi Germany", "German-occupied Europe", Poland
		(by) Germans, Nazis, civilians, soldiers	"Nuremburg Trials"
		(against) Jews	

You will not use ALL these words in each of your searches—you will get no results! However, you can combine them to get specific results.

- **Boolean Operators:** connects your keywords to broaden or narrow your results.

AND: use AND to narrow your search. If you were to search for just "Stanley Milgram," you will find thousands of results, even if you start with your library's catalog. However, Milgram did many types of experiments, and not all of them were shock experiments related to genocide in World War II. To be more specific, add another keyword or two to your search. Use the operator AND to find results that have ALL the keywords. Write out your search phrase like this:

Genocide AND "Stanley Milgram" AND "World War II"
(Note, it is important that you capitalize AND as well as the other Boolean operators as demonstrated)

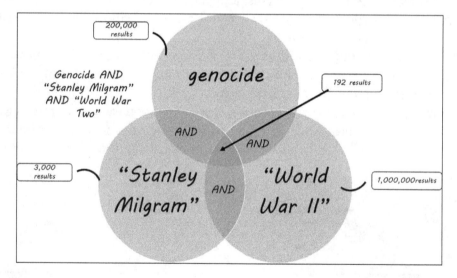

Instead of thousands of unrelated results, this search shows us less but more specific results, all that mention Stanley Milgram, genocide, and World War II. You can continue to narrow down your results by adding more keywords with AND until you have a number that you are comfortable with skimming the titles (to start with, we'll talk about choosing sources in Evaluating Information).

Genocide AND "Stanley Milgram" AND "World War II" AND "Nuremberg Trials"

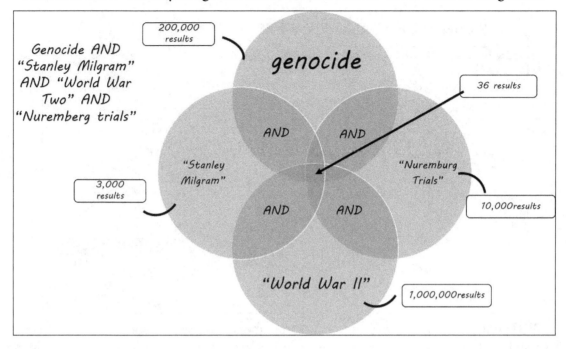

OR: use OR to broaden your search. If you do not have enough results or none at all, try using your alternate keywords instead of your main keywords. You can also use the operator OR to find more results. OR will find results that use either keyword you connect with it. When you write OR search phrases, put the terms in parentheses:

("World War II" OR "World War Two")

You can combine the AND and OR operators to make a unique search phrase.

"Stanley Milgram" AND ("World War II" OR "World War Two")

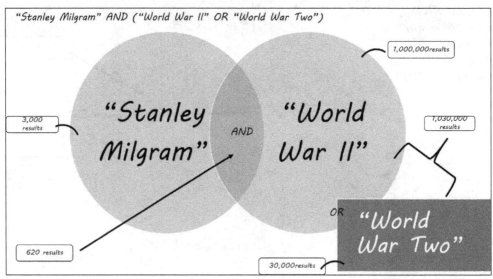

NOT: use NOT to narrow your search. Sometimes as you search, you will find results that have nothing to do with your search—they contain one of your keywords, but with a different meaning. For example, a search for "mustang" may come up with results about the horse, or about the car. If you are writing a research paper about preserving the wild horses' natural habitat, results about muscle cars are not going to help you! In cases like these, use the operator NOT to limit your search to just the results about horses. Use parentheses to separate that phrase.

mustang AND (horse NOT Ford)

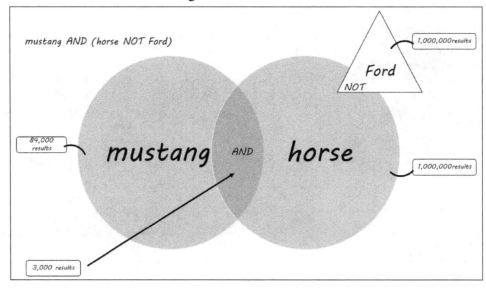

Using keywords instead of natural language searching will help you have a much more specific search, and connecting your keywords with Boolean operators such as AND, OR, and NOT will help get you more or fewer results, as needed. Although it might seem clunky at first, once you search this way a few times, it will become second nature, and you will be much more pleased with your specific results, instead of having to wade through hundreds of results that are not right for your research paper. You can combine keywords with operators in many different ways. If you are not having success with a search phrase in an information source, try adding or removing keywords, and different combinations of operators.

Research Log.   As you search, keep a research log of where you search, how you searched, and your search results. You can keep a research log in a paper notebook, on index cards, using word processing software, or online note-taking programs. This log will help you see what keywords are the best, how to combine them, and know where to pick up your searching if you have stepped away from it for a period.

Where	How	Results	Notes
FHSU Forsyth catalog	Genocide AND "Stanley Milgram" AND "World War II"	192	
	("Stanley Milgram" OR "Phillip Zimbardo") AND (obedience OR conformity) AND (Genocide OR Holocaust OR Shoah OR murder) AND ("World War II" OR "World War Two" OR Second World War")	609	Too many results. Too much in search phrase!
	Genocide AND "Stanley Milgram" AND "World War II" AND "Nuremberg Trials"	36	
EBSCO PsycARTICLES	"Stanley Milgram" AND (holocaust OR shoah)	2	Diff theories: Ernest Becker, Gustave Gilbert
	("obedience to authority" OR conformity AND Milgram)	15	
Sage Premier	(genocide OR holocaust OR shoah) AND Milgram	235	Need to narrow down by article type

Once you gathered potential information sources, you can then move on to evaluating them for use in your research project.

Evaluating Information

Now that you have a list of results from your searches, you may be tempted to start at the top and use each article in your research paper. Although each result listed may fulfill your keyword requirements, it is up to you, the living, breathing, thinking human, and not the computer program, to decide which information sources are best for your paper. Ask yourself, can the programmed logic of Boolean searching tell you if:

- Is the author an authority on the subject?
- The information in the source is relevant for your specific research project?
- Your sources represent diverse points of view?

These are common questions you should ask when Evaluating Information and this section will help you evaluate information and critically select sources to incorporate into your research projects.

The Five W's.   *The scenario: In your psychology class, your assignment is to write a 10 a page paper on the topic of your choice. You focused on the idea of social influence and compliance. You chose the research question: Do Stanley Milgram's shock experiments provide an explanation of acts of genocide during World War II? You created and followed a research plan with keywords and operators and kept a log of your work.*

When creating your research question, you asked yourself the Five W's to help focus your topic. You can use these questions again to focus in on each source and decide if it is appropriate for you to use in your paper. When answering these questions you may not be able to answer every question, but add the information you find to your research log. Keep in mind that you do not have to read the entire article from beginning to end to find these answers—feel free to jump around the sections of scholarly articles and skim when needed. You can read more in depth once you have determined that the source is appropriate for your research project.

- **Who?** Who is the author? Who is their employer? Are they experts in this field? In psychology? Do the authors represent diverse worldviews? Have they written about this subject before? Search for the authors, their universities and companies, and their previous writing.
- **What?** What type of information is in the source? Is it qualitative or quantitative data? Is this primary or secondary research? Is it scholarly and based on research or basic information for the public? Does the information present more than one view on the topic? Look at the abstract, introduction, and results sections of scholarly articles.
- **When?** When was the information published? When was the research conducted? Is the information up-to-date for the current period? Does the period affect if the findings are still relevant or correct? Look at the publication date and methods of scholarly articles.

- **Where?** Is there an area of the world or country that is the focus of this research focuses? Was this published in connection to a certain research institute or university? Are certain populations or points of view included or excluded because of this? Look at the publication location, where the authors work, and in what languages the article was written or published.

- **Why?** What were researchers trying to find out? Was the research sponsored or paid for by an institute, university, or corporation? Is the purpose of the information to educate or to persuade someone to change their view on the topic? Look at the abstract, results, and discussion sections of scholarly articles.

Here is an evaluation for one of the articles (Slater et al., 2006) found using keywords and operators from the research plan above.

"A Virtual Reprise of the Stanley Milgram Obedience Experiments"
https://doi.org/10.1371/journal.pone.0000039

Title:	A Virtual Reprise of the Stanley Milgram Obedience Experiments	Notes
Who?	Mel Slater, Angus Antley, Adam Davison, David Swapp, Christoph Guger, Chris Barker, Nancy Pistrang, Maria V. Sanchez-Vives	Most at University College London, Computer Science & Psychology Depts, United Kingdom, Austria, Spain
What?	Quantitative, primary research, scholarly	
When?	Published in 2006	Obedience connections may not have changed since 2006- but virtual reality has and those findings may be outdated
Where?	United Kingdom/Europe	
Why?	Replicating original Milgram experiment in a virtual environment- focus on virtual interaction not obedience	

Authority.   When working on a scholarly project, you will want to ensure that your sources are authorities on the subject. You can define authority in several ways, depending on what you require for your current information needs. Scholarship and education can provide subject expertise, public office or titles are indicators of authority in society, and participating in historical events can give firsthand experience in topics.

When writing for a research project, scholarly peer-reviewed articles are an accepted standard in demonstrating authority in a subject. However, keep in mind that not everyone who writes an article (scholarly or for the public) is an authority, nor do authorities only write for these publications. They may also write for news publications, give interviews, blog, or use social media to disseminate information.

It is up to you, working within the parameters of your research project, to determine the criteria for authority—this "who" context may change from project to project. For example, Dr. Mel Slater, one of the authors of "A Virtual Reprise of the Stanley Milgram Obedience Experiments," has many scholarly publications and books about virtual reality and clinical psychology. These demonstrate his authority through scholarship. However, his views on those topics are also on his blog (http://presence-thoughts.blogspot.com/), web page (http://www.melslater.me/), and his Twitter account (@melslater). In your scenario, you would probably determine that it is most appropriate to use Dr. Slater's articles and books in your research paper, as those are the types of sources expected (and often required) by your instructors. However, you could use his blog and social media posts in your class discussions and to learn more about virtual reality and psychology.

Relevance.   If you have searched using keywords and operators, your list of results should at least have something to do with your research question—such as this programmed Boolean logic search phrase:

"Stanley Milgram" AND (obedience OR authority)

Many search engines and library catalogs will list those results in order of relevance. The program attempts to determine how likely the result contains what it is you want. However, only you can make the final decision to use an information source, and if it is truly relevant to your research project.

To help determine this, look back to your research question. What are the most important points? These may be the same as your main keywords. Think ahead to your paper outline and the points you want to discuss. Compare these "what" and "why" criteria to your information source to determine if it is relevant for your paper. The main criteria for the research question "Do Stanley Milgram's shock experiments provide an explanation of acts of genocide during World War II?" are Milgram, shock experiments, and genocide during World War II.

For example, by looking at the abstract of "A Virtual Reprise of the Stanley Milgram Obedience Experiments," you can learn that the authors did not intend that the experiment study obedience, but to study human responses to virtual characters. Therefore, although the article is relevant to the ideas of Milgram and shock experiments, it does not discuss genocide and World War II. You would probably determine that this article is less relevant than others you have found that do discuss genocide, as well as Milgram's experiments. You may decide not dismiss it entirely, instead saving it to use if you find you need further information, or if you decide to discuss modern versions of the experiments.

Experiment methods, technology, and established theories may also have an impact on the relevance of an information source. Virtual reality is a key part of the experiments in "A Virtual Reprise of the Stanley Milgram Obedience Experiments"; however, the research is from 2006. Reading the article over a decade later may lead you to decide that the information is no longer relevant, due to the advances and changes in the technology of virtual reality.

Points of View.   Many points of view can be—and should be—represented in the information sources for your research project. These perspectives can take many forms.

Counterarguments. Make sure that some sources have ideas counter to your own. Including arguments against your thesis will allow you to address those concerns in your own words. Explaining other ponts of view strengthens your credibility and helps you to avoid confirmation bias—the tendency to search for, choose, and use information that only reinforces or repeats your ideas.

Underrepresented authorities. Through the publishing process and biases to race, gender, religion, sexual orientation, and other diverse aspects, scholarly articles and other information sources exclude some points of view. Ask yourself if you are writing about a topic that deals with a marginalized group. If so, make sure to use authors that belong to that group to represent those voices in your work. For example, if you are researching gender equality, make sure that you include transgender and asexual points of view. Including these underrepresented authorities will help break the cycle of bias and work toward greater equality in authorship.

Diverse authorities. Look over your information sources. Are the authors predominantly male? Then make a point to include more female authorities. Are your sources based on traditional Western (Europe and North America) thinking? Search your perspectives from Asian, African, or South American sources. For example, in "A Virtual Reprise of the Stanley Milgram Obedience Experiments," the majority of authors are men. They are all based in Europe and conducted their research there. Seeing this, you may then search for information sources that include research done in non-Western parts of the world, as well as more articles written by women around the world. By carefully evaluating the sources you have gathered, according to criteria you set in context for your research project, you will be able to identify the best information sources to use.

Using Information

The scenario: In your psychology class, your assignment is to write a 10 a page paper on the topic of your choice. You focused on the idea of social influence and compliance. You chose the research question: Do Stanley Milgram's shock experiments provide an explanation of acts of genocide during World War II? You created and followed a research plan with keywords and operators and kept a log of your work. You have evaluated the information sources you found to include counterarguments, underrepresented, and diverse viewpoints.

Now that you have gathered and evaluated your information resources for your research project, you are ready to use them in your paper. Using resources effectively and responsibly is often stressed as using the correct citation format—usually APA Style in psychology. Chapter 8 covers the basics of APA Style. However, there are several reasons behind your instructor's insistence to use proper style conventions. Have you ever wondered:

- Why is it important to cite the research you have used?
- Why does it matter which citation style you use?
- Why is my research paper important?

Information has Value.   One of the main reasons that you cite sources in your research is to give credit to others' work. Citation shows your reader that the work is not your own and that someone else put in the time, effort, and money to produce the ideas (ACRL, 2015). Even if the information is free through open access or public domain, there is still the hours of work behind it before it reached the user. Giving credit to the authors shows that you respect that time and effort.

There are also legal ramifications to the value of information, with copyright restrictions and fair use prompting lawsuits. In higher education, without properly crediting your sources you risk failure on assignment, a course, removal from a degree program, or expulsion from the school. In the workplace, plagiarism can result in demotions, dismissals, loss of respect in an industry, and other legal consequences. Terms to consider related to copyright issues are:

- **Copyright:** legal right to determine whether, and how, others may use an original work
- **Plagiarism:** violation of copyright using someone else's work or ideas without crediting them
- **Fair Use:** legal doctrine in US copyright law that, in specific circumstances, lets you use excerpts of copyrighted material without permission or payment
- **Open Access:** scholarly movement where research is made available free to the public
- **Public Domain:** original works not protected by copyright laws, can be used without permission

Information Creation as a Process.   There are several different types of citation styles—APA, MLA, and Chicago Style are three of the most popular. Different academic disciplines, publishers, and careers will use different styles, depending on what is important to that field of study, and how that information is created and represented in their publications (ACRL, 2015). Not only does citing your sources show that you can follow copyright laws and avoid plagiarism, using the specified citation style shows that you are a contributing member of a field and that you respect their rules and standards.

An example of this is interview for a job. Even if the everyday job involves wearing jeans, work boots, and a hard hat (as in the construction industry), when you go to the interview for the job, the expected standard is that you will wear more formal business wear, such as a blouse and skirt, dress pants, or a suit jacket and tie. Wearing formal interview clothes signals to the hiring panel that you are a professional and ready for the job. By "dressing up" your work in the approved citation style, you are signaling to your readers that you are also a professional in the field and able to follow their process to create information. In the psychology field, the American Psychology Association (APA) has established APA Style as the industry standard (APA, n.d.).

Scholarship as a Conversation.   If you are struggling with using your information sources responsibly, you may be asking yourself, "What does it matter? Who cares about my paper?" You might think that the only person who will ever care about your research project is the instructor who is grading it this semester. However, the work that you do now while learning about psychology can have a much further impact on your academics, psychology career, and the education and careers of others.

When attributing the work of others in your research, you are entering into a scholarly conversation. It can be a slow, quiet, conversation, but it is the steady exchange of ideas back and forth between experts and students in the field. You have read the ideas of others in their scholarly articles, and adding them to your ideas sends those ideas out to new readers. You are also responding to their ideas with your own opinions (especially if those ideas are different from your own, as in counterarguments). Many authorities in the field will track their citations in other papers, and this gives them the opportunity to respond to your ideas about their work and to be exposed to new ideas and opinions. You can do something similar and trace ideas through the works of others, connecting the works used as references in research and seeing how it forms a web of connections. Scholarly ideas are also parts of more active, louder conversations in blogs, social media, news stories, conference presentations, and professional speakers (ACRL, 2015).

For example, in "A Virtual Reprise of the Stanley Milgram Obedience Experiments," the authors cited 32 other authorities in their paper. Several of these directly mention Milgram's shock experiments, and Milgram himself is the author of three of the references. Because the authors credited these works as part of the conversation, you can track these back to the authorities, finding additional information resources to use in your current or future research projects. In turn, when you cite this article, future readers will be able to track those ideas back to the source, pulling them into the larger conversation with you.

Information Literacy in Everyday Life

This chapter focused on how to Gather, Evaluate, and Use Information. As a psychology student, this means that you should be able to determine the nature of the information you need for a research project, access that information, critically evaluate it, and use it effectively (ACRL, 2010). However, you will find yourself using these information literacy skills in more than just your psychology courses. Information literacy helps combat the negative effects of misinformation, as well as deepens your understanding of the information you receive from news, social media, and professional literature. You can apply these abilities in all of your academic coursework, in scholarly conversations in your career and life, and in finding the answers to those everyday questions that pop up, whenever you find yourself searching for information.

References

American Psychological Association (APA). (n.d.). *What is APA Style?* Retrieved from https://www.apastyle.org/learn/faqs/what-is-apa-style

Association of College and Research Libraries (ACRL). (2015). *Framework for information literacy for higher education.* Retrieved from http://www.ala.org/acrl/standards/ilframework

Association of College and Research Libraries (ACRL). (2010). *Psychology information literacy standards.* Retrieved from http://www.ala.org/acrl/standards/psych_info_lit

Slater, M., Antley, A., Davison, A., Swapp, D., Guger, C., Barker, . . . Sanchez-Vives, M. (2006). A virtual reprise of the Stanley Milgram obedience experiments. *PLOS ONE, 1,* e39. doi:10.1371/journal.pone.0000039

12

Database Searching for Psychology Topics

by MaryAlice Wade, MS, MLS

In Chapter 11, *Information Literacy*, you learned how to choose a manageable topic, write a research question, identify the types of sources you need, and broaden and narrow your searches. In this chapter, we will go into more depth about where and how to find the information you need and demonstrate many practical, time-saving approaches and strategies.

The First Step: Understand Your Assignment

Read the assignment carefully, as soon as you receive it. This will allow you time to ask your instructor about anything that is unclear. There is nothing worse than spending hours, days, or weeks on an assignment, only to lose points or even fail because your paper, although perhaps interesting and well written, did not meet the criteria of the assignment.

As mentioned in Chapter 13, you may want to use an *assignment calculator*, which lays out the steps with a time frame, explanation, and links to helpful resources for each step, or you may just want to make careful notes. However you approach it, the point is to identify the important criteria in your assignment and take these into account as you plan your research. Most assignments include rules about the topic, type and number of sources, required content and length, and of course the all-important due date. Here are some points to consider as you plan your research:

- **Topic.** If a topic is unfamiliar to you, start by getting some background information. Jumping in to find articles on a topic you do not really understand usually only results in more confusion and a frustrating search process. Finding basic information, also called *pre-search*, helps you get a good foundation of knowledge on your research topic and prepares you to springboard into a more in-depth investigation. Pre-search needs might include: (a) definitions of terms and basic concepts, which can be found in in reference books like psychology dictionaries or encyclopedias, your textbook, or scholarly books, and (b) an overview of key research studies, available in journal articles with literature reviews or systematic analyses.

- **Sources.** What type of sources are acceptable? How many do you need? Do you know how to identify source types? The good news is that databases identify source types for you, so it is usually just a matter of knowing how to limit your search. If you are searching the web, however, you will need to be able to determine if a source is peer-reviewed or meets whatever source criteria you have.

- **Content and length.** Keep the amount and depth of information you need in mind when choosing your sources.

- **Due date.** Give yourself plenty of time to do your research. You may need to locate sources in other libraries, work with a librarian, or get writing assistance. Often students think they are "doing it wrong" if they do not quickly find the perfect article, or even a relevant one. The truth is that research is not linear. Rather, it is an iterative process of experimenting with search terms, evaluating what you find, making changes, and trying again. The solution might be as simple as changing your keywords, or switching to a different database, or perhaps a more significant change is needed. Do not be afraid to narrow, broaden, or even change your topic, based on what you discover as you search.

Accessing the Information You Need

In most cases, the best sources of reliable information are peer-reviewed journal articles and scholarly books. These can most easily be found in electronic databases and online catalogs available through university libraries. In addition, there are a growing number of publicly available databases. Databases vary widely in subject matter, content, source types, and accessibility. Understanding these variations will help you choose the best places to find information suitable for your assignment.

Levels of Accessibility.

Subscription databases. University libraries generally have the largest collections of databases. Because these databases require very costly subscriptions, access is usually restricted to current students (both on-campus and virtual) and faculty, with a campus log-in. Check the library's website or contact a librarian at your school if you need help accessing your library's resources.

Libraries' database collections vary according to the size of the population they serve, what programs or degrees the university offers, and the amount of available funding. But even the largest libraries will not own every issue of every journal, newspaper, or magazine you may need. *You may not have immediate access to a particular source.* **Starting early, planning your research, and allowing enough time to find quality sources are the keys to producing the best papers.**

A note about cost: Because the subscription costs of the databases have been paid by the library or university, students should not have to pay for access. This is one reason it is important to access library databases through the library's links. If you try to access an article via an internet search, you may hit a pay-wall that requires a fee to read or download the article. Going through the library's site and signing in with your student log-in will allow you free access to the article, if it is available. If not, you can often request the material from another library. This process is called Interlibrary Loan (ILL) and is available at most university and public libraries, often for free. Check with your librarian.

Some university libraries also allow members of the public to utilize their databases from within the building, but not remotely (i.e., from outside the library). Public libraries often offer a smaller collection of databases that may be remotely accessible. Some state libraries, such as the State Library of Kansas, offer free access to databases to state residents.

A Selective List of the Best Subscription Databases for Psychology.

- **PsycINFO**: The most comprehensive psychology database. Published by the American Psychological Association (APA), it contains article citations and abstracts (often with links to the complete article) from nearly 2,500 journals, of which 99% are peer-reviewed, as well as citations for books and dissertations. Content covers the 1880s to the present and is updated twice weekly (APA, 2019c). Start here!

- **PsycArticles**: Contains nearly 200,000 full-text articles from all the peer-reviewed journals published by APA. Updated weekly (APA, 2019a).

- **Psychology and Behavioral Science Collection**: Produced by EBSCOhost, this database contains more than 480 full-text scholarly journals covering psychology, psychiatry, counseling, as well as other social sciences. It is especially useful for child and adolescent psychology and counseling topics (EBSCO Industries, Inc., 2019).

- **Academic Search Premier** (ASP; EBSCOhost): This database contains articles from thousands of magazines, newspapers, and peer-reviewed journals. Although ASP is a general database covering a huge range of topics, its psychology coverage is excellent.

Open access databases. Have you ever thought about how articles get published? You may have assumed that your professors are paid for publishing their articles in scholarly journals and that publishers provide free or low-cost access to libraries. In truth, libraries must spend many hundreds of thousands of dollars to purchase access to the databases, and the authors of articles do not receive *any* payment. In fact, they are often required to pay the publisher a fee, or sign away all rights to their work. The inequity of this situation has caused a growing demand for *open access*.

Scholarly Publishing and Academic Resources Coalition (SPARC) defines *open access* as "the free, immediate, online availability of research articles combined with the rights to use these articles fully in the digital environment" (SPARC, n.d.). SPARC further states:

"...our current system for communicating research is crippled by a centuries old model that hasn't been updated to take advantage of 21st century technology:

1) Governments provide most of the funding for research—hundreds of billions of dollars annually—and public institutions employ a large portion of all researchers.

2) Researchers publish their findings without the expectation of compensation. Unlike other authors, they hand their work over to publishers without payment, in the interest of advancing human knowledge.

3) Through the process of peer-review, researchers review each other's work for free.

4) Once published, those that contributed to the research (from taxpayers to the institutions that supported the research itself) have to pay again to access the findings. Though research is produced as a public good, it isn't available to the public who paid for it" (SPARC, n.d.).

Academic libraries and librarians can help you locate open resources, online as well as those within the library's collections. Some library catalogs have a filter for open access content, as do many databases and journal sites.

These open access databases are useful for psychology topics:

- **Google Scholar (https://scholar.google.com/):** Search for scholarly literature from all disciplines, including article citations and some full-text articles, book citations, theses, and more. *NOTE*: not all content in Google Scholar is peer-reviewed, so evaluate carefully.

- **PubMed (https://www.ncbi.nlm.nih.gov/pubmed).** Published by the U.S. National Library of Medicine, these databases focus on biomedical literature, but also contain some psychology content.

- **PubMed Central (https://www.ncbi.nlm.nih.gov/pmc/)** is the full-text subset of PubMed.

- **Directory of Open Access Journals (https://doaj.org):** An "independent database which contains approximately 12,000 open access journals covering all areas of science, technology, medicine, social science, and humanities" (Directory of Open Access Journals [DOAJ], 2019, para. 1) from over 100 countries and published in many languages. At the time of this writing, DOAJ contained over 150 peer-reviewed, English-language journals covering the subject of psychology.

- **ProQuest Dissertations and Theses Open (PQDT Open): (https://pqdtopen.proquest.com/search.html).** This database provides free access to complete dissertations and theses covering a wide range of disciplines, whose authors have published as open access. Although dissertations and theses are not peer-reviewed, their extensive bibliographies are sources for peer-reviewed articles. These works sometimes contain copies of psychological tests and measures, though these should not be utilized for publication without permission from the copyright holder.

- **Scholarly Repositories**: Free online collections of documents, both published and unpublished, that are often scholarly, but not necessarily peer-reviewed. Many universities have their own repositories containing research done by staff or students, for example, FHSU's Scholars Repository (https://scholars.fhsu.edu/). Often these individual repositories are part of a larger network such as the Digital Commons Network (http://network.bepress.com/). Published research articles in repositories may not be identical to the version published in the journal.

- **PTSDpubs (https://www.ptsd.va.gov/ptsdpubs/search_ptsdpubs.asp)**: Provided by the U.S. Dept. of Veterans Affairs, this database contains citations and abstracts covering Posttraumatic Stress Disorder and related consequences of trauma. Sources include journal articles, books, dissertations, reports, and newsletters. More information is available at the National Center for PTSD at www.ptsd.va.gov

- **WorldCat.org:** WorldCat lets you search the catalogs of over 10,000 libraries all over the world. You can enter your zip code, and find out what nearby libraries, if any, have the item you need. You can then work with your library to request the item.

Table 1 shows a selection of both subscription and open access databases that contain psychology research in a variety of source types.

Online library catalogs. Although a catalog is basically a list of what the library owns, university libraries and many public libraries have catalogs that allow you to search across source types and in many electronic databases as well. Most catalogs can be searched by anyone, but access to the items themselves may be restricted to those affiliated with the library. If the full-text of the item is available, you will find a link to it in the online catalog. If it is a tangible item like a print book or an article available only in a print journal, the catalog will give you the information you need to locate the item. Librarians are happy to help you find what you need—just ask!

The library catalog can be a good place to start your search, especially if you are just beginning to explore your topic. Once you have a clearer idea of what you are looking for, it is often beneficial to switch to searching directly in a psychology database.

Types of Database Content

Article databases. Most databases contain articles from a variety of sources, including (a) scholarly, peer-reviewed journals that contain primary research and secondary research like literature reviews and systematic analyses; (b) popular (nonscholarly) magazines; (c) newspapers, and (d) trade journals, which are written for workers in a particular field and generally not peer-reviewed.

General versus subject-focused. Some databases, such as EBSCOhost's *Academic Search Premier* or Gale's *InfoTrac*, are general, multidisciplinary collections that cover a

Table 1 Content of Selected Subscription and Open Access Databases

Database	Psychology-focused or general?	Peer-Reviewed Articles	Magazine Articles	News Articles	Book Citations	Full-Text E-Books	Dissertations and Theses	Pro/Cons of Current Topics	Any Open Access Content?	Primarily Open Access
Library Catalog	General	✓	✓	✓	✓	✓	✓		✓	
PsycINFO	Psychology	✓			✓		✓		✓	
PsycArticles	Psychology	✓							✓	
Psychology and Behavioral Science	Psychology	✓	✓	✓						
Academic Search Premier	General	✓	✓	✓						
Opposing Viewpoints	General	✓	✓	✓				✓		

Google Scholar	General	✔			✔				✔
DOAJ	General	✔							✔
PQ Dissert. and Theses Open	General							✔	✔
PTSDpubs	Psychology & related	Citations only							Free to search
PubMed & PubMed Central	Some psychology content	✔			✔			✔	✔
Scholarly Repositories	General	✔					✔		✔
WorldCat	General	✔	✔	✔	✔	Citations only			Free to search

wide variety of topics. Subject databases, as you might guess, focus on a single discipline such as psychology, nursing, chemistry, etc. Usually it is best to use databases that focus on your discipline, as these are most likely to contain articles from the top journals in the field and to have specially designed search interfaces with limiters relevant to the discipline. However, do not overlook the general databases, as they frequently contain useful articles as well.

Full-text versus abstracts.   Sometimes database titles can be confusing; for example, not all the articles in *Social Sciences Full-Text* are in fact, full-text. Most databases contain some articles that are *full-text* (that is, the complete article is immediately accessible) and others for which only the citation and abstract are available. The search interfaces include filters that allow you to limit your results to full-text articles, if desired.

Indexes.   An index, whether electronic or print, contains citations, usually with abstracts, but no full-text content. If an electronic database has the word Index or Abstract in the title, it contains no full-text. At some university libraries, full-text articles not available in the database you are searching may have a link to search the university's other databases for the complete article. If it is available, a link will be provided; if not, you can request it via ILL.

Books and e-books.   If you need background information on your topic, definitions of terms, or more in-depth information than an article can provide, explore what books your library has to offer. Both print and e-books can be found by searching the library's online catalog. E-books can be read online and possibly downloaded, and often allow note-taking, highlighting, and limited printing and copying. E-books can also be found in specialized databases such as *ProQuest E-Book Central*, *Credo Reference E-Book Collection*, and *Gale Virtual Reference Collection*.

If your library does not have books on your topic, try searching WorldCat.org to identify relevant titles and request them from another library through ILL. WorldCat.org is a freely available online database that allows you to search the collections of over 10,000 libraries worldwide.

Other types of database content.   Databases may also include streaming videos, music, government documents, theses and dissertations, and more. A few, such as *Opposing Viewpoints*, *CQ Researcher* and *Issues & Controversies,* focus on current controversial topics and contain in-depth reporting on the key debates and pro/con arguments. If you are stumped for a topic, try browsing these databases and considering the psychological aspects of today's hot-button issues.

Information Research in Action

Let us explore the process of information research by imagining the steps someone might take as they tackle a research paper. We will call our researcher Ann. Ann's assignment reads as follows:

> Write a 10- to 12-page paper that answers the research question, "Is social media use psychologically harmful to college students?" Since **social media** and **psychologically harmful** are broad terms, you must define what each concept means in the context of your paper. You must cite at least 10 peer-reviewed, primary research sources, published in the last 10 years. Your rough draft is due in 3 weeks.

Ann starts by carefully reading her assignment as soon as she receives it, so she can ask her instructor about anything that is unclear. Then she identifies the most important elements, to ensure her paper meets the requirements of the assignment.

- **Length**: 10 to 12 pages
- **Topic/Research Question**: Does social media use cause psychological harm to college students?
- **Source Requirements:** 10 **peer-reviewed** articles reporting **primary research**, published in the last **10** years.
- **Style and Formatting**: APA Style. See Chapter 8 for more on APA style.
- **Due:** Rough draft due in 3 weeks.

To keep track of where and how she has searched, Ann starts a research log, as described in Chapter 11. She first identifies the keywords or phrases in her topic: *social media, psychological harm,* and *college students*. Using the search box on the library's website, Ann begins by searching the library's catalog for *social media* AND *psychological harm* AND *college students*. (In the catalog, capitalize connecting words like AND, OR, or NOT; otherwise, they will be treated as search terms).

This search yields over 99,000 results. For a moment, Ann is overwhelmed at the thought of having to sort through all those results, but then remembers the specific source types required by her assignment: *peer-reviewed, primary research* articles published within the last *10 years*. Using the filters in the catalog, she limits her search results to *peer-reviewed journals*, to the Resource Type *articles*, to the Topic of *psychology*, and the Date Range of *2009 to 2019*. Since there is no filter here for primary research, she will need to examine the articles and decide for herself if they are primary or secondary sources. This reduces her results to about 1,400.

Ann takes a quick look at the titles on the first page of results, and notices several articles are not relevant. For example:

Boysen, G. A. (2013). Confronting math stereotypes in the classroom: Its effect on female college students' sexism and perceptions of confronters. *Sex Roles, 69*(5–6), 297–307. doi:10.1007/s11199-013-0287-y

Judging by the title, this article does not appear to have anything to do with Ann's topic, except that it focuses on college students. She opens the document and reads the abstract, which does not mention social media. She uses the "find" tool on her computer to search for the word *social*; it appears 30 times in the article. A search for *social media* yields 0 results, which verifies Ann's suspicion that this article is not relevant to her topic.

To improve the relevance of her search results, Ann modifies her search slightly by putting quotation marks around "*social media.*" This should bring up only those articles in which that *phrase,* not just individual words, appear somewhere in the citation, text, or description.

If she finds her results are still not very relevant, Ann could select Advanced Search and choose to search only in the title or subject. Terms located in either of those sections are usually the main topics of the article. Revising her search removes her previous limits, so she again filters to peer-reviewed, by date range, and to the topic of psychology. This reduces her results to about 200.

Ann begins to scan the article titles and discovers that a wide range of behaviors and attitudes have been studied in relation to social media. There are articles on social media and smoking, political activism, weight loss, depression, dating. . . .and that is just on the first page of results! "Social media" also means different things in different articles. In some, the phrase is a broad, comprehensive term. In others, it means only Facebook, or a combination of specific social media platforms. This variation helps Ann understand her instructor's requirement that she defines what she means by *social media* and *psychological harm* in her paper.

She remembers hearing reports about the significant increase in anxiety disorders among young people (Schrobsdorff, 2016) and the theory that increased use of technology, like social media, is a leading cause. Browsing her search results, she notices several anxiety-related terms, like *social anxiety, avoidance, worry,* and *insecurity.* Ann wants to save a few of these articles related to anxiety. To do this, she could use a citation manager like Zotero or the folder system available in the online catalog. She clicks "sign in" at the top of the catalog screen and logs in with her university ID. (Ann knows that if she does not sign in, any articles she saves will be lost once she closes out of the online catalog). She clicks the pin icon next to the articles she wants to save. Ann records her search methods and results in her research log.

Armed with an idea of how she might narrow her topic, Ann decides to search the library's databases next. She goes to the list of research databases and selects *psychology* in the subject menu to find the best library databases for her topic. These could include

PsycINFO, PsycArticles, Psychology and Behavioral Sciences Collection, and *Academic Search Premier.*

Ann starts with PsycINFO and selects the key terms she wants to combine in her search: *anxiety, social media,* and *college students.* She enters each term in a separate search box, connected by the Boolean operator "and": anxiety AND social media AND college students. After limiting to peer-reviewed/academic journals and by date, she finds about 20 articles, of which only a few look relevant and interesting to her. Ann notices that the database has a folder system to save articles, which is similar to the pin function in the online catalog. She creates an account, signs in, and saves a few articles.

One seems especially relevant:

Lee-Won, R. J., Herzog, L., & Park, S. G. (2015). Hooked on Facebook: The role of social anxiety and need for social assurance in problematic use of Facebook. *Cyberpsychology, Behavior, and Social Networking, 18,* 567–574. doi:10.1089/cyber.2015.0002

She checks to make sure this article meets her source requirements. Is it peer-reviewed? Ann limited her search to peer-reviewed articles, and she is searching PsycINFO, a scholarly database. Also, the article includes a list of works cited—a required component of peer-reviewed articles—and includes the authors' scholarly credentials. These characteristics all indicate that the article is peer-reviewed. Is it recent? The article was published in 2015, so it falls within the 10-year date range requirement.

Is it a primary research article? By reading the abstract, Ann notes that the article is describing a single study and its results. Scanning the body of the paper, she finds the "Methods" section, which describes how the study was conducted, the number of subjects and how they were chosen, followed by a "Results" section in which the study's findings are analyzed. She can see that this is indeed a primary research article. Therefore, this article would meet the source requirements of the assignment, and it is relevant to her topic. Its results indicate that problematic Facebook use does have a positive correlation with social anxiety in college students.

Ann also finds this article:

Seabrook, E. M., Kern, M. L., & Rickard, N. S. (2016). Social networking sites, depression, and anxiety: A systematic review. *JMIR Mental Health, 3*(4), e50. doi:10.2196/mental.5842

Ann verifies that this article is peer-reviewed, and it was published in 2016, so it fits the date range. But the article is not reporting primary research. A red flag for this article is the phrase *systematic review* in the title. A systematic review is a type of literature review, in which the authors gather all the relevant studies that fit their established criteria, and compare the results. By quickly browsing the article, Ann sees that the article discusses multiple studies, and there is no Method section. Therefore, this is a *secondary* source, so she puts it aside. Although it does not fit the source criteria for this assignment, this article is still useful. It could lead Ann to primary research articles, since it likely cites many of these. We will discuss more about finding articles with citations later in this chapter.

How to Broaden Your Search to Find More Results

Use Synonyms.   Ann believes she should be able to find more articles on this topic than her initial search has yielded. She noticed that when she was typing in her terms, the database was suggesting synonyms connected by "or." For example, typing in *anxiety or* resulted in many search suggestions, including:

> anxiety or depression
> anxiety or stress
> anxiety disorders or generalized anxiety disorders
> anxiety or fear or panic or worry or stress

She could experiment with any of these to see which produces the most relevant results. Ann chooses option four. She types "or" after her other terms to discover synonyms for them, until her search looks like this:

> social media or Facebook or Twitter or Instagram
> AND
> anxiety or fear or panic or worry or stress
> AND
> college students or undergraduates or university students

The purpose of adding these synonyms of our original keywords is to broaden the search and pick up additional relevant results. An article that only talks about a particular type of social media like Facebook, or uses the term *worry* instead of *anxiety*, might still be relevant but would be missed if these synonyms were left out of the search. This broader search increases her results from 20 to 100.

Search More than One Database.   Another method of finding more articles is to add databases to your search. If you think of databases like individual drawers in a dresser, this method allows you to look in multiple drawers at once. Several companies that produce databases (such as EBSCOhost and ProQuest) allow you to cross-search their databases. To add additional databases, Ann clicks "Choose Databases" just above the search box. A menu of other EBSCOhost databases pops up. Hovering over the page icon next to each title tells her what it contains. Ann chooses psychology-related options, such as *Psychology and Behavioral Sciences Collection* and *PsycArticles*. Since her topic has to do with students, she also adds *Education Source*. Adding these databases increases the number of her results significantly.

A word about choosing databases. Consider adding databases that do not focus solely on psychology. Think about the different aspects of your topic when considering where to search. For example, if you were researching mental illness among young people in the juvenile justice system, a database that focuses on criminal justice could be useful. If you were researching the emotional effects of traumatic brain injury, then a medical or nursing database might have the most relevant articles.

Narrowing Your Search

If your pool of results is too large to work with, you may need to narrow your topic and/or date range, exclude irrelevant terms, search a different database, or try a combination of these strategies.

As noted in Chapter 11, you can use the operators AND and NOT to narrow your topic or exclude irrelevant results. Ann employed the AND operator when she added AND anxiety to her search, to focus on just that type of psychological harm. She could narrow it further by focusing on a particular subgroup of college students, such as AND (female or women). Sometimes "social network" is given as a synonym for social media, but "social network" can also mean the friends, family, acquaintances or organizations "to whom an individual is tied socially, usually by shared interests and, in many cases, values, attitudes, and aspirations" (Gregory, Johnston, Watts, Pratt, & Whatmore, 2012). A search for *anxiety* AND *"social media"* NOT *"social network"* would exclude results which contain the phrase "social network." If you are searching a general database, you could narrow your results by searching a subject-focused database, or use the "publication" limiter to search only certain journals.

Presenting a Balanced Selection of Evidence

When browsing her search results, Ann notices this article about the stress-*reducing* effects of social media use:

Zhang, R. (2017). The stress-buffering effect of self-disclosure on Facebook: An examination of stressful life events, social support, and mental health among college students. *Computers in Human Behavior, 75,* 527–537. doi:10.1016/j.chb.2017.05.043

Ann remembers from Chapter 11 that good research includes evidence showing more than one side of a question. She needs to be open to many viewpoints and research findings and avoids cherry-picking only those studies that support what *she* thinks is the answer to her research question. She also wants to include research that has been conducted by diverse authors or that involve underrepresented groups, so that she is presenting as complete a picture of the evidence as possible.

For this topic, it will be important to include articles that show a positive correlation between social media use and anxiety, as well as those that show no correlation, or that indicate social media use may actually improve mental health. Most questions in psychology do not have black and white, yes or no answers; the reality is more nuanced and will be affected by many variables. In this case, variables could include the amount or type of social media use, the personality characteristics of the user, pre-existing psychological conditions, and cultural influences, among others.

Include Diverse Sources.   There are a few ways to do find research by or about underrepresented groups. One method is to add additional keywords related to race, religion, culture, sexual orientation, gender, or other characteristics to your search. Continuing to search the group of databases she chose earlier, Ann tries the search string below. *Note:* Putting an asterisk at the end of a word stem will pick up all forms of that word. So anxi* will capture results using the words anxiety, anxieties, anxious, anxiolytic, etc. It is a simple way to broaden your search.

anxi* or stress or worry AND **college student or university student**

AND **race or religion or Black or African American or Latin* or Asian or LGBTQ**

Ann could also focus on a particular aspect of diversity, such as religion (e.g., Christian* or Muslim or Islam* or Buddhist or atheist or agnostic, etc.) depending on your topic and focus. Your choices may be affected by how much research has been done on the intersection of your research topic and various aspects of diversity.

Here are two examples of articles found with this search:

Stanton, A. G., Jerald, M. C., Ward, L. M., & Avery, L. R. (2017). Social media contributions to strong Black woman ideal endorsement and Black women's mental health. *Psychology of Women Quarterly, 41*(4), 465–478. doi:10.1177/0361684317732330

Park, N., Song, H., & Lee, K. M. (2014). Social networking sites and other media use, acculturation stress, and psychological well-being among East Asian college students in the United States. *Computers in Human Behavior, 36,* 138–146. doi:10.1016/j.chb.2014.03.037

A second method is to search journals that focus on diversity. Table 2 shows a list of journals that focus on various underrepresented populations or aspects of diversity.

Once you have identified a particular journal you would like to explore, search the online catalog for the journal name in quotation marks. If it is found, pay attention to the details; it might be available in print, microform, and/or online. Certain publication years may be available in one format but not in another, and online access can vary depending on the database. For example, a library may currently own the *Journal of Black Studies* on microfilm (1984 to 2009), in JSTOR database from 1970 to 2015, and in Sage Premier database from 1999 to the present.

If the journal is available online, click the *online access* link in the catalog and search by keyword, just as you would in a database containing many different journals. If a journal is not owned by the library in any format, or if the available issues are too old for your research, try going to the journal website. You may not be able to access any complete articles, but you can often view citations and abstracts, and then use ILL to obtain the article.

Ann searches for her topic in the journal *Violence Against Women* and locates this article:

Woodlock, D. (2017). The abuse of technology in domestic violence and stalking. *Violence Against Women, 23*(5), 584–602. doi:10.1177%2F1077801216646277

Table 2 Selected Journals Which Focus on Diverse or Underrepresented Groups

Journal Name	Focus: Gender	Sexual Orientation	Age	Race	Religion	Culture
Aging and Mental Health						
Archives of Sexual Behavior	✓	✓				
Asian American Journal of Psychology				✓		✓
Cultural Diversity and Ethnic Minority Psychology				✓		✓
GeroPsych			✓			
Hispanic Journal of Behavioral Sciences				✓		
Journal of Black Psychology				✓		
Journal of Black Studies				✓		
Journal of Cross-Cultural Psychology						✓
Journal of Gay & Lesbian Mental Health	✓	✓				
Journal of Gender Studies	✓	✓				
Journal of Homosexuality	✓	✓				
Journal of Lesbian Studies	✓	✓				
Journal of LGBT Youth	✓	✓	✓			

Journal of Multicultural Counseling and Development						✓
Journal of Psychology and Christianity					✓	
Journal of Psychology and Theology					✓	
Journal of Religion, Spirituality, and Aging			✓		✓	
Journal of Women and Aging	✓		✓			
Mental Health, Religion, and Culture					✓	✓
Psychology and Aging			✓			
Psychology of Men and Masculinity	✓					
Psychology of Religion and Spirituality					✓	
Psychology of Sexual Orientation and Gender Div.	✓	✓				
Psychology of Women Quarterly	✓					
Sage: A Scholarly Journal on Black Women				✓		
Sex Roles	✓					
Violence Against Women	✓					✓

Searching for Diverse Content in PsycINFO.   PsycINFO has a unique feature that makes it easier to search by categories, including some which are relevant to diversity. PsycINFO (APA, 2019b; https://www.apa.org/pubs/databases/training/class-codes.pdf) assigns each item a code that describes its primary subject matter. As stated on the APA website, these codes were "designed to describe the content of the PsycINFO database, not the field of psychology."

To limit your search to a particular classification, use the Advanced Search and select the desired code in the "Classification Codes" limiter. Hold down the Control Key or Command Key to select more than one classification. They may be listed by their code numbers rather than alphabetically, so the list available at the site mentioned above can be useful. If you know the code you want, you can just type it in the search box and select the field "CC: Classification." The code(s) under which an article is classified can be found in its detailed description, or *record*; click the article title to see this information. Once you have selected the code limiters, search by keywords just as you normally would, and the limiter(s) will be applied to your results. Several codes in section 2900 *Social Processes and Social Issues* are relevant to diversity, including 2920: Religion, and 2970: Sex Roles and Women's Issues, among others.

Citation Mining

If you have not found enough articles or still have gaps in your research, try these additional strategies.

Researching Backward.   In Chapter 11, scholarly research was described as a conversation. You could also think of it as a trail that leads both backward and forward. When an author provides a list of works cited in an article, they are essentially sharing a hard-fought exploration with you—all the relevant sources they collected as they hacked their way through the information jungle. So take advantage of it! As you read an article, pay attention to which of the cited sources are relevant to your topic and search them out. Since references cited in a study are older than that study (you cannot cite studies that do not exist yet), this technique is known as "researching backward."

Remember the systematic review Ann found earlier? She put it aside because it did not fit the assignment's source requirements. However, its bibliography of 148 articles is a gold mine of potentially relevant sources. She looked through the article quickly, then used the "find" feature on her computer to search for the word *anxiety*. There were many articles about anxiety, since that is a major focus of the review. Here is a source she found in the bibliography that is relevant, within the allowed date range, and a primary research article:

Shaw, A. M., Timpano, K. R., Tran, T. B., & Joormann J. (2015). Correlates of Facebook usage patterns: The relationship between passive Facebook use, social anxiety symptoms, and brooding. *Computers in Human Behavior, 48,* 575–580. doi:10.1016/j.chb.2015.02.003

Since she does not know in which database this article might be found, Ann uses the online catalog. She begins by searching for the first few words of the article title, in quotes: "correlates of Facebook usage patterns" and finds that the article is available in the database *Science Direct*.

Tip: if searching for the article title does not work, search for the name of the journal, which in this case is *"Computers in Human Behavior."* If it is found, then search for the article title within the journal, or navigate to the correct volume. Because not all journals are indexed at the article level in the catalog (i.e., you cannot find an article by searching for the article title, even though it is in fact available), you may have to use a sort of back-door approach by looking for the journal name instead.

Researching Forward.

If the Shaw et al. (2015) article proves useful, Ann could continue following this trail by mining *its* bibliography, and so forth. But what if she wants to find newer articles? She would need to find out what later articles cited the Shaw et al. (2015) article by using tools like the *cited reference search* in the specialized database *Web of Science*. She could also use a similar feature in Google Scholar.

Using Google Scholar to Find Citing Articles.

Ann searches Google Scholar for the article title in quotation marks. Under the abstract is the "Cited By" information from both Google and Web of Science. She clicks on *Cited by 101* to view the citing articles.

Figure 1   Using Google Scholar to find works which cite an article. Google and the Google logo are registered trademarks of Google LLC, used with permission.

She can now browse the list or check the box to "search within citing articles" and enter keywords to find the most relevant articles. The citing articles can also be limited by publication date using the menu on the left. If the complete article is available, there is a link on the right, sometimes provided by your library.

Among the list of citing articles, Ann finds a relevant article on the positive effects of social media use:

Rus, H. M., & Tiemensma, J. (2018). Social media as a shield: Facebook buffers acute stress. *Physiology & Behavior, 185,* 46–54.

Figure 2 Searching within citing articles. Google and the Google logo are
registered trademarks of Google LLC, used with permission.

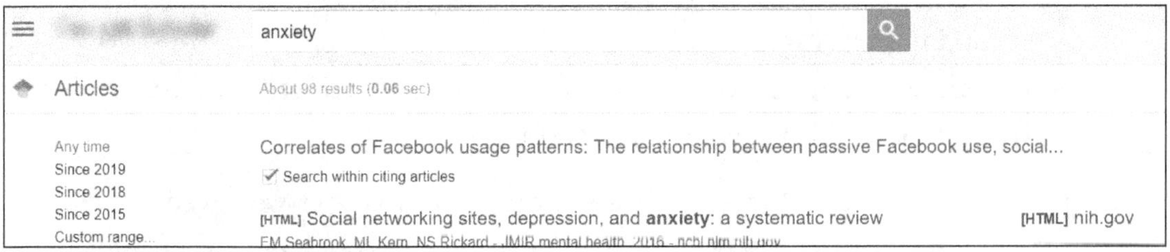

Only the abstract of this article is available through Google Scholar, and Ann cannot find it using the library's online catalog. Therefore, she submits an ILL request to get the article from another library, after contacting a librarian to learn the simple procedure.

A note of caution: Not every source that cites a scholarly article is necessarily peer-reviewed itself. For example, the Shaw article is cited by a paper titled, "Relationship between social media use and social anxiety among emerging adults," (Hughes, 2017), contained in the Digital Commons at Liberty University. As noted in the description above, university repositories contain both published and *unpublished* research. A closer look at the Hughes paper shows that it is a research proposal written for a course at Liberty University. It has not been published in a journal and therefore is not peer-reviewed. Also, it is not primary research, because it is only a proposal; no study has been carried out. Therefore this would not be a reputable or appropriate source for Ann to use in her paper. Remember that it is up to each individual to be a careful reader and consumer of information, especially information that is freely available online.

Troubleshooting Your Search

Tips to Help you Overcome Common Research Roadblocks

1) **I can't access the library's databases.**
   - Make sure you are signed in with your student ID, and that it has been activated.
   - Use the library's database link, rather than going in through a web search or a link provided by your instructor.
   - If you are on a work computer, there may be a firewall that is interfering with the campus login system. The IT staff at your workplace may be able to resolve this.
   - Try using a different browser; for example, if you are using Firefox, try Chrome.
   - Clear your browser's cache.

2) **The article I want is not full-text.**

- If there is not a link to the complete article in the database, there may be a "find it" link (or something similar) that will search other databases for the article.
- Try an internet search.
- Sometimes articles have been published as open access and are freely available.
- Request the article via your library's ILL service.

3) **I found an article on the web, but I'm not sure if it is peer-reviewed.**

- Examine the article. Peer-reviewed articles always cite their sources and contain a bibliography.
- They usually provide the credentials of the author and may also provide information about when the article was submitted, reviewed, and published.
- Search the web for the name of the journal. On the journal site, look for a description or an "about" section. Peer-reviewed status is often one of the first things mentioned. The term *refereed* may be used instead. The section that provides submission information for authors often describes the peer-review process.
- Or, ask a librarian!

4) **I can't find a single scholarly article on my topic!**

- *Change your search terms.* Often the difference between a successful search and an unsuccessful one is your search terms. First, check your spelling. Second, think of other ways to phrase your search. If you can find articles that are about a closely related topic, look at the subject terms provided. Some databases provide a thesaurus which will help you identify the best terms for your topic. Do a search in Google Scholar or just on the web and look at your results—can you find alternate terms?
- *Broaden your topic.* For example, if your research question is: "What coping mechanisms are used by first-generation female college juniors at Midwestern universities during final exams?" there may be no research on that. But if you broadened it a bit to "How do first-generation college students cope with test anxiety?" you would likely find scholarly research studies.
- *Is your topic too recent?* Scholarly research can take months or years to be published, so there won't be any peer-reviewed articles about an event that happened very recently.
- *Is your topic nonscholarly?* Think about how likely it is that your topic has been studied scientifically. If you are looking for information on your favorite football player or musician, information is more likely to be found in magazines, newspapers, and websites rather than academic journals.

If you are searching for a reasonably broad topic suitable for academic research, consider these questions:

- *Are you looking in the right place?* Select a scholarly database that focuses on a field most related to your topic. Some databases contain only news and magazine articles. Check the description of the database in the library's list or look at what filters are available in the database—can you limit by source type? Are academic/scholarly journals listed?

- *Would you like some help?* If you are unable to locate the information you need, consult a librarian.

5) **I don't know how to cite my sources.**

- First, verify what citation style your instructor wants you to use. Psychology and other social sciences usually use APA style.

- Secondly, identify what type of source you are trying to cite. Is it a journal article, a book, a dissertation, a website, or something else? Citation format is determined by the type of source, so correctly identifying the source is crucial.

If you found a source in the online catalog or in a database, there may be a citation helper. But, be aware that the citations provided by these tools are frequently incorrect. They can be a good place to start, since they usually contain the necessary elements. But they often have incorrect punctuation, capitalization, and page number formatting. For example, here is an article citation provided by a database citation tool:

HUNT, M. G., MARX, R., LIPSON, C., & YOUNG, J. (2018). No More FOMO: Limiting Social Media Decreases Loneliness and Depression. *Journal of Social & Clinical Psychology,* *37*(10), 751. https://doi.org/10.1521/jscp.2018.37.10.751

Mistakes in this citation include (a) author names are in all capital letters; (b) every word in the article title is capitalized, rather than just the first word, the first word following a colon, and proper nouns; (c) the issue number is not needed; (d) only the beginning page number is given, (e) the doi should not include https://doi.org/; and (f) there is no hanging indent. The corrected citation is:

Hunt, M. G., Marx, R., Lipson, C., & Young, J. (2018). No more FOMO: Limiting social media decreases loneliness and depression. *Journal of Social & Clinical Psychology, 37,* 751–768. doi:10.1521/jscp.2018.37.10.751

Be sure to check your citation formatting with your APA manual or a reputable online guide such as the Purdue Online Writing Lab or the APA Style Blog. These sources can also help with other formatting such as in-text citations, margins, headings, etc.

Conclusion

The search strategies described in this chapter will be effective in any database, whether subscription or open access, and with any topic. Although information literacy skills are necessary in any field, they are vital to a career in a research-based discipline like psychology, in which our knowledge is constantly evolving. Mastering these skills will serve you well throughout your college career as well as in your professional life, and make finding the information you need faster, easier, and much more effective.

References

American Psychological Association (APA). (2019a). *PsycArticles quick facts.* Retrieved from https://www.apa.org/pubs/databases/psycarticles?tab=3

American Psychological Association (APA). (2019b). *PsycINFO classification categories and codes.* Retrieved from https://www.apa.org/pubs/databases/training/class-codes

American Psychological Association (APA). (2019c). *PsycINFO quick facts.* Retrieved from https://www.apa.org/pubs/databases/psycinfo?tab=3

Boysen, G. (2013). Confronting math stereotypes in the classroom: Its effect on female college students' sexism and perceptions of confronters. *Sex Roles, 69*(5), 297–307.

Directory of Open Access Journals (DOAJ). (2019). *About DOAJ.* Retrieved from https://doaj.org/about

EBSCO Industries, Inc. (2019). *Psychology and behavioral sciences collection.* Retrieved from https://www.ebsco.com/products/research-databases/psychology-behavioral-sciences-collection

Gregory, D., Johnston R., Pratt G., Watts M. J., & Whatmore S. (2012). *The dictionary of human geography.* Chichester, England: Wiley-Blackwell.

Hughes, D. L. (2017). *Relationship between social media use and social anxiety among emerging adults [research proposal]. Liberty University.* Retrieved from https://digitalcommons.liberty.edu/research_symp/2017/Oral_Presentations/52/

Hunt, M. G., Marx, R., Lipson, C., & Young, J. (2018). No more FOMO: Limiting social media decreases loneliness and depression. *Journal of Social & Clinical Psychology, 37,* 751–768. doi:10.1521/jscp.2018.37.10.751

Lee-Won, R. J., Herzog, L., & Park, S. G. (2015). Hooked on Facebook: The role of social anxiety and need for social assurance in problematic use of Facebook. *Cyberpsychology, Behavior, and Social Networking, 18,* 567–574. doi:10.1089/cyber.2015.0002

Park, N., Song, H., & Lee, K. M. (2014). Social networking sites and other media use, acculturation stress, and psychological well-being among East Asian college students in the United States. *Computers in Human Behavior, 36,* 138–146. doi:10.1016/j.chb.2014.03.037

Scholarly Publishing and Academic Resources Coalition (SPARC). (n.d.). *Open access.* Retrieved from https://sparcopen.org/open-access/

Schrobsdorff, S. (2016). Teen depression and anxiety: Why the kids are not alright. *Time, 188*(19). Retrieved from http://time.com/magazine/us/4547305/november-7th-2016-vol-188-no-19-u-s/

Seabrook, E. M., Kern, M. L., & Rickard, N. S. (2016). Social networking sites, depression, and anxiety: A systematic review. *JMIR Mental Health, 3*(4), e50. doi:10.2196/mental.5842

Shaw, A. M., Timpano, K. R., Tran, T. B., & Joormann J. (2015). Correlates of Facebook usage patterns: The relationship between passive Facebook use, social anxiety symptoms, and brooding. *Computers in Human Behavior, 48,* 575–580. doi:10.1016/j.chb.2015.02.003

Stanton, A. G., Jerald, M. C., Ward, L. M., & Avery, L. R. (2017). Social media contributions to strong Black woman ideal endorsement and Black women's mental health. *Psychology of Women Quarterly, 41*(4), 465–478. doi:10.1177/0361684317732330

Woodlock, D. (2017). The abuse of technology in domestic violence and stalking. *Violence Against Women, 23*(5), 584–602. doi:10.1177%2F1077801216646277

Zhang, R. (2017). The stress-buffering effect of self-disclosure on Facebook: An examination of stressful life events, social support, and mental health among college students. *Computers in Human Behavior, 75,* 527–537. doi:10.1016/j.chb.2017.05.043

13

Technology for Developing and Writing a Research Project

by H. Andrew Tincknell, MS

Writing a research project can be a daunting undertaking. Fortunately, technology is available to make organization and writing easier. Many applications and online tools exist to assist with tasks, including project management, the organization of data, composition, and editing, as well as citations and collaboration. This chapter will offer ideas and recommendations for several of these helpful technologies. The suggestions will also gear toward being either free or so ubiquitous, like Microsoft Office, that researchers will have little trouble gaining access.

Project Management

Getting organized is a significant factor in getting research projects off the ground. It can also make your projects less intimidating. Creating schedules are valuable first steps in preparing to write. Assignment calculators provide outlines of steps to complete various kinds of projects. Timelines based on the assignment type and deadline establishing dates for each goal's completion are created. These tools provide many tips for success for each milestone; from pointers for understanding your assignment to things to consider when polishing your final paper. They even recommend a percentage of your total work time you should apportion for each step. Assignment calculators are becoming popular features on the websites of many libraries. Most are based upon the one created by the University of Minnesota Libraries, which can be found at www.lib.umn.edu/ac ("Assignment Calculator · University of Minnesota Libraries," n.d.). Some academic libraries also provide credentialed users with email reminders as you near the suggested date for completion of a task, so check the libraries at your institution for this service.

For further scheduling work, there are a plethora of project management tools to help coordinate group work or provide a self-generated to-do list and timeline for completion of objectives toward your final goal. One popular example is Trello. Trello defaults to three lists; "To Do," "Doing," and "Done," but these labels can be modified to suit other purposes and more lists can be added if needed. Cards are added to these lists representing each task. The cards could denote

Figure 1 University of Minnesota's Assignment Calculator

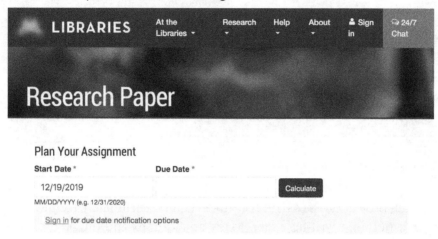

nodes carried forward from the assignment calculator or created independently. Cards can contain additional information including comments, attachments, and even checklists. When a task changes status, it can easily be moved to another list. Boards can also be shared for collaborative work, which is very useful for keeping team members on the same page. Each team member can be assigned a card, or task, which they can use to update their status as they proceed through the project ("Getting started with Trello video demo—Trello Help," n.d.). Another useful feature is the Calendar Power-Up that helps with the visualization of milestones and due dates with a traditional calendar view ("Power-Ups | Trello," n.d.).

Figure 2 Trello Board with 3 lists

Figure 3 Trello Calendar Power-Up

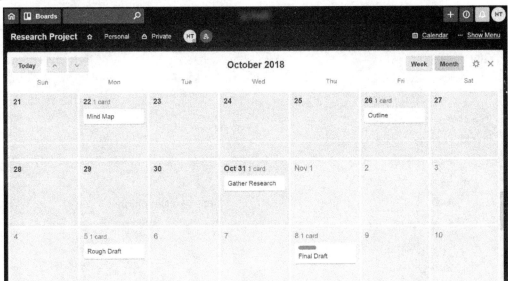

Concept Organization

It is important to brainstorm keywords and fundamental phrases for your topic early in the organization process, including ideas you want to search, explore, and possibly elaborate on in your text. This forms the skeleton of the body of work that will be fleshed out over time. Mind mapping is one technique for doing this. Online applications such as MindMup (www.mindmup.com) allow you to add a variety of keywords and short concepts onto a board in random order. You can

Figure 4 Mind map created with MindMup

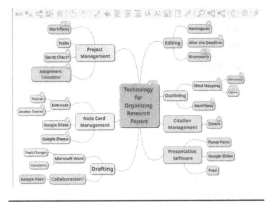

then start to arrange and attach these nodes to form the basis of an outline. Nodes can be color-coded and there are often capabilities for notes, web links, and images ("Mind-Mup," n.d.).

It may be helpful after creating a mind map, or possibly instead of one, to create an outline to put order to concepts and expand upon ideas. Of course, this can be completed using a simple word processing application, but WorkFlowy (workflowy.com) takes outlining to the next level. WorkFlowy's outline bullets are easily collapsible and expandable, allowing users to view the big picture or focus on the details. Items can easily be moved around by clicking

Figure 5 Example of Workflowy outline

- Technology for Organizing Research Papers
  - Organization
    - Assignment Calculator
    - Project Management
      - Gantt Chart
      - Trello
      - Workflowy
    - Outlining
      - Mindmapping
      - Workflowy
    - Note Card Management
  - Citation Management
  - Drafting
  - Editing
  - Presentation Software

and dragging bullet points. Adding hashtags to topics provides more filtering and organization options. The application's features can also be useful for project management in a similar fashion to Trello ("Try WorkFlowy Instantly," n.d.).

Figure 6 Evernote notes on a smart phone

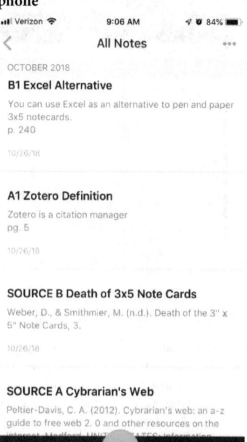

Note Creation

In the days before computers became a useful tool for preparing and writing, most researchers used paper note cards to document small amounts of information. These cards would later be sorted over and over until eventually forming paragraphs, sections, and pages. They also contained citation information that was useful in building a reference list. Some people still prefer the pen and paper method, but many people look to analogs of familiar practices when exploring useful technologies. Although few, if any, applications emulate the note card method exactly, there are a few ways to make familiar programs do the job.

Everyday applications used for word processing, such as Microsoft Word and Google Docs, can be used to simply write notes and then select sections to drag and drop or copy and paste. Just getting words on a page is a kick start to writing and can be a major benefit to this method. Alternatively, some individuals may prefer slide presentation applications like PowerPoint or Google Slides, which provide more of the feel of note cards and still provide the ability to sort at will and copy and paste into a document (CockrumVideos, n.d.)

There are a few other methods for accomplishing the note card techniques such as spreadsheets including Excel and Google Sheets, that do not allow for the same freedom of arrangement but can be automatically sorted alphabetically, numerically, or by date of creation (Weber & Smithmier, n.d.). Evernote is also an application that allows notes to be sorted automatically and it works equally well on a computer or a mobile device. In fact, notes are easily interchangeable between the two platforms. Adding letters and numbers to a final outline that correlate to the topics on these virtual note cards helps to aid automatic sorting (mrhawkinsclass, n.d.; Weber & Smithmier, n.d.).

Citations Creation and Tracking

Citing sources is often a source of trepidation when writing. Technologies, like Zotero, are evolving to make it easy to collect and organize citations ("Zotero | your personal research assistant," n.d.). The Zotero download also includes extensions to your favorite browsers like Chrome and Firefox which allow you to document a source by simply clicking the extension icon while browsing items including online journals, e-books, web links, and more. When using information from one of those sources in a document, use the included Zotero add-in for Microsoft Word or Google Docs to easily cite each source and then to create a reference list automatically when the paper is completed. Zotero supports many popular citation styles, including APA, MLA, and the Chicago Manual of Style. Although Zotero excels at interpreting the information it is given for citing resources, it is important to double-check each citation and reference for accuracy. When using quotes in your paper, page or paragraph numbers also must be entered manually if needed ("Word processor plugin usage [Zotero Documentation]," n.d.).

Figure 7 A Zotero library

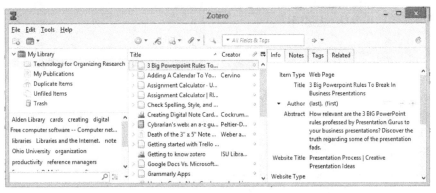

Document Creation

It is hard to imagine authoring a paper today without some sort of word processing application. Microsoft Word is the most popular, but Google Docs is nipping at its heels. The best application is a matter of opinion with many people switching back and forth depending on their need at the time. Word offers more features for the more advanced user, whereas Google Docs is the go-to app for collaboration ("Google Docs Vs. Microsoft Word," n.d.). Google autosaves constantly to the cloud, which is a blessing during computer glitches when the user has not saved in a while. Word comes with a price tag that varies based upon the plan level chosen, whereas Google Docs is free. There is a free version of Word called Word Online, but features are scaled down from its pay counterpart. Many students may also be eligible for a free license for the Office 365 suite, which includes Word, through their universities.

No matter which word processing application is preferred, similarities can be found. For example, inserting headers, footers, and page numbers. Almost all word processing programs have tools for external editors to review the author's work by tracking changes and inserting comments. It is important to have these other perspectives when writing and other's feedback can be recorded through features such as "Track Changes" or "Suggesting Mode" and "Comment."

Editing Your Work

Before having a second pair of eyes review your work, online applications can help with the editing process. Using one or a combination of these can help fix more obvious errors and provide feedback on style choices. Grammarly provides a lot of feedback on sentence structure for free, and even more with a paid account. You can get a grammar check by copying and pasting text into their website or using their add-in for Word or Chrome extension for

Figure 8 Grammarly suggestion

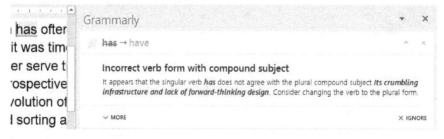

Figure 9 After the Deadline demonstration screen

Google Docs. Grammarly also allows you to set performance goals such as intent, audience, and style. Using these criteria, your work is scored against other works submitted by Grammarly users with similar goals ("Grammarly Apps," n.d.).

To supplement Grammarly with more free writing advice, try After the Deadline. The easiest way to use it is to go to the "Demonstration" tab at www.afterthedeadline.com, copy and paste a passage, and click "Check Writing." The site will offer feedback including style and grammar suggestions, as well as a spell check ("Check Spelling, Style, and Grammar with After the Deadline," n.d.).

Presentations

Once the paper is completed, it may be necessary to present its information in class or even at a professional conference. Although a slide presentation is not always required, most presenters find it useful for providing extra information to their audience. This information may include simple talking points and visual aids such as charts, graphs, and photos. The presenter should have enough familiarity with the content to not depend on the slides for more than a basic outline. No one wants to sit through a presentation where a speaker reads slides verbatim. Although the general rule for slide presentations is "less is more," always keep the audience in mind when designing slides. Use them to help the audience understand the concept, even if that means more words on a slide. This is often the case in the hard sciences (Garrett, 2016). However, when possible, break concepts down into multiple slides.

As with word processing, there are many products available for creating slide presentations. Two of the leading providers are also the same, Microsoft and Google. The comparisons are roughly the same too. Microsoft PowerPoint is more robust, whereas Google Slides specializes in collaboration. Prezi is another player in the presentation game. It offers a free educational plan that provides tools for providing dynamic presentations, but users should proceed with caution ("Presentation Software | Online Presentation Tools | Prezi," n.d.). If used poorly, the animations within Prezi have been known to give audiences something akin to motion sickness. "Conversational Delivery" is a major focus of Prezi, making it easy to jump around from topic to topic instead of the linear progression of more traditional slide presentations ("Conversational Presenting | Sales Dialogues | Prezi Business | Prezi," n.d.)

Poster presentations are another popular way to present research. This is another instance where slide presentations software, specifically PowerPoint, can come in handy. PowerPoint is the most simple way to create a poster. Guidelines for poster design differ from those for slide presentations. Much more content is added to the one slide that will become the poster. Before beginning a poster design, be sure to change the slide size to fit the requirements or recommendations of the conference. The "Text Box" tool under the "Insert" tab will be very helpful for aligning text elements. Charts and graphs can be inserted as images or copied from Excel. After printing, the font sizes should be legible from 4 to 5 ft away. Viewers should be able to read and comprehend the poster's message within 5 to 10 minutes (Ramsewak, 2012).

Writing can be challenging, but using even a portion of the tools discussed in this chapter should make the process more organized and easier. Not every application will be useful for every assignment. Pick and choose the one that works best for your work habits and style of writing (See Table 1 for a summary of tools). After all, the technology exists to make life easier, not to add more work.

Tutorials

- Trello: https://www.youtube.com/watch?v=zzwovrD0vM4
- MindMup: https://www.youtube.com/watch?v=NeR8dcls4qQ
- Workflowy: https://www.youtube.com/watch?v=qPMVtkNrquU
- Evernote: https://www.youtube.com/watch?v=RiaNfejKfi0
- Zotero: https://www.youtube.com/watch?v=gR3djTAZH9g
- Grammarly: https://www.youtube.com/watch?v=mqVbQ8gM6qw

Table 1

App	Website	Features	Platforms	Cost
Assignment Calculator	https://www.lib.umn.edu/ac	Schedule milestones to complete an assignment on time	Web	Free
Trello	https://trello.com/home	Create "to do" lists and schedules, collaborate with team members	Web, Mobile	Free or Premium
MindMup	https://www.mindmup.com/	Create mind maps	Web, Mobile	Free or Premium
Workflowy	https://workflowy.com/	Create an expandable outline	Web, Mobile	Free or Premium
Evernote	https://evernote.com/	Emulate note cards	Web, Desktop, Mobile	Free or Premium
Zotero	https://www.zotero.org/	Collect, organize, and create citations and bibliographies	Desktop	Free or Premium
Microsoft Word	https://www.office.com/	Organize, write, and edit	Desktop, Mobile, Web	Academic plans available for free or reduced pricing. Consult with your university's technology center.
Google Docs	https://www.google.com/docs/about/	Organize, write, edit, and collaborate	Web, Mobile	Free
Grammarly	https://www.grammarly.com	Grammar, spelling, and word choice suggestions	Download, Web	Free or Premium
After the Deadline	https://www.afterthedeadline.com/	Grammar, spelling, and word choice suggestions	Web	Free
PowerPoint	https://www.office.com/	Create slideshow and poster presentations	Desktop, Mobile, Web	Academic plans available for free or reduced pricing. Consult with your university's technology center.
Prezi	https://prezi.com	Conversational presentation delivery	Web, Mobile	Free (education) or Premium

References

Assignment Calculator · University of Minnesota Libraries. (n.d.). Retrieved October 19, 2018, from https://www.lib.umn.edu/ac

Check Spelling, Style, and Grammar with After the Deadline. (n.d.). Retrieved November 2, 2018, from https://www.polishmywriting.com/

CockrumVideos. (n.d.). *Creating digital note cards using Evernote or Google Presentation.* Retrieved from https://www.youtube.com/watch?v=RiaNfejKfi0

Conversational Presenting | Sales Dialogues | Prezi Business | Prezi. (n.d.). Retrieved November 2, 2018, from https://prezi.com/business/conversational-presenting/

Garrett, N. (2016). How do academic disciplines use PowerPoint? *Innovative Higher Education, 41*(5), 365–380. Retrieved from https://doi.org/10.1007/s10755-016-9381-8

Getting started with Trello video demo—Trello Help. (n.d.). Retrieved October 22, 2018, from https://help.trello.com/article/899-getting-started-video-demo

Google Docs Vs. Microsoft Word: Everything You Need to Know. (n.d.). Retrieved November 1, 2018, from https://www.goskills.com/Microsoft-Office/Articles/Google-Docs-Microsoft-Word-comparison

Grammarly Apps. (n.d.). Retrieved November 1, 2018, from https://app.grammarly.com/apps

MindMup. (n.d.). Retrieved October 19, 2018, from https://www.mindmup.com/ mrhawkinsclass. (n.d.). *How to create note cards in Evernote.* Retrieved from https://www.youtube.com/watch?v=YjHE2SS3hM8

Power-Ups | Trello. (n.d.). Retrieved October 22, 2018, from https://trello.com/power-ups/55a5d917446f517774210011/calendar

Presentation Software | Online Presentation Tools | Prezi. (n.d.). Retrieved November 2, 2018, from https://prezi.com/pricing/#edu

Ramsewak, A. (2012). How to.create a poster presentation. *Education for Primary Care, 23*(5), 360–361. doi:10.1080/14739879.2012.11494140

Try WorkFlowy Instantly. (n.d.). Retrieved October 19, 2018, from https://workflowy.com/demo/embed/

Weber, D., & Smithmier, M. (2008). Death of the 3" x 5" note cards. *English Journal, 98*(2), 37–39. Retrieved from http://www.ncte.org/library/NCTEFiles/Resources/Journals/EJ/0982-nov08/EJ0982Death.pdf

Word processor plugin usage [Zotero Documentation]. (n.d.). Retrieved October 26, 2018, from https://www.zotero.org/support/word_processor_plugin_usage#inserting_and_editing_citations

Zotero | your personal research assistant. (n.d.). Retrieved October 1, 2018, from https://www.zotero.org/

14

Can you Cure a Psychopath?

by Kim A. Gorgens, PhD & Emily Goodwin

Everyone is familiar with the portrayal of psychopaths in film, literature, and popular culture. Typically, the psychopath is a handsome man whose callous, detached persona hints at sadistic, murderous impulses. According to this outsized public perception, "psychopaths are archetypes of evil: incorrigible, remorseless, cold-blooded criminals" (Gonzalez-Tapia, Obsuth, & Heeds, 2017, p. 1). In truth, though, psychopathic personality traits exist along a continuum where the near end includes people who cheat on romantic partners and exams in school or who opt not to return incorrect change at the grocery store. The far end, however, is defined by the total absence of empathy or conscience. Arguably, not everyone on the far end of this continuum is a dangerous offender–in fact, there is some research to suggest that psychopathic traits are overrepresented among especially successful business and political leaders (Babiak & Hare, 2006; Boddy, 2011; Clarke, 2005; Dutton, 2012; Morse, 2004; Smith & Lilienfeld, 2013). These "successful psychopaths" are highly functioning individuals who are able to navigate society despite symptoms of impulsivity and remorselessness (Gonzalez-Tapia et al., 2017; Kiehl & Hoffman, 2011).

Contrary to popular belief, psychopathy is not synonymous with sociopathy and antisocial personality disorder (ASPD; Walsh & Bolen, 2012). Psychopathy may have been first described by Biblical references (Horley, 2014), but the first psychiatric cases were published by French psychiatrist and humane-psychiatric-treatment-pioneer Philippe Pinel in 1806. Pinel called this callous, remorseless behavior "manie sans de´lire," referring to the kind of mania without delusional thinking he observed in a group of patients under his care at the hospital. His initial case description was of a young, continuously angry man known to physically assault anyone or anything that provoked him. Soon after, British physician Harold Arthur Prichard (1842) coined the term "moral insanity" to describe "a disorder which affects only the feelings and affections, or what are termed the moral powers of the mind, in contradistinction to the powers of the understanding or intellect" (p. 19). At the turn of the 20th century, Kraepelin (1907) wrote about "psychopathic personalities," the first subtype of which was the "professional criminal" which he reported to include a trajectory of increasing criminality throughout life, as well as selfish, cunning, deceitful, and callous personalities. Finally, American psychiatrist Hervey Cleckley is credited with writing one of the most descriptive accounts of the essential characteristics of psychopathy in "The Mask of Sanity" (1941). His account includes the following vivid description:

> They possessed superficial charm in order to manipulate others but generally lacked any real social intelligence or ability to learn from their mistakes at all. Psychopaths lie constantly to those around them in order to manipulate or manage impressions; indeed, Cleckley went so far as to state that they lack the ability to perceive the difference between truth and falsehood. They are without any sense of responsibility and any sense of guilt, lacking an ability to accept any blame for their own actions. In short, the psychopath is a manipulative, dissembling, self-absorbed and possibly dangerous individual, maybe interesting and pleasant to be around but only briefly (Horley, 2014, p. 100).

Psychopathy has more recently been described as a lack of empathy, callousness, a lack of remorse, limited emotions and shallow effect, a lack of responsibility, and intact cognitive abilities with no capability of acting morally (Gonzalez-Tapia et al., 2017; Kiehl & Hoffman, 2011). In the general population, the prevalence of individuals at the far end of the continuum, those with significantly elevated levels of psychopathic features, is estimated to be approximately 1 to 2% of men and 0.3 to 0.7% of women (Hare & Neumann, 2008; Sörman et al., 2014). The rates are higher among incarcerated populations, as high as 25% of the individuals in an incarcerated male offender population (Hare, 2003). The rates of psychopathy among female offenders are reported to be substantially lower, 16%, in prison populations (Salekin, Rogers, & Sewell, 1997). Some data suggest that about "93% of adult male psychopaths in United States are in prison, jail, parole, or probation" (Kiehl & Hoffman, 2011, p. 2).

Psychopaths are also more likely to remain in prison. Research suggests that psychopaths receive longer and harsher sentences than other offenders because they are considered more violent and more likely to recidivate (Umbach, Berryessa, & Raine, 2015). Recidivism by psychopathic offenders is estimated to cost "approximately $460 billion per year in criminal social costs" (Kiehl & Hoffman, 2011, p. 16). Further, since there is limited evidence for the effectiveness of treatment with psychopaths, they often receive maximum sentences in the service of reducing risk to public safety (Kiehl & Hoffman, 2011; Polaschek & Daly, 2013; Umbach et al., 2015). In fact, incarceration programs are generally considered successful if psychopaths are "held fully responsible in the eyes of the law" (Gonzalez-Tapia et al., 2017, p. 57).

In those eyes, psychopaths are fully "bad," not "mad." We generally hold the perception that all people have free will and make conscious decisions to commit antisocial acts and must, therefore, be held fully accountable (Kiehl & Hoffman, 2011). However, there is growing research to suggest a neurological or psychobiological basis for psychopathy, and those results complicate criminal responsibility. For instance, if neurological deficits impact someone's responses to external stimuli, should that individual be held to the same degree of accountability for his or her actions (Ortega-Escobar, Alcázar-Córcoles, Puente-Rodríguez, & Peñaranda-Ramos, 2017)? Impairments in brain areas affecting emotional responses and moral perception may one day be recognized as qualifying for the insanity defense (Gonzalez-Tapia et al., 2017). Today, though, offenders with psychopathic traits are sentenced with greater impunity since they are assumed to pose a long-term danger to the public. Gonzalez-Tapia et al. (2017) wrote, "The aim of criminal law is to protect society from dangerousness and transgression against ethical and moral values; it cannot do this by focusing on 'individual peculiarities,' such as those who do not care about the moral implications of their actions or the potential material consequences" (p. 57).

All told, our collective penchant for punishment over rehabilitation has largely been driven by research on treatment outcomes, not the biological bases of behavior. There is currently not a strong enough scientific basis for "reconsidering the current legal treatment of psychopaths" (Gonzalez-Tapia et al., 2017, p. 57). Research to support or refute the efficacy of therapies for psychopathy will literally dictate the management of as many as one in four adult offenders, whether in favor of habilitation and restoration efforts designed to promote community reintegration or in favor of long-term, secure containment designed to protect public safety.

To the Best of Our Knowledge, There Is No Cure for Psychopathy

Cannot Create Empathy.   Traditional rhetoric about treatment failures for psychopathic populations includes the recognition that psychology and psychiatry have no intervention that can consistently generate empathy in deficient persons. Such treatment failures have been outlined for decades (e.g., Hare, 1970). Cason and Pescor detailed the study of 500 prisoners in a special unit for psychopaths in Missouri in 1946. The male inmate patients continued to show a remarkable lack of regard for other people's property after "unspecified psychotherapy," and the 3-year reoffense rate to be 37%.

Symptoms May Worsen.   In addition to the reported persistence of callous personality and risk for reoffense, there is a troubling indication that treatment may actually exaggerate poor outcomes. One notable study of the most intensive therapeutic community interventions for incarcerated psychopaths found little difference between the "standard" reoffense rates of participants in the program relative to people not receiving treatment. Importantly though, their research suggested that those who received intensive group therapy actually had higher "violent" recidivism rates than those who were not treated at all (Harris, Rice, & Cormier, 1991). The training paradoxically equipped psychopaths with the skills necessary to mimic emotionality and, thus, to become better at manipulating people. Hare quoted one psychopath as saying, "These programs are like a finishing school.

They teach you how to put the squeeze on people" (Hare, 1993, p. 199). Overall, psychopaths are "four to eight times more likely to violently recidivate compared to nonpsychopaths" (Kiehl & Hoffman, 2011, p. 1).

Brain Anomalies.   One important feature of psychopathy is a disregard for rules and punishment. It might be assumed that without an appreciation of consequences, successful treatment is impossible. Advances in neurobiological research have identified neurotransmitter imbalances and structural brain abnormalities in areas of the brain responsible for moral reasoning, desire, impulse control, and behavioral inhibitions (Perez, 2012). Dysfunction in the prefrontal cortex, for example, is associated with poor treatment outcomes (Ortega-Escobar et al., 2017).

Difficult to Assess.   Finally, it may be impossible to gauge the effectiveness of therapy with a population of psychopaths mandated to receive treatment, since, by virtue of their very nature, they are considered to be master manipulators and to have the "expert ability to 'read' other people" and "exploit them" (Polaschek & Daly, 2013, p. 595).

Maybe We've Been Going About This All Wrong

The research highlighted above is fraught with methodological error and includes an over-emphasis on small case designs and anecdotal reports from practicing clinicians. There are very few well-designed large-scale studies and no double-blind, placebo-controlled studies on the effectiveness of treatment. That said, there are a few robust studies to suggest that treatment actually improves some outcomes for psychopathic participants.

Hope for Young Offenders.   Lipsey and Wilson (1998) were the first social science researchers to report that some aspects of treatment for psychopaths were actually valuable, especially for younger offenders. That optimism is reflected in results generated by the Decompression Model developed by the Mendota Juvenile Treatment Center (MJTC) in Wisconsin (Caldwell & Van Rybroek, 2001). In the decompression model program, psychopathic juvenile offenders participate in one-on-one programming several hours per day for 6 to 121 months focused on rebuilding social connection and engagement. In several follow-up studies, results suggest that violent, psychopathic offenders who undergo decompression treatment are more successful in social adjustment and less likely to recidivate than those who engage in other mental health treatments or only assessments (Kiehl & Hoffman, 2011). The recidivism rates, in particular, are significantly lower among participants in the decompression therapy (56% vs. 78%), including violent recidivism previously reported to increase with intensive treatment (18% vs. 36%; Caldwell, McCormick, Umstead, & Van Rybroek, 2007). Overall, results suggest that decompression therapy is twice as effective as traditional therapy which the authors report may actually be helpful if juvenile psychopaths are identified and treated early (Caldwell et al., 2007).

Brains can be Repaired.   There is also some indication that the treatment of psychopathic behaviors may actually result in neurobiological changes. Specifically, recent advances suggest that brain abnormalities in a psychopathic offender's amygdala and prefrontal cortex could be identified and targeted in treatment for improvement in structural and functional deficits (Ortega-Escobar, et al., 2017; Perez, 2012; Umbach et al., 2015). Psychopathy is often associated with a reduction in gray matter in the brain; specifically, an overall reduction in gray matter in the brain as well as regional gray matter alterations in the amygdala and basal ganglia (Vieira et al., 2015). Several techniques have been correlated with significant increases in gray matter volume in the brain. For instance, meditation and mindfulness practices are linked to gray matter neurogenesis (Last, Tufts, & Auger, 2017) and physical activity and overall fitness is related to increased gray matter in the prefrontal cortex (Erickson, Leckie, & Weinstein, 2014). If these interventions can increase gray matter in the brains of psychopaths, there could be a related reduction in psychopathic traits. In this way, brain imaging evidence could be used to demonstrate the need for and ultimately to document the response to treatment (Umbach et al., 2015).

Aging out of Psychopathy.   Lastly, there is literature to suggest that psychopathic behaviors decline with age. In one study, Gill and Crino (2012) found that age was inversely related to psychopathic traits including interpersonal manipulation, callousness, and self-reported psychopathy. Age-related changes in the behavioral and cognitive features of psychopaths can be accounted for by a number of variables. For example, there are naturally occurring neurobiological changes with advancing age, including declines in the levels of cortisol and testosterone, variations in the serotonergic system, and structural transformations in the brain (Gill & Crino, 2012). Given that psychopathy has been linked to structural and functional abnormalities in the brain, age-related changes in neurobiological systems may cause a reduction of psychopathic features. In addition, psychopathic individuals may accumulate knowledge and experiences with age, such as an understanding of the consequences of maladaptive behaviors (Gill & Crino, 2012). Advancing age is also factor in predicting recidivism risk for psychopathic offenders (Olver & Wong, 2015).

Conclusion

More than anything, the arguments presented here in favor of opposing incarceration over rehabilitation should serve as a call to action for both emerging and seasoned scholars. The study of *how* the symptoms of psychopathy interact with treatment methods to impact effectiveness is in its infancy, and research to better understand how psychopathic personalities differ along the continuum is nearly absent from the literature (Polaschek & Daly,

2013). The operational definition of "effective," the assignment of participants to experimental studies in jail settings, and the temporal and practical limitations of outcome measurement are all pressing methodological issues that warrant attention despite being outside the scope of this chapter. This chapter closes with a reminder about consensus. Scholars and practitioners agree that early identification and proactive management of aggressive behavior holds tremendous promise in reducing risk for violence and, ultimately, for improving treatment and community outcomes (Kimonis, Kennealy, & Goulter, 2016).

References

Babiak, P., & Hare, R. D. (2006). *Snakes in suits: When psychopaths go to work.* New York: HarperCollins.

Boddy, C. R. (2011). Corporate psychopaths, bullying, conflict and unfair supervision in the workplace. *Journal of Business Ethics, 100,* 367–379. doi:10.1057/9780230307551_3

Caldwell, M. F., McCormick, D. J., Umstead, D., & Van Rybroek, G. J. (2007). Evidence of treatment progress and therapeutic outcomes among adolescents with psychopathic features. *Criminal Justice and Behavior, 34,* 573–587. doi:10.1177/0093854806297511

Caldwell, M. F., & Van Rybroek, G. J. (2001). Efficacy of a decompression treatment model in the clinical management of violent juvenile offenders. *International Journal of Offender Therapy and Comparative Criminology, 45,* 469–477. doi:10.1177/0306624X01454006

Cason, H., & Pescor, M. J. (1946). A statistical study of 500 psychopathic prisoners. *Public Health Reports, 61,* 557–574. doi:10.2307/4585634

Clarke, J. (2005). *Working with monsters: How to identify and protect yourself from the workplace psychopath.* Sydney: Random House.

Cleckley, H. (1941). *The mask of sanity: An attempt to reinterpret the so-called psychopathic personality.* St. Louis: Mosby.

Dutton, K. (2012). *The wisdom of psychopaths: What saints, spies, and serial killers can teach us about success.* New York, NY: Scientific American Books.

Erickson, K. I., Leckie, R. L., & Weinstein, A. M. (2014). Physical activity, fitness, and gray matter volume. *Neurobiology of Aging, 35,* S20–S28. doi:10.1016/j.neurobiolaging.2014.03.034

Gill, D. J., & Crino, R. D. (2012). The relationship between psychopathy and age in a non-clinical community convenience sample. *Psychiatry, Psychology and Law, 19,* 547–557. doi:10.1080/13218719.2011.615810

Gonzalez-Tapia, M. I., Obsuth, I., & Heeds, R. (2017). A new legal treatment for psychopaths? Perplexities for legal thinkers. *International Journal of Law and Psychiatry, 54,* 46–60. doi:10.1016/j.ijlp.2017.04.004

Hare, R. D. (1970). *Psychopathy: Theory and research.* New York, NY: John Wiley.

Hare, R. D. (1993). *Without conscience: The disturbing world of the psychopaths among us.* New York, NY: Pocket Books.

Hare, R. D. (2003). *Manual for the revised psychopathy checklist* (2nd ed.). Toronto: Multi-Health Systems.

Hare, R. D., & Neumann, C. S. (2008). Psychopathy as a clinical and empirical construct. *Annual Review of Clinical Psychology, 4,* 217–246. doi:10.1146/annurev.clinpsy.3.022806.091452

Harris, G. T., Rice, M., & Cormier, C. A. (1991). Psychopathy and violent recidivism. *Law and Human Behavior, 15,* 625–637. doi:10.1007/BF01065856

Horley, J. (2014). The emergence and development of psychopathy. *History of the Human Sciences, 27,* 91–110. doi:10.1177/0952695114541864

Kiehl, K. A., & Hoffman, M. B. (2011). The criminal psychopath: History, neuroscience, treatment, and economics. *Jurimetrics, 51,* 355–397.

Kimonis, E. R., Kennealy, P. J., & Goulter, N. (2016). Does the self-report Inventory of Callous-Unemotional Traits predict recidivism? *Psychological Assessment, 28,* 1616–1624. doi:10.1037/pas0000292

Kraepelin, E. (1907). *Textbook of psychiatry.* London: Macmillan.

Last, N., Tufts, E., & Auger, L. E. (2017). The effects of meditation on grey matter atrophy and neurodegeneration: A systematic review. *Journal of Alzheimer's Disease, 56,* 275–286. doi:10.3233/JAD-160899

Lipsey, M. W., & Wilson, D. B. (1998). Effective intervention for serious juvenile offenders: A synthesis of research. *Serious & Violent Juvenile Offenders: Risk Factors and Successful Interventions,* 313–345. doi:10.4135/9781452243740.n13

Morse, G. (2004). Executive Psychopaths. *Harvard Business Review.* Retrieved from https://hbr.org/2004/10/executive-psychopaths

Olver, M. E., & Wong, S. C. P. (2015). Short- and long-term recidivism prediction of the PCL-R and the effects of age: A 24-year follow-up. *Personality Disorders: Theory, Research, and Treatment, 6,* 97–105. doi:10.1037/per0000095

Ortega-Escobar, J., Alcázar-Córcoles, M. Á, Puente-Rodríguez, L., & Peñaranda-Ramos, E. (2017). Psychopathy: Legal and neuroscientific aspects. *Anuario De Psicología Jurídica, 27,* 57–66. doi:10.1016/j.apj.2017.01.003

Perez, P. R. (2012). The etiology of psychopathy: A neuropsychological perspective. *Aggression and Violent Behavior, 17,* 519–522. doi:10.1016/j.avb.2012.07.006

Pinel, P. (1806). *A treatise on insanity.* Sheffield: Cadell and Davies.

Polaschek, D. L., & Daly, T. E. (2013). Treatment and psychopathy in forensic settings. *Aggression and Violent Behavior, 18,* 592–603. doi:10.1016/j.avb.2013.06.003

Prichard, J. C. (1842). *On the different forms of insanity in relation to jurisprudence.* London: Bailliere.

Salekin, R. T., Rogers, R., & Sewell, K. W. (1997). Construct validity of psychopathy in a female offender sample: A multitrait-multimethod evaluation. *Journal of Abnormal Psychology, 106,* 576–585. doi:10.1037//0021-843x.106.4.576

Smith, S. F., & Lilienfeld, S. O. (2013). Psychopathy in the workplace: The knowns and unknowns. *Aggression and Violent Behavior, 18,* 204–218. doi:10.1016/j.avb.2012. 11.007

Sörman, K., Edens, J. F., Smith, S. T., Svensson, O., Howner, K., Kristiansson, M., & Fischer, H. (2014). Forensic mental health professionals' perceptions of psychopathy: A prototypicality analysis of the Comprehensive Assessment of Psychopathic Personality in Sweden. *Law and Human Behavior, 38,* 405–417. doi:10.1037/lhb0000072

Umbach, R., Berryessa, C. M., & Raine, A. (2015). Brain imaging research on psychopathy: Implications for punishment, prediction, and treatment in youth and adults. *Journal of Criminal Justice, 43,* 295–306. doi:10.1016/j.jcrimjus.2015.04.003

Vieira, J. B., Ferreira-Santos, F., Almeida, P. R., Barbosa, F., Marques-Teixeira, J., & Marsh, A. A. (2015). Psychopathic traits are associated with cortical and subcortical volume alterations in healthy individuals. *Social Cognitive and Affective Neuroscience, 10,* 1693–1704. doi:10.1093/scan/nsv062

Walsh, A., & Bolen, J. D. (2012). *The neurobiology of criminal behavior: Gene-brain-culture interaction.* Farnham, UK: Ashgate Publishing.

15

Should Children Be Allowed to Participate in Contact Sports?

by Jordan Sparrow, Carol Patrick, PhD, & Skylar Hayes

The issue of whether children should be allowed to participate in team contact sports has become hotly debated in recent years. There are many benefits of sports participation that have been empirically supported (Marsh & Kleitman, 2003). However, more recently, concerns about physical and psychological harm to the children involved have arisen, and more and more parents are expressing concerns about allowing their children to participate in contact sports (Fishman et al., 2017). In this chapter, you will read about three positive outcomes of sports participation indicated by research, as well as three areas of concern.

Contact Sports Have Many Benefits for Children

Prosocial Growth. Positive social development is seen through participation in sports, including contact sports. Social growth directly related to contact sports includes relationships formed through the team and the coaching staff. One study investigated the effect team sports has on female adolescents' self-esteem (Pedersen & Seidman, 2004) Self-esteem levels of the adolescent girls showed significant increases over the course of the study. This finding was supported in male and female Latino subgroups (Erkut & Tracy, 2002). A positive relationship between sports and self-esteem was significant and observed in both female and male Mexican-Americans, Puerto Rican girls, and Cuban-American boys. Therefore, team sport participation was linked to a significant increase in global self-esteem for adolescent females.

Aside from self-esteem, there are many other social growth benefits that occur through sports participation. The perceptions of low-income parents and their children of the benefits of youth participation in sports suggested that there were perceived social benefits, including the positive effects of coach/participant relationships, peer relationships, and teamwork/social skills (Holt, Kingsley, Tink, & Scherer, 2011).

Health-related quality of life differences and social functioning among athletes and non-athletes was examined (Snyder et al., 2010). Athletes were healthier mentally, emotionally, and socially than peers who do not participate in sports. Furthermore, the researchers reported significantly higher levels of social functioning in athletes as opposed to those who did not participate in sports. In addition, the social functioning of children participating in different amounts and types of school activities was assessed. Sport-focused youth demonstrated increased positive behaviors compared to youth who were less involved in sports (Linver, Roth, & Brooks-Gunn, 2009). Together, these studies indicate children may benefit from participation in contact sports by experiencing positive social growth. Health may also be positively affected.

Academic Achievement.

In addition to prosocial growth, there is a vast amount of research on the effects of sport participation and academic achievement. Academic achievement can have several different definitions. One way of measuring academic achievement is through the use of a grade point average (GPA). For example, one study examined the effects of sports participation on the academic performance of middle school students (Stephens & Schaben, 2002). Athletes had a significantly higher GPA than nonathletes. Further, this significance was observed across gender; however, in comparison to boys, girls who participated in athletics had significantly higher GPAs. Also for both males and females, middle schoolers' participation in extracurricular activities (like sports) resulted in significantly higher GPAs compared to students who did not participate in extracurricular activities (Boatwright, 2009; Schlesser, 2004).

More evidence supporting higher levels of academic achievement was found in a study of the link between frequency of physical activity in elementary school–aged children and academic performance (Syvaoja, 2014). Children with higher GPAs were physically active for 60 minutes a day for 5 to 6 days a week, whereas, children with lower GPAs were only physically active 0 to 2 days a week.

Another study suggested that students participating in interscholastic sports achieve higher levels academically than those who do not participate in sports (White, 2005). Teachers of the students at the school were asked for their beliefs of the effects of athletic participation on academic achievement. Participation in sports was reported by teachers positively affecting students' academic achievement and attitude toward school.

Therefore, there seems to be a relation between sports participation and academic achievement. Whether the relationship is causative; that is, whether sports makes you a better student, remains to be seen.

Emotional Well-Being and Mental Health.

Along with prosocial growth and academic success, sports have also been shown to increase at-risk youth's emotional well-being, as well as decrease symptoms of a mental illness. A meta-analysis (Lubans, Plotnikoff & Lubans, 2012) suggested that at-risk youth (children or adolescents who live in a negative environment and/or do not possess the skills and values that assist them in becoming responsible members of society) who engaged in team sports and individual sport competitions were better able to understand their emotions compared to at-risk youth who did not engage in similar activities. When youth are better able to understand their own emotions, they are better able to regulate their emotions leading to a decrease in physical and verbal outbursts. This is important, especially for youth who are deemed "at risk," since emotion regulation is an important component of successful daily functioning and overall temperament.

Children with social cognitive and disruptive behaviors who engaged in sports for a 10-month period of time were able to improve their overall temperament (Palermo et al., 2006). Thus, they were better able to interact in socially appropriate ways after participating in the sports program, increasing their chances of making friends with same age peers. Furthermore, this study indicates that children who participate in sports can increase their overall emotional functioning in daily living.

More recent studies suggest that sports can not only improve emotional well-being but also can decrease symptoms of mental illness. Children who experienced symptoms of social anxiety (as reported by parents and teachers) were enrolled in an extracurricular sport (Dimech & Seiler, 2011). Children's levels of social anxiety were measured before they started the sport, then again 1 year after the initial enrollment in the extracurricular sport. Results suggested that children who participated in team sports were lower on all measures of social anxiety after the 1-year participation in sports compared to their initial reports.

A similar study examined the relationship between sports and emotional functioning of children who were diagnosed with Attention Deficit Hyperactivity Disorder (ADHD; Kiluk, Weden, & Culotta, 2009). The children who participated in three or more sports displayed significantly fewer anxiety or depression-related symptoms than the children who participated in fewer than three sports. Thus, these results are consistent with the previous literature suggesting that the participation in sports can decrease symptoms of mental illness.

In conclusion, there are many benefits for children who play contact sports. However, this research constitutes just some of the evidence supporting the benefits of contact sports. There is also evidence that there are negatives associated with contact sports for children.

Contact Sports Can Harm Children Physically and Psychologically

Aggression.   Participation in contact sports is an integral part of American society and is encouraged at a young age. Although these contact sports can be beneficial in a multitude of areas, they can also have serious detrimental impacts, particularly in regard to encouraging aggressive behaviors. Aggressive behaviors (overt actions intended to injure oneself or another physically or physiologically) are not only taught, but are encouraged in contact sports, such as football and hockey.

The perpetuation of aggression within the context of sport encourages young athletes to engage in aggressive behaviors outside of their respective sports and in their daily lives. For example, college athletes have more reported cases of being the perpetrator of sexual assault compared to the general population of college students (Humphrey & Kahn, 2000). Individuals who were on the football team were the most common perpetrator for these aggressive crimes.

Not only are these athletes engaging in aggressive behaviors more frequently, but they are also experiencing acts of aggression more frequently. That is, adolescents have been exposed to hazing rituals as part of the "right of passage" onto the team, as well as being verbally and physically abused by their peers and coaches. Recent research showed that adolescents who participated in sports were at risk for physical and emotional harm (Stafford, Alexander, & Fry, 2013). These risks include verbal and sexual harassment from coaches and other team members, being forced to play through injuries, and being forced to play while exhausted. These risks foster the culture of aggression within the youth who participate in sports at a young age. Although future aggressive behaviors are a major concern for individuals who participate sports at a young age, these sports also foster a culture of risky behavior.

Risky Behaviors.

Risky behaviors can be defined as actions whose results are unknown and which may impact negatively on health, life quality, and/or life expectancy (De Guzman & Bosch, 2007). These risky behaviors encompass a multitude of acts, such as excessive gambling, substance use, and sexual assault/rape attempts and completions. Indeed, athletes were more likely to have obsessive–compulsive rituals, and engage in obsessive gambling, infidelity, substance abuse (i.e., alcohol, cannabis, anabolic steroids) and suicidal ideation compared to the general population (Stillman, Brown, Ritvo, & Glick, 2016).

In October of 2018, the backup quarterback for the Denver Broncos, Chad Kelly, was arrested for criminal trespassing after a night of excessive drinking and alleged substance use. This is just one of many cases every year of athletes (of all levels) who are arrested in connection with criminal activity stemming from risky behavior (Foody & Stapleton, 2018).

A more prevalent problem, namely among younger athletes, is the increased rates of sexual assault/rape. Men who participated in contact sports (primarily football) were more likely to endorse rape-supportive attitudes, were significantly more sexually aggressive, and were more likely to commit sexual assaults than nonathletes (Humphrey & Kahn, 2000).

Brain Damage (CTE).

One of the most significant arguments against contact sports in young children is the possible long-term damage it may do to their brains. Although the study of chronic traumatic encephalopathy (CTE) may be in its infancy, there is plenty of evidence that real and substantial risks to children are possible. CTE is caused by multiple diagnosed and/or nondiagnosed traumatic brain injuries (TBIs), also known as concussions or subclinical (nondiagnosed) concussions.

Symptoms of CTE include changes in behavior (such as depression, agitation, impulsivity, and aggression), cognition (including problems with memory, executive functioning, decision making, inhibition of impulses, attention, and language), and also motor functioning, including Parkinson's Disease-like symptoms (Love & Solomon, 2014). Incidences of violence to self or others is common. These symptoms may not start until decades after the damage is done, and are directly related to observable damage in the brain.

The story of pro football player Aaron Hernandez is a cautionary tale about CTE and early involvement in contact sports. Hernandez was convicted of one murder and tried for two others, before committing suicide in his prison cell at the age of 27. Hernandez started playing football at a young age, and was the youngest player drafted in the 2010 draft. His brain was examined postmortem and he had extensive CTE damage (at a Stage 3, out of 4 possible), according to Anne McKee, Director of the CTE center at Boston University. Never had anyone under the age of 46 been diagnosed with such serious brain damage (Carey, 2017).

Initial studies began to examine adult athletes of different contact sports, particularly boxing and American football, for long-term damage to the brain. Postmortem brain studies of 51 athletes (mostly boxers and professional football players) showed damage consistent with CTE (McKee et al., 2009). When 85 people with a history of mild TBI were examined (mostly football players), 50 were found to have CTE-related brain damage, though none in a control group without TBI were found with CTE-related brain damage (McKee et al., 2013). Omalu et al. (2011) discovered that seven of eight professional football players showed CTE pathology postmortem.

MRI and DTI comparisons of pre- and post-season college athletes from several contact sports indicated damage from the season in the corpus callosum, which connects the two hemispheres of the brain and damage in this area is a key indicator of TBI (Lao et al., 2015). Damage was particularly noted in the areas of the corpus callosum which provide communication between the areas of the brain that process executive function, and is linked to impaired learning ability.

Attention has recently been focused on whether the age at which one starts playing a contact sport has an effect on CTE later in life. This message is certainly getting out to parents. A poll of pediatricians showed that 77% of parents would not allow their sons to play football and 35% would not allow their sons or daughters to play hockey because of fears of concussions (Fishman et al., 2017). Research shows there may be reason to worry. The brain is still in a period of rapid development through the child and adolescent years, particularly in the area of the brain that supports executive functioning and may possibly, therefore, be more susceptible to long-term damage from concussive injuries.

Research supports that early contact sport involvement may increase CTE risk. NFL players who started playing football before the age of 12, when compared to those who began playing after age 12, showed more impairment in executive functioning, memory, and intelligence, even though the two groups of players had similar numbers of overall concussions (Stamm et al., 2015). Two groups (high vs. low contact sports) of youth athletes, who had no reported concussions were compared on neuropsychological subconcussive effects (Tsushima, Geling, Arnold, & Oshiro, 2016). The high contact athletes had significantly poorer reaction times and processing speeds compared to the low contact athletes. A replication study also examined the neuropsychological test scores of high school athletes (aged 12 to 18) in high contact sports were compared with high school athletes in low contact sports (Tsushima, Siu, Yamashita, Oshriro, & Murata, 2018), and it was discovered that their reaction time and visual motor speed were significantly lower than the high contact group. When executive functions from a battery of neuropsychological tests were studied across 3 years in 211 youth hockey players between the ages of 8 and 15, significant negative impacts were found in cognitive flexibility and psychomotor speed, and the frequency and severity of concussion was predictive of these changes (Lax et al., 2015).

References

Boatwright, T. C. (2009). Comparison of grade point averages and dropout rates of students who participate in extracurricular activities and students who do not participate. *Dissertation Abstracts International Section A: Humanities and Social Sciences, 70,* 3403.

Carey, B. (2017). *Yes, Aaron Hernandez suffered brain injury.* Retrieved from https://www.nytimes.com/2017/09/21/sports/aaron-hernandez-cte-brain.html

De Guzman, M. R., & Bosch, K. R, (2007). High risk behaviors among youth. *NebGuide.* Retrieved from https://digitalcommons.unl.edu/cgi/viewcontent.cgi?article=5123&context=extensionhist

Dimech, A. S., & Seiler, R. (2011). Extra-curricular sport participation: A potential buffer against social anxiety symptoms in primary school children. *Psychology of Sport and Exercise, 12*(4), 347–354. doi:10.1016/j.psychsport. 2011.03.007

Erkut, S., & Tracy, A. (2002). Predicting adolescent self-esteem from participation in school sports among Latino subgroups. *Hispanic Journal of Behavioral Science, 4,* 409–429. doi:10.1177/0739986302238212

Fishman, M., Taranto, A. B., Perlman, M., Quinlan, K., Benjamin, H. J., & Ross, L. F. (2017). Attitudes and counseling practices of pediatricians regarding youth sports participation and concussion risks. *The Journal of Pediatrics, 184,* 19–24. doi:10.1016/j.jpeds.2017.01.048

Foody, K., & Stapleton, A. (2018). *Broncos backup QB Chad Kelly arrested in trespassing case.* Retrieved from https://www.apnews.com/2c4e70cc871a447393d6c1e1b1184cfc

Holt, N., Kingsley, B., Tink, L., & Scherer, J. (2011). Benefits and challenges associated with sport participation by children and parents from low-income families. *Psychology of Sport and Exercise, 12,* 490–499. doi:10.1016/j.psychsport.2011.05.007

Humphrey, S. E., & Kahn, A. S. (2000). Fraternities, athletic teams, and rape: Importance of identification with a risky group. *Journal of Interpersonal Violence, 15,* 1313–1323.

Kiluk, B. D., Weden, S., & Culotta, V. P. (2009). Sport participation and anxiety in children with ADHD. *Journal of Attention Disorders, 12*(6), 499–506. doi:10.117/1087054708320400

Lao, Y., Law, M., Shi, J., Gajawelli, N., Hass, L., Wang, Y., & Lepore, N. (2015). AT1 and DTI fused 3D corpus callosum analysis in pre- vs. post-season contact sports players. *10th International Symposium on Medical Information Processing and Analysis, 9287.* doi:10.1117/12.2-72600

Lax, I. D., Paniccia, M., Agnihotri, S., Reed, N., Garmaise, E., Azadbakhsh, M., . . .Taha, T. (2015). Developmental and gender influences on executive function following concussion in youth hockey players. *Brain Injury, 29,* 1409–1419. doi:10.3109/02699052.2015.1043344

Linver, M., Roth, J., & Brooks-Gunn, J. (2009). Patterns of adolescents' participation in organized activities: Are sports best when combined with other activities? *Developmental Psychology, 45,* 354–367. doi:10.1037/a0014133

Love, S., & Solomon, G. S. (2014). Talking with parents of high school football players about chronic traumatic encephalopathy. *The American Journal of Sports Medicine, 43,* 1260–1264. doi:10.1177/0363546514535187

Lubans, D. R., Plotnikoff, R. C., & Lubans, N. J. (2012). A systematic review of the impact of physical activity programmes on social and emotional wellbeing in at risk youth. *Child and Adolescent Mental Health, 17,* 2–13. doi:10.1111/j.1475-3588.2011.00623.x

Marsh, H., & Kleitman, S. (2003). School athletic participation: Mostly pain with little gain. *Journal of Sport and Exercise Physiology, 25,* 205–228. doi:10.1123/jsep.25.2.205

McKee, A. C., Cantu, R. C., Nowinski, A. J., Hedley-Whyte, E. T., Gavett, B. E., Budson, A. E., . . . Stern, R. A. (2009). Chronic traumatic encephalopathy in athletes: Progressive tauopathy after repetitive head injury. *Journal of Neuropathology and Experimental Neurology, 68,* 709–735. doi:10.1097/NEW.0b013e3181a9d503

McKee, A. C., Stein, T. D., Nowinski, C. J., Stern, R. A., Daneshvar, D. H., Alvarez, V. E., . . . Cantu, R. C. (2013). The spectrum of disease in chronic traumatic encephalopathy. *Brain, 136,* 43–64. doi:10.1093/brain/aws307

Omalu, B., Bailes, J., Hamilton, R. L., Kamboh, M. I, Hammers, J., Case, M., & Fitzsimmons, R. (2011). Emerging histomorpholgic phenotypes of chronic traumatic encephalopathy in American athletes. *Neurosurgery, 69,* 173–183. doi:10.1227/NEU.0b013e318212bc7b

Palermo, M. T., Di Luigi, M., Dal Forno, G., Dominici, C., Vicomandi, D., Sambucioni, A., . . . Rasqualetti, P. (2006). Externalizing and oppositional behaviors and Karate-do: The way of crime prevention: A pilot study. *International Journal of Offender Therapy and Comparative Criminology, 50,* 654–660. doi:10.1177/0306624X06293522

Pedersen, S., & Siedman, E. (2004). Team sports achievement and self-esteem development among urban adolescent girls. *Psychology of Women Quarterly, 28,* 412–422. doi:10.1111/j.1471-6402.2004.00158.x.

Schlesser, C. E. (2004). The correlation between extracurricular activities and grade point average of middle school students. *The Graduate School University of Wisconsin-Stout, Menomonie.*

Snyder, A., Martinez J. C., Bay R. C., Parsons J. T., Sauers, E. L., & McLeod, T. C. V. (2010). Health-related quality of life differs between adolescent athletes and adolescent non-athletes. *Journal of Sports Rehabilitation, 19,* 237–248. doi:10.1123/jsr.19.3.237

Stafford, A., Alexander, K., & Fry, D. (2013). Playing through pain: Children and young people's experiences of physical aggression and violence in sport. *Child Abuse Review, 22,* 287–299. doi:10.1002/car.2289

Stamm, J. M., Bourias, A. P., Baugh, C. M., Fritts, N. G., Daneshvar, D. H., Martin, B. M., . . Stern, R. A. (2015). Age of first exposure to football and later-life cognitive impairment in former NFL players. *Neurology, 84,* 1114–1119. doi:10.1212/WNL.0000000000001358

Stephens, L. J., & Schaben, L. A. (2002). The effect of interscholastic sports participation on academic achievement of middle level school students. *NASP Bulletin, 86*(630), 34–41. doi:10.1177/019263650208663005

Stillman, M. A., Brown, T., Ritvo, E. C., & Glick, I. D. (2016). Sport psychiatry and psycho-therapeutic intervention. *International Review of Psychiatry, 28,* 614–622. doi:10.1080/09 540261.2016.1202812

Syvaoja, H. (2014). *Physical activity and sedentary behaviour in association with academic performance and cognitive functions in school-aged children* (Doctoral dissertation). Retrieved from http://www.likes.fi/filebank/1427-Dissertation_Heidi_Syvaoja_tiivis.pdf

Tsushima, W. T., Geling, O., Arnold, M., & Oshiro, R. (2016). Are there subconcussive neuropsychological effects in youth sports? An exploratory study of high- and low-contact sports. *Applied Neuropsychology, 5,* 149–155. doi:10.1080/21622965.2015.1052813

Tsushima, W. T., Siu, A. M., Yamashita, N., Oshriro, R. S., & Murata, N. M. (2018). Comparison of neuropsychological test scores of high school athletes in high and low contact sports: A replication study. *Applied Neuropsychology: Child, 7,* 14–20. doi:10.1080/21622 965.2016.1220860

White, N. B. (2005). *The effects of athletic participation on academic achievement* (Doctoral dissertation). Retrieved from http://rave.ohiolink.edu/etdc/view?acc_num=marietta1124134979

16

Is Parental Divorce and/or Marital Conflict Harmful to Children?

by Janett M. Naylor-Tincknell, PhD & Kaylan J. Lagerman

The American Psychological Association (2018) states that between 40 and 50% of marriages in America end in divorce. Around 21 million children reside with one parent in the United States, whether from divorce or the death of a parent (Vespa, Lewis, & Kreider, 2013) and around 50% of children in the United States experience the divorce of their parents (Lansford, 2009). How, if at all, are children developmentally affected when divorce or parental conflict occurs?

Defining Parental Conflicts

According to Sarrazin and Cyr (2007), six different characteristics apply when defining parental conflict, including frequency, content, level of involvement of the child, intensity, parents' behavior, and presence or absence of resolution. Because of the complexity of parental conflict, research related to its impact on children is mixed. Some results indicate negative impacts on future relationships (Braithwaite, Doxey, Dowdle, & Fincham, 2016), children's well-being (Hertzmann et al., 2017), and academic achievement (Potter, 2010). However, other research suggests that the negative impact of divorce and marital conflict is inconsistent and their effects more nuanced (Emery, 1982; Lansford, 2009). In the next section, research regarding the impact of parental divorce/marital conflict on children is reviewed.

Divorce/Marital Conflict Has Harmful Effects

Marital conflict and divorce can have short-term and long-term negative effects on children and adolescents. Overall, children whose parents are divorced show relationship difficulties later in adulthood (Cui & Fincham, 2010). Additionally, depression and anxiety rates are higher in children with divorced parents than children with intact families (Hertzmann et al., 2017). Ample research also supports parental divorce's impact on academic achievement (Potter, 2010).

Negative Impact on Romantic Relationships.   Parental conflict, especially divorce, can have an effect on the romantic relationships of young adults. The link between parental divorce/marital conflict and young adult romantic relationship quality is well established. For example, young adults who held negative attitudes toward marriage and divorce also had lower levels of relationship dedication in their own romantic relationships (Cui & Fincham, 2010). Furthermore, young adult marriages are at a higher risk for divorce when influenced by parental divorce and conflict (Braithwaite et al., 2016). Children who witness their parents' conflicts can begin to hold negative views about marriage and relationships in general. Overall, adolescents and adults whose parents divorced do not view their relationships with the same commitment and positivity because of the impact of witnessing marital conflict and divorce when younger.

Negative Impact on Well-Being.   Parental conflict can not only affect romantic relationships, it can also affect well-being in multiple aspects. Poor emotional and psychological development can result from intense parental conflicts because children may experience intense stress, leading to mistrust and negative behaviors among other outcomes. These damages can last for the children's entire life (Hertzmann et al., 2017). Although developmental harm may not be detected until children are older, every day health problems can arise due to ongoing parental conflict. For example, children displayed the physical symptoms of stress, such as low body temperature, increased cardiac rhythm, and elevated blood pressure, when dealing with fighting parents (Sarrazin & Cyr, 2007). Parental conflict and divorce negatively impact emotional and physical well-being, which are important factors for parents to remember when they feel tensions rising in front of their children.

Negative Impact on Academic Achievement.   Research shows that divorce can specifically affect academic achievement, in that children who experience parental divorce typically do not perform as well as children from intact families (Potter, 2010). Children's diminished psychosocial well-being resulting from divorce impacted academic achievement and lower success in school. Children's poor academic outcomes and increased problematic behavior can also result from extreme conflicts between children's parents (Sarrazin & Cyr, 2007). Research findings highlight the severe academic repercussions that parental conflict can have on the children caught in the middle.

Harmful Effects Summary.   Romantic relationships, well-being, and academic achievement are important parts of children's lives and, when negatively impacted by parental divorce/marital conflict, can affect overall development of children who experience such events. If children are unable to function adequately in these areas, they may experience difficulties later in life.

Divorce continues to affect millions of children in both short-term and long-term ways, but research suggests that divorce may be more harmful to children in cultures where divorce is highly stigmatized (Lansford, 2009). Continued research on the effects of parental conflict and divorce allows for families in such circumstances to responsibly weigh all options before deciding how to handle major conflicts. Policies related to determining fault or no fault in a divorce, child custody, and child support are set by each state to try to determine the "best interests of the child" and parents in every case. Married and divorced parents who educate themselves on appropriate ways to handle their conflicts responsibly can decrease the possibility of negative effects on their children.

Divorce/Marital Conflict Does Not Have Harmful Effects

Divorce impacts children and families in different ways with varying outcomes of which not all are long-term negative outcomes. Divorce may not necessarily be the cause of problems, but is best thought of as a process of family disruption ending in marital separation (Furstenberg & Teitler, 1994), which allows the impact of individual components (e.g., marital conflict, family relations, attachment) of the process to be studied. In fact, examination of individual components have demonstrated positive outcomes (Amato & Anthony, 2014; Lansford, 2009), possible moderators (Bastaits & Mortelmans, 2016; Modecki, Hagan, Sandler, & Wolchik, 2015), and methodological flaws (Emery, 1982), indicating that divorce may not be as devastating as previous research suggests.

Divorce is Not the Cause.   Divorce is not the cause of negative outcomes. Problematic behaviors actually start to occur well before divorce (Furstenberg & Teitler, 1994) and continue as a gradual disintegration of behavior. In fact, divorce may actually be the starting point for family healing to begin. The marital conflict before, during, and after divorce could better explain the negative impact on children (Emery, 1982) than the actual divorce event. Resulting negative effects are most likely due to troubled family relationships rather than divorce (Amato & Anthony, 2014). For example, predivorce marital conflict and tension in the home cause children's lack of sleep, which leads to lower academic achievement (El-Sheikh, Buckhalt, Keller, & Cummings, 2007). When considered a process and not a single event, divorce is not the cause of negative outcomes. The cause may be marital conflict, tension, lack of sleep, and other problematic family interactions.

Examining the Complexities of Divorce.   The process of divorce involves several components: martial conflict and resolution, involvement of parents postdivorce, and parenting effectiveness postdivorce, ending with marital dissolution. Examination of the complex components of martial conflict and conflict resolution indicates that children of divorce may actually have better long-term outcomes. Harmonious endings to marital conflict resulted in children demonstrating less negative emotionality and increased emotional security (Davies, Myers, & Cumming, 1996). When parents use positive problem-solving strategies to resolve conflict, adolescents are more likely to use positive problem-solving strategies to solve parent–adolescent dispute strategies (Van Doorn, Branje, & Meeus, 2007).

Once divorce is settled, parental involvement and parental effectiveness can moderate any potential negative outcomes. When compared to children in highly conflictual marriages, children of divorce have fewer negative long-term outcomes or no negative long-term outcomes (Lansford, 2009). Additionally, children of divorce whose noncustodial fathers are involved (with low conflict) have higher academic achievement and less externalizing behavior than children of divorce whose parents continue to display highly conflictual relations (Modecki et al., 2015). Postdivorce parenting effectiveness can alter the negative impact. Parents who use parenting techniques that are supportive and highly controlled is linked with children's increased self-esteem and life satisfaction (Bastaits & Mortelmans, 2016). Overall, when parents remain engaged in and supportive of their children's lives, the impact of divorce lessens or even shows improvement indicating that divorce may be the start of healing rather than a time of more strife and trouble.

Methodological Concerns.
Finally, methodology concerns must be considered when attributing negative outcomes to divorce because the effects of divorce are confounded with other dysfunctional factors resulting in inaccurate estimates of negative outcomes (Arkes, 2017). Most studies do not control for confounding variables like parent–child attachment (El-Sheikh, et al., 2007), children's appraisal of responsibility taking and self-blame for parental conflict (Cummings, Davies, & Simpson, 1994), and children's emotional security (Davies & Cummings, 1994). When effects were found, they were modest because of variability in children and the process of divorce (Amato, 2001), suggesting that many other variables should be considered. The impact of divorce is only a small aspect of a complex process of divorce. These methodological flaws change the magnitude of effects because of biased sampling, nonindependent data, and nonreliable and valid measures (Emery, 1982). Given the methodology concerns, the negative effects of divorce on children cannot be soundly established.

No Harmful Effects Summary.
Divorce is not a onetime event. When researchers investigate the impact of divorce on children, the complexity of the process and enormity of the variables involved are often overlooked. Although a simple explanation may be appealing, marital dissolution is not a simple concept. Without understanding the entirety of the situation, divorce cannot be considered the cause of negative outcomes.

References

Amato, P. R. (2001). Children of divorce in the 1990s: An update of the Amato and Keith (1991) meta-analysis. *Journal of Family Psychology, 15,* 355–370. doi:10.1037//0893-3200.15.3.355

Amato, P. R., & Anthony, C. J. (2014). Estimating the effects of parental divorce and death with fixed effects model. *Journal of Marriage and Family, 76,* 370–386. doi:10.1111/jomf.12100

American Psychological Association. (2018). *Marriage and divorce.* Retrieved from https://www.apa.org/topics/divorce/

Arkes, J. (2017). Separating the harmful versus beneficial effects of marital disruptions on children. *Journal of Divorce and Remarriage, 58,* 526–541. doi:10.1080/105002556.2017.1344500

Bastaits, K., & Mortelmans, D. (2016). Parenting as a mediator between post-divorce family structure and children's well-being. *Journal of Child and Family Studies, 25,* 2178–2188. doi:10.1007/s10826-016-0395-8

Braithwaite, S. R., Doxey, R. A., Dowdle, K. K., & Fincham, F. D. (2016). The unique influences of parental divorce and parental conflict on emerging adults in romantic relationships. *Journal of Adult Development, 23,* 214–225. doi:10.1007/s10804-016-9237-6

Cui, M., & Fincham, F. D. (2010). The differential effects of parental divorce and marital conflict on young adult romantic relationships. *Personal Relationships, 17,* 331–343. doi:10.1111/j.1475-6811.2010.01279.x

Cummings, E. M., Davies, P. T., & Simpson, K. S. (1994). Marital conflict, gender, and children's appraisal and coping efficacy as mediators of child adjustment. *Journal of Family Psychology, 8,* 141–149. doi:10.1037/0893-3200.8.2.141

Davies, P. T., & Cummings, E. M. (1994). Marital conflict and child adjustment: An emotional security hypothesis. *Psychological Bulletin, 116,* 387–411. doi:10.1037/0033-2909.116.3.387

Davies, P. T., Myers, R. L., & Cumming, E. M. (1996). Responses of children and adolescents to marital conflict scenarios as a function of the emotionality of conflict ending. *Merrill-Palmer Quarterly, 42,* 1–21. Retrieved from http://www.jstor.org/stable/23090518

El-Sheikh, M., Buckhalt, J. A., Keller, P. S., & Cummings, E. M. (2007). Child emotional insecurity and academic achievement: The role of sleep disruptions. *Journal of Family Psychology, 21,* 29–38. doi:10.1037/0893-3200.21.1.29

Emery, R. E. (1982). Interparental conflict and the children of discord and divorce. *Psychological Bulletin, 92,* 310–330. doi:10.1037/0033-2909.92.2.310

Furstenberg, F. F., & Teitler, J. (1994). Reconsidering the effect of marital disruption: What happens to children of divorce in early childhood. *Journal of Family Issues, 15,* 173–190. doi:10.1177/0192513X94015002002

Hertzmann, L., Abse, S., Target, M., Glausius, K., Nyberg, V., & Lassri, D. (2017). Mentalisation-based therapy for parental conflict—parenting together: An intervention for parents in entrenched post-separation disputes. *Psychoanalytic Psychotherapy, 31*, 195–217. doi:10.1080/02668734.2017.1320685

Lansford, J. E. (2009). Parental divorce and children's adjustment. *Perspectives on Psychological Science, 4*, 140–152. doi:10.1111/j.1745-6924.2009.01114.x

Modecki, K. L., Hagan, M. J., Sandler, I., & Wolchik, S. A. (2015). Latent profiles of non-residential father engagement six years after divorce predict long-term offspring outcomes. *Journal of Clinical Child and Adolescent Psychology, 44*, 123–136. doi:10.1080/15374416.2013.865193

Potter, D. (2010). Psychosocial well-being and the relationship between divorce and children's academic achievement. *Journal of Marriage and Family, 72*, 933–946. doi:10.1111/j.1741-3737.2010.00740.x

Sarrazin, J., & Cyr, F. (2007). Parental conflicts and their damaging effects on children. *Journal of Divorce & Remarriage, 47*, 77–93. doi:10.1300/J087v47n01_05

Van Doorn, M. D., Branje, S. J. T., & Meeus, W. H. J. (2007). Longitudinal transmission of conflict resolution styles from marital relationships to adolescent-parent relationships. *Journal of Family Psychology, 21*, 426–434. doi:10.1037/0893.3200.21.3.426

Vespa, J., Lewis, M. J., & Kreider, R. M. (2013). America's families and living arrangements: 2012 population characteristics. *Current Population Reports, U.S. Census Bureau*. Retrieved from https://www.census.gov/content/dam/Census/library/publications/2013/demo/p20-570.pdf

17

Are Monogamous Relationships Optimal?

by April Phillips, PhD

Monogamy, defined as an exclusive sexual relationship between one man and one woman (Stone, Goetz, & Shackelford, 2005), is currently accepted by contemporary Western societies as the optimal relationship pattern (Conley, Ziegler, Moors, Matsick, & Valentine, 2012). In fact, over 90% of both men and women marry at some point in their lives. When asked, the majority of people identified a monogamous marriage as their ideal mating arrangement (Stone et al, 2005). However, there is considerable evidence that many of these supposedly monogamous relationships are plagued by infidelity. Estimates of marital infidelity range from 15% to 70% for women and 25% to 50% for men (Gangestad & Thornhill, 1997; Shackelford & Buss, 1997; Simmons, Firman, Rhodes, & Peters, 2004). Based on these data, it appears that despite our current societal norms and beliefs about the benefits of monogamy, humans are not actually very good at maintaining long-term monogamous relationships. Of course, we often pursue goals that are challenging because the benefits of achieving these goals are so great. For example, the difficulties of exercising and maintaining a healthy weight can be offset by the health benefits of these activities. Thus, we must ask ourselves two questions: What are the benefits of monogamy and are these benefits specific to monogamous relationships?

In one large-scale study, monogamy was perceived to provide benefits in three broad areas: relationship quality, health, and family benefits (i.e., child rearing; Conley, Moors, Matsick, & Ziegler, 2013). However, monogamy may not be the only relationship pattern that provides these and other benefits. For example, recently there has been interest in examining polyamorous or consensually nonmonogamous relationships (CNM) as an alternative to monogamy. CNM relationships have been defined as any relationship in which both partners have agreed that engaging in sexual and/or romantic relationships with other individuals is allowed and even encouraged. Recent estimates indicate that approximately 4% to 5% of Americans are currently involved in CNM relationships (Conley et al., 2012). Although this is a small overall percentage, it still represents a sizable minority and is comparable to estimations of the number of gay, lesbian, and bisexual individuals in the population

(Conley et al., 2013). This chapter will present evidence and arguments both for and against the supposition that monogamy is the optimal relationship pattern.

Monogamous Relationships Are Optimal

Relationship Quality.   Multiple researchers have examined various factors that affect relationship quality in romantic relationships. In one survey, "faithfulness" was ranked as the most important predictor of successful marriages indicating support for the idea that monogamy is best (Pew Research Center, 2007). When asked what they perceived the benefits of monogamy to be, participants overwhelmingly cited factors associated with relationship quality and satisfaction (i.e., commitment, emotional security, trust, and meaningfulness, less jealousy), revealing that participants perceived monogamous relationships to be higher quality (Conley et al., 2013). Jealousy in particular, which occurs when a valued relationship is threatened by a rival (Pines, 1992), is usually seen as a destructive force in relationships, leading to conflict and potential dissolution (Guerrero & Andersen, 1998). Not surprisingly, actual or suspected infidelity is the leading cause of spousal abuse and homicide, as well as the most frequently cited reason for divorce among married couples (Shackelford & Buss, 1997). Due to the presence of other partners (potential rivals), jealousy is a common concern in CNM relationships (Rubel & Bogaert, 2015). Many people see monogamy as a way to prevent or reduce jealousy by increasing trust and commitment (Conley et al., 2012).

Health Benefits.   There is ample evidence that maintaining close relationships with others is essential to our health, adjustment, and overall well-being, indicating that humans have a strong fundamental need to form and maintain close interpersonal relationships (Baumeister & Leary, 1995). For example, social isolation is a major risk factor for mortality, equivalent to others such as smoking, high blood pressure, and obesity (House, Landis, & Umberson, 1988). Since marriage is the central relationship for the majority of adults, it is not surprising that married people enjoy better physical and mental health compared to the unmarried (Kiecolt-Glasser & Newton, 2001). Of course, this effect is dependent on relationship quality in that only those who are happily married experience positive health effects. In fact, unmarried people are often better off than those in unhappy marriages (Glenn & Weaver, 1981).

In addition to evidence that stable committed relationships (monogamy) are associated with higher levels of well-being, there is also a pervasive belief among both mental health experts and the general public that individuals who practice CNM are neurotic, or otherwise mentally unstable (Conley et al., 2013; Hymer & Rubin, 1982, p. 2004). In support of this belief, research has shown that swingers reported higher levels of anxiety and depression (Levitt, 1988). In addition, CNM has been linked to at least three other indicators of poorer well-being. Specifically, researchers have found that people in CNM relationships reported less happy childhoods, more distant relationships with their parents, and a greater history of seeking counseling services (Gilmartin, 1974; Rubel & Bogaert, 2015). Finally, due to the pervasive bias that society tends to hold toward CNM, social pressure and stigma may also negatively affect the well-being of individuals engaging in these marginalized relationships (Conley et al., 2013; Rubel & Bogaert, 2015). For example, swinging couples in Thailand reported fears that they would be stigmatized or blackmailed if others found out about their activities (Viwatpanich, 2010).

In addition to increased psychological well-being, monogamous relationships might provide protection from sexually transmitted infections (STIs) and other benefits to sexual health. As part of a study on the perceived benefits of monogamy, participants listed a variety of positive outcomes related to sex and sexual health. Specifically, participants believed that monogamous relationships would result in higher sexual frequency, more exciting and meaningful sex, and safer sex (i.e., a lower risk of STIs; Conley et al., 2013). Indeed, engaging in multiple and concurrent sexual relationships (nonmonogamy) is associated with higher levels of STIs and unplanned pregnancies (Kogan, Yu, & Brown, 2016).

Family Benefits (Child Rearing).   Family benefits were widely perceived as an important positive aspect of monogamous relationships (Conley et al., 2013). Specifically, participants judged monogamous relationships as providing a stable family structure for raising children. There is a large body of research to support the idea that children benefit by being raised in a stable two-parent home. For example, children living in two-parent homes displayed higher levels of academic achievement across a variety of measures than children from single-parent homes. Furthermore, family structure was shown to be a better predictor of student success than the types of parental involvement usually encouraged by educators (O'Malley, Voight, Renshaw, & Eklund, 2015). The importance of investment and care being provided by both parents have led evolutionary psychologists to conclude that monogamy may have evolved because it solves problems our ancestors likely faced, such as paternity uncertainty and facilitated parental care by fathers (Geary, 1998; Stone et al., 2005).

Consensually Nonmonogamous Relationships Are Just as Good (or Better)

Relationship Quality.   Most of the studies examining relationship quality and satisfaction have focused exclusively on relationships that are heterosexual and monogamous, reflecting an overall bias in favor of monogamy, both culturally and within the academic literature (Conley et al., 2012). As a result, most of the available data directly comparing monogamous relationships with CNM relationships examine other nonnormative relationship patterns such as gay, lesbian, and bisexual relationships. Despite this potential limitation, current studies indicate that individuals involved in CNM relationships report similar levels of psychological well-being and relationship quality as those in traditional monogamous relationships (Rubel & Bogaert, 2015). In two studies, researchers found that both gay men who were in open relationships and those in sexually faithful monogamous relationships had higher levels of relationship adjustment than men in relationships in which at least one partner had broken the agreement to be monogamous (LaSala, 2004; Wagner, Remien, & Carbella-Dieguez, 2000). Thus, it appears that whether couples abide by their individual agreement matters more than whether they engage in relationships outside their primary partnership.

There is also some evidence that couples who are struggling to remain monogamous might benefit by mutually agreeing to open their relationship to other partners. In two studies, participants reported that adopting a CNM relationship style had improved their marital happiness and/or satisfaction (Rubel & Bogaert, 2015). When asked directly about the benefits their relationships provided, CNM individuals reported three categories of benefits that were not mentioned in previous studies of monogamous relationships: need fulfillment, variety of nonsexual activities, and personal growth and development (Moors, Matsick, & Schechinger, 2017). It appears that individuals in CNM relationships see their relationship structure as allowing them to meet a variety of their needs including those for personal growth. They also value the potential to enjoy a variety of social activities that having multiple relationship partners affords them.

As mentioned in the previous section, jealousy is common in CNM relationships (Rubel & Bogaert, 2015); however, studies have suggested that the level of jealousy experienced is similar across both types (CNM and monogamous) of relationships (Rubin & Adams, 1986). In at least one study of gay men, those in CNM relationships reported lower levels of sexual jealousy (Parsons, Starks, Gamarel, & Grov, 2012). Couples in CNM relationships may also perceive jealousy differently, conceptualizing it as something that is easily managed and can provide opportunities for positive growth within the relationship (de Visser & McDonald, 2007). Additionally, the negative effects of jealousy in CNM relationships may be offset by feelings of compersion. Compersion is a term used within the polyamorous community that describes the experience of taking pleasure in seeing your partner's happiness with his/her other relationships and is generally perceived as a positive benefit of CNM relationships (Deri, 2015; Ritchie & Barker, 2006).

Health Benefits.   As discussed previously, maintaining close relationships with others is essential to our health, adjustment, and overall well-being (Baumeister & Leary, 1995). However, the question remains as to whether these benefits to health and well-being are specific to monogamous relationships. Although there is not as much research examining CNM relationships, there is some evidence that individuals involved in stable CNM relationships might enjoy many of the same benefits to their health and well-being as those in monogamous relationships. For example, in one study of swingers, 97.5% reported higher levels of excitement in their lives and decreased levels of boredom as a result of swinging (Levitt, 1988). CNM relationships might also provide individuals with a closer social network. In one study, swingers reported closer relationships with their friends than members of a comparison group (Gilmartin, 1974). Thus, it is reasonable to conclude that CNM might provide some individuals with both excitement and increased social support (Rubel & Bogaert, 2015).

As discussed earlier, monogamous relationships are believed to result in higher sexual frequency, more exciting and meaningful sex, and safer sex (i.e., a lower risk of STIs; Conley et al., 2013). However, a large body of research has shown that sexual frequency and satisfaction actually decreases over the course of a long-term monogamous relationship (Brewis & Meyer, 2005; Clement, 2002). In fact, lack of sexual arousal is one of the most common reasons given for seeking marriage therapy (Conley et al., 2012). In contrast, many people in CNM relationships report that engaging in outside relationships results in improved sex with their primary partner (Rubel & Bogaert, 2015; Viwatpanich, 2010).

In terms of protection from STIs, it does seem logical to assume that monogamous relationships would result in safer sex practices. However, this would be true only for those relationships in which both partners test negative for STIs at the beginning of the relationship and remain sexually faithful (Conley et al., 2012). Unfortunately, as discussed earlier, that is often not the case. Infidelity is a frequent occurrence in many "monogamous" relationships (Gangestad & Thornhill, 1997; Shackelford & Buss, 1997; Simmons et al., 2004). Further, when looking at safer sex practices, individuals in CNM relationships are more likely to use condoms and other barrier methods with all partners and to discuss their STI testing history prior to engaging in sex than sexually unfaithful individuals in monogamous relationships (Swan & Thompson, 2016).

Family Benefits (Child Rearing).   Although there is considerable support for the idea that growing up in a stable two-parent household is beneficial for children, there is very little research examining the outcomes for children whose parents are involved in CNM relationships. In this case, the type of relationship might matter. For example, some couples (i.e., swingers) engage in outside relationships in which their children do not meet or interact with their other partners (Conley et al., 2012). In these relationships, we would not expect to see any differences in parenting or family dynamics connected to the parents' relationship style. However, some individuals in polyamorous relationships involve all of their partners in their children's lives. In these cases, the structure of the parents' relationship could potentially impact the children (Conley et al., 2012). Currently, there is very little research investigating this topic. However, in one longitudinal study, polyamorous parents who are engaged in co-parenting reported a number of benefits to their children. Due to the presence of additional adults who were invested in the welfare of the children, these families reported less reliance of day care and exposure to a diversity of interests and perspectives (Sheff, 2010). Based on the available evidence, it appears that CNM results in similar outcomes for children compared to monogamy, and that other aspects of the parents' relationship, such as stability, matter more (Conley et al., 2012).

References

Baumeister, R. F., & Leary, M. R. (1995). The need to belong: Desire for interpersonal attachments as a fundamental human motivation. *Psychological Bulletin, 117,* 497–529. doi:10.1037/0033-2909.117.3.497

Brewis, A., & Meyer, M. (2005). Marital coitus across the life course. *Journal of Biosocial Science, 37,* 499–518. doi:10.1017/S002193200400690X

Clement, U. (2002). Sex in long-term relationships: A systemic approach to sexual desire problems. *Archives of Sexual Behavior, 31,* 241–246. doi:10.1023/A:1015296718952

Conley, T. D., Moors, A. C., Matsick, J. L., & Ziegler, A. (2013). The fewer the merrier?: Assessing stigma surrounding consensually non-monogamous romantic relationships. *Analyses of Social Issues and Public Policy (ASAP), 13,* 1–30. doi:10.1111/j.1530-2415.2012.01286.x

Conley, T. D., Ziegler, A., Moors, A. C., Matsick, J. L., & Valentine, B. (2012). A critical examination of popular assumptions about the benefits and outcomes of monogamous relationships. *Personality and Social Psychology Review, 17,* 124–141. doi:10.1177/1088868312467087

de Visser, R., & McDonald, D. (2007). Swings and roundabouts: Management of jealousy in heterosexual 'swinging' couples. *British Journal of Social Psychology, 46,* 459–476. doi:10.1348/014466606X143153

Deri, J. (2015). *Love's refraction: Jealousy and compersion in queer women's polyamorous relationships.* Toronto, ON: University of Toronto Press. Retrieved from https://search.ebscohost.com/login.aspx?direct=true&db=psyh&AN=2015-25795-000&site=ehost-live

Gangestad, S. W., & Thornhill, R. (1997). The evolutionary psychology of extrapair sex: The role of fluctuating asymmetry. *Evolution and Human Behavior, 18,* 69–88. doi:10.1016/S1090-5138(97)00003-2

Geary, D. C. (1998). *Male, female: The evolution of human sex differences.* Washington, DC: American Psychological Association. doi:10.1037/10370-000. Retrieved from https://search.ebscohost.com/login.aspx?direct=true&db=psyh&AN=2000-07043-000&site=ehost-live

Gilmartin, B. G. (1974). Sexual deviance and social networks: A study of social, family, and marital interactions among co-marital sex participants. In J. R. Smith & L. G. Smith (Eds.), *Beyond monogamy* (pp. 291–323). Baltimore, MD: John Hopkins University Press.

Glenn, N. D., & Weaver, C. N. (1981). The contribution of marital happiness to global happiness. *Journal of Marriage and the Family, 43,* 161–168. doi:10.2307/351426

Guerrero, L. K., & Andersen, P. A. (1998). The dark side of jealously and envy: Desire, delusion, desperation, and destructive communication. In B. H. Spitzberg & W. R. Cupach (Eds.), (pp. 33–70). Mahwah, NJ: Lawrence Erlbaum Associates Publishers. Retrieved from https://search.ebscohost.com/login.aspx?direct=true&db=psyh&AN=1998-08064-002&site=ehost-live

House, J. S., Landis, K. R., & Umberson, D. (1988). Social relationships and health. *Science, 241*, 540–545. doi:10.1126/science.3399889

Hymer, S. M., & Rubin, A. M. (1982). Alternative lifestyle clients: Therapists' attitudes and clinical experiences. *Small Group Behavior, 13*, 532–541. doi:10.1177/104649648201300408

Kiecolt-Glaser, J. K., & Newton, T. L. (2001). Marriage and health: His and hers. *Psychological Bulletin, 127*, 472–503. doi:10.1037/0033-2909.127.4.472

Kogan, S. M., Yu, T., & Brown, G. L. (2016). Romantic relationship commitment behavior among emerging adult African American men. *Journal of Marriage and Family, 78*, 996–1012. doi:10.1111/jomf.12293

LaSala, M. C. (2004). Extradyadic sex and gay male couples: Comparing monogamous and nonmonogamous relationships. *Families in Society, 85*(3), 405–412. doi:10.1606/1044-3894.1502

Levitt, E. E. (1988). Alternative life style and marital satisfaction: A brief report. *Annals of Sex Research, 1*, 455–461. doi:10.1007/BF00878109

Moors, A. C., Matsick, J. L., & Schechinger, H. A. (2017). Unique and shared relationship benefits of consensually non-monogamous and monogamous relationships: A review and insights for moving forward. *European Psychologist, 22*, 55–71. doi:10.1027/1016-9040/a000278

O'Malley, M., Voight, A., Renshaw, T. L., & Eklund, K. (2015). School climate, family structure, and academic achievement: A study of moderation effects. *School Psychology Quarterly, 30*, 142–157. doi:10.1037/spq0000076

Page, E. H. (2004). Mental health services experiences of bisexual women and bisexual men: An empirical study. *Journal of Bisexuality, 4*, 137–160. doi:10.1300/J159v04n01_11

Parsons, J. T., Starks, T. J., Gamarel, K. E., & Grov, C. (2012). Non-monogamy and sexual relationship quality among same-sex male couples. *Journal of Family Psychology, 26*, 669–677. doi:10.1037/a0029561

Pew Research Center. (2007). *Modern marriage: "I like hugs. I like kisses. But what I really love is help with the dishes."* Retrieved from http://www.pewsocialtrends.org/2007/07/18/modern-marriage/

Pines, A. M. (1992). Romantic jealousy: Five perspectives and an integrative approach. *Psychotherapy: Theory, Research, Practice, Training, 29*, 675–683. doi:10.1037/0033-3204.29.4.675

Ritchie, A., & Barker, M. (2006). 'There aren't words for what we do or how we feel so we have to make them up': Constructing polyamorous languages in a culture of compulsory monogamy. *Sexualities, 9*, 584–601. doi:10.1177/1363460706069987

Rubel, A. N., & Bogaert, A. F. (2015). Consensual nonmonogamy: Psychological well-being and relationship quality correlates. *Journal of Sex Research, 52*, 961–982. doi:10.1080/00224499.2014.942722

Rubin, A. M., & Adams, J. R. (1986). Outcomes of sexually open marriages. *Journal of Sex Research, 22,* 311–319. doi:10.1080/00224498609551311

Shackelford, T. K., & Buss, D. M. (1997). Anticipation of marital dissolution as a consequence of spousal infidelity. *Journal of Social and Personal Relationships, 14,* 793–808. doi:10.1177%2F0265407597146005

Sheff, E. (2010). Strategies in polyamorous parenting. In M. Barker & D. Langridge (Eds.), *Understanding non-monogamies* (pp. 169–181). New York, NY: Routledge.

Simmons, L. W., Firman, R. C., Rhodes, G., & Peters, M. (2004). Human sperm competition: Testis size, sperm production and rates of extrapair copulations. *Animal Behavior, 68,* 297–302. doi:10.1016/j.anbehav.2003.11.013

Stone, E. A., Goetz, A. T., & Shackelford, T. K. (2005). Sex differences and similarities in preferred mating arrangements. *Sexualities, Evolution & Gender, 7,* 269–276. doi:10.1080/14616660500335391

Swan, D. J., & Thompson, S. C. (2016). Monogamy, the protective fallacy: Sexual versus emotional exclusivity and the implication for sexual health risk. *Journal of Sex Research, 53,* 64–73. doi:10.1080/00224499.2014.1003771

Viwatpanich, K. (2010). Swinging: Extramarital sexuality in Thai society. *Anthropological Notebooks, 16,* 57–70. Retrieved from http://www.drustvo-antropologov.si/AN/PDF/2010_2/Anthropological_Notebooks_XVI_2_Viwatpanich.pdf

Wagner, G. J., Remien, R. H., & Carballo-Diéguez, A. (2000). Prevalence of extradyadic sex in male couples of mixed HIV status and its relationship to psychological distress and relationship quality. *Journal of Homosexuality, 39,* 31–46. doi:10.1300/J082v39n02_02

18

Is Gender a Binary Construct?

by Carrie Nassif, PhD

In the United States, gender has long been defined as being either male or female; however, this appears to be in flux. At least seven states (Arkansas, California, Colorado, Maine, New York, Oregon, and Washington), as well as the District of Columbia, have some legal provision for third gender, gender neutral, or intersex designations on state-issued government identification and/or birth certificates. However at the federal level, the Department of Health and Human Services, under President Trump, has threatened to redefine gender in Title IX as being according to only the sex assigned at birth, either male or female—essentially rolling back transinclusive guidelines for children in schools. This is happening at a time when teens are more likely to identify themselves with nontraditional gender labels; up to 2.7% in 2016 (Rider, McMorris, Gower, Coleman, & Eisenberg, 2018).

Meanwhile, research on gender has historically focused on the differences between men and women, with only little acknowledgment of gender diversity. As a result, much of the literature is marked by the biases of a gender binary lens. In fact, a brief published by the Williams Institute's GenIUSS Group (Gender Identity in U.S. Surveillance) in 2013 discussed the dearth of major federally supported surveys that collect data on gender diversity.

Finally, in 2015, the American Psychological Association's Guidelines for Psychological Practice with Transgender and Gender Nonconforming People indicates, in its first guideline, that "gender is a non-binary construct that allows for a range of gender identities and that a person's gender identity may not align with sex assigned at birth" (p. 834). Why do they believe that this is the case? In such a divisive social and cultural context, what does the research show about how we should conceptualize gender? Is it a binary construct, or is gender more accurately represented on a spectrum?

Gender as a Binary Construct

Mainstream culture in the United States ascribes to traditional masculine and feminine gender roles, with men being expected to be more dominant, and women, more nurturing. There is often a harsh social penalty for deviance from these culturally determined gender norms, which may range from school-yard bullying to violent hate crimes. The vast majority of individuals, if they were familiar with the term, would consider themselves as being "cisgender," which means that their sex assigned at birth is consistent with who they see themselves as being on an internal level, or with their "gender identity." In fact, most were classified at birth as either male or female based on a combination of their anatomy, hormones, and/or chromo-somal testing. We have even begun to assign babies' gender before they are born at gender reveal events, which often have themes perpetuating gender stereotypes based on extremes of traditional gender roles, like "trucks or tiaras." On the whole, our social environment provides extensive evidence of the gender binary; that is, that the human experience is either male or female, and that these two discrete, nonoverlapping categories are the only valid options.

Gender Roles are Traditionally Masculine or Feminine.

With regard to gender roles, our societal standards and expectations have traditionally been more pervasively binary, but what about in current times? Because gender roles are culturally defined, it is appropriate to evaluate what a representative sample reports in a survey of gender differences. A large-scale survey by the Pew Research Center (2017) indicates that most Americans believe that men and women have very different interests, skills, ways of feeling and behaving, and different parenting and work styles. In general, men were valued more for their honesty, morality, financial success, leadership, strength, and good work ethic; and women for their physical appearance and their nurturing and empathy skills. These findings also indicated that Americans emphasize different parenting approaches as being appropriate for boys than for girls. Overall, most respondents did not see these gender differences as being negative; and many (56%) said they were a good thing.

Men and Women have Different Innate Personalities.

The stereotype that men tend to be more aggressive than women is borne out in U.S. crime rates, and the stereotype that women are more nurturing is seen in the gender disparity among child care providers and nurses. But if we look further back, before the impact of culture, evolutionary theories can explain the function of these differences with regard to reproductive strategies. Aggression is useful in men who compete for mates by hunting and protect their mates and offspring from harm, and nurturing is important for women who bear the children and are limited to foraging with their young.

In a large-scale study, Del Guidice, Booth, and Irwing (2012) compared the results of a personality assessment, the 16PF, in over 10,000 U.S. adults. Statistically significant differ-ences were found between genders when comparing each trait with the other: Women were found to have higher levels of Sensitivity, Warmth, and Apprehension, whereas men had higher Emotional Stability, Dominance, Rule Consciousness, and Vigilance. These findings are consistent with other research in the field of gender differences (and with evolutionary theory). However, the authors also created a more complex model that allowed for multiple group differences to be compared in multiple steps, and found two distinct patterns of distri-bution with "very large" effect sizes using this methodology. A male and female pattern over-lapped by only 10%, indicating very little similarity between the sexes. They posit that previous findings underestimate sex differences because of their uses of less discriminating personality tests and/or less advanced data analytic methods. This finding of strongly discrete patterns of personality variables between the sexes supports the gender binary construct.

Men and Women have Different Brains.   Researchers study sex differences in the brain in attempts to identify structural features that explain evolutionary, developmental, and/or hormonally driven biological differences in behavior among men and women. A 2014 meta-analysis indicated significant brain differences by gender for global brain volume and for tissue volume and density in several areas of the brain relevant to the functioning of psychiatric disorders, which disproportionately affect men and women such as autism, depression, schizophrenia, and ADHD (Ruigrok et al., 2014).

One large-scale study conducted since then was intended to address some of the limitations cited by that meta-analysis with enough power to detect even small effect sizes (Ritchie et al., 2018). The largest such study to date examined sex differences in over 5,000 participants in terms of the structure and function of their brains. Even though there was significant overlap, male brains had higher volume and surface area than female brains on average; a significant difference that persisted even when accounting for body height. In contrast, female brains had thicker cortexes than men in nearly all areas measured. Depending on task given, the functional connectivity differed between genders as well, indicating specialized function for the two genders.

Gender as a Spectrum

Although the gender binary clearly describes the experiences of the majority of Americans, it does not account for a minority of the population who are transgender, who are intersex, or who consider themselves to be otherwise "gender nonconforming". Transgender is an adjective used to describe someone whose sex assigned at birth is at variance with their gender identity; that is, their sense of self as male, female, or something else (e.g., androgynous, "gender queer," two-spirit, etc.). Gender identity is about one's self-perception. Intersex, on the other hand, is about one's physical body. Intersex is a label for someone who is born with male and female biological characteristics, something that occurs in about 1% to 2% of births in the United States (Blackless et al., 2000). In the past, when the sex at birth was observably ambiguous, it was common practice to surgically "correct" the anatomy to fit the gender binary—often without the children ever being informed. There is a growing consensus that this is, at best, a medically unnecessary practice, potentially harmful, and ethically problematic because the children living with the consequences is unable to consent to the procedure. Differences in sex development can occur even when biological markers appear consistent with a single gender at birth because some chromosomal abnormalities and hormonal syndromes may not become evident until puberty, or incidentally discovered, if at all (World Health Organization: Genomic Resource Centre, 2018). The very existence of such diversity within human biology makes a case for a more varied classification of gender.

Furthermore, being considered outliers, deviants, or invalids by the prevalent gender binary appears to put people at risk. Because they are often not identified in research, very little health outcomes research is specific to people who do not identify as male or female (Rider et al., 2018). Transgender and gender nonconforming youth reported poorer health, less preventative care, and more nurse visits than cisgender youth. Additionally, those whose gender identity was less consistent with their sex assigned at birth also reported having more negative consequences. Furthermore, suicide attempts are reported disproportionately more often among transgender adolescents: 50.8% of female to male transgender teens, 41.8% of nonbinary transgender teens, and 29.9% for male to female transgender teens; compared to 9.8% for cisgender male and 17.6% for cisgender female adolescents (Toomey, Syvertsen. & Shramko, 2018).

Cross-Cultural Research Provides Nonbinary Models of Gender Roles.

Anthropologists tend to take an etic view that is one from outside of our own perspective. They often conduct fieldwork to describe how other groups of people function to provide insight into understanding the range of human possibility. For example, Nanda (2012) studied sex and gender systems in multiple cultures and describes several variations inconsistent with the U.S. binary. The author described an "alternative gender" in India, called the *hijra*, a class of self-identified people with a distinct and multifaceted way of being that allows for participation in Hindu practices, taking on an ascetic role within the culture. Hijra are considered neither male nor female, but a complicated variation with a rich and historical context. Nanda's fieldwork also documented the evolution of the Thai *kathuey*, a third gender comprising of those with both male and female aspects. Kathuey were a part of Thailand's early origin stories and consistent with Buddhist perspectives, which did not clearly differentiate among sexes, gender identities, or sexualities. Cultural variation was noted in the degree to which some societies practice an acceptance of gender variance as being natural with no need for specific recognition, in contrast with those who utilize a distinct, third gender which is traditionally given specific and often sacred roles in the society. In some cases, they include the presence of alternative genders applied predominantly to either males or females, in others, alternative genders apply to both. The prevalence of third or other genders in other cultures makes it hard to argue that our prevalent gender binary is the natural human condition.

Personality is More Alike Across Genders than it is Different.

In contrast with the gender differences model, Hyde (2005) proposed a Gender Similarity Hypothesis following a meticulous examination of meta-analyses on psychological gender differences. No support was found for gender differences in motor differences (which advantage males after puberty when their muscle mass and bone size increases over that of females), in sexuality (in which differences occurred in frequency of masturbation and in attitudes about casual sex), and in physical aggression (with men in the lead). However, for the vast majority of variables that had been investigated and included in the 124 meta-analyses conducted under a gender difference model, effect sizes were actually negligible. In fact, most gender differences are small or close to zero and indicated that these overinflated claims of gender difference in the research can cause real-world harm in terms of falsely reinforcing stereotypes and self-fulfilling (or self-limiting) prophecies in which lower expectations hinder growth and ability to reach full potential.

Brain Structure and Function is not Attributable to Gender.   Researchers continue to fine tune their descriptions of gender differences in brain structure and function; however, Joel et al. (2015) proposed that current findings are not sufficient to conclude that human brains belong to two distinct categories because models of male and female differences have too much in common with each other (they overlap too much to distinguish male from female brains well) and because they are not internally consistent (they are not made of features that occur only in male or only in female brains). Their study of more than 1,400 MRIs of human brains analyzed gray matter, white matter, connectivity, and even brain volume. Findings suggested that even when including all of the available comparisons at once, substantial overlap made it impossible to determine a prototypical male brain structure from a prototypical female brain structure. Even attempts to isolate just the extreme ends of male and female distributions did not provide usable models. Conclusions were that the field should focus not on gender differences, which treat variability in the human brain as noise, but on the noise itself, the complexity and variability of individual differences.

Conclusion

Gender is a complicated construct. Trying to unspool the impacts of evolutionary and reproductive pressures or of cultural conditioning on gender roles, the nature and nurture of personality and/or brain differences, the complexity of gender identity, or the difficulty of assigning sex assigned at birth quickly becomes overwhelming. The majority of U.S. culture is at least superficially well served by the gender binary, it is what people know and how they identify; it is much simpler in black and white. It is clear that there are some observable differences between the genders. However, if our models comparing men and women have so much overlap and inconsistency, it is difficult to see whether we are really cleaving reality at its joints, or if we are forcing a continuous entity to fit a binary model.

References

American Psychological Association (2015). Guidelines for psychological practice with transgender and gender non-conforming people. *American Psychologist, 70,* 832–864. doi:10.1037/a0039906

Blackless, M., Charuvastra, A., Derryck, A., Fausto-Sterling, A., Lauzanne, K., & Lee, E. (2000). How sexually dimorphic are we? Review and synthesis. *American Journal of Human Biology, 12,* 151–166. doi:10.1002/(SICI)1520-6300(200003/04)

Del Guidice, M., Booth, T., & Irwing, P. (2012). The distance between Mars and Venus: Measuring global sex differences in personality. *PLoS One, 7,* e29265. doi:10.1371/journal.pone.0029265

Hyde, J. S. (2005). The gender similarities hypothesis. *American Psychologist, 60,* 581–592. doi:10.1037/0003-066X.60.6.581

Joel, D., Berman, Z., Tavor, I., Wexler, N., Gaber, O., Stein, Y., … Assaf, Y. (2015). Sex beyond the genitalia: The human brain mosaic. *Proceedings of the National Academy of Sciences of the USA, 112,* 15468–15473. doi:10.1073/pnas.1509654112

Nanda, S. (2012). Cross-cultural issues. In D. L. Rowland & L. Incrocci (Eds.), *Handbook of sexual and gender identity disorders.* Retrieved from https://doi.org/10.1002/9781118269978.ch15

Pew Research Center. (2017). *On gender differences, no consensus on nature vs. nurture: Americans say society places a higher premium on masculinity than femininity.* Retrieved from http://www.pewsocialtrends.org/2017/12/05/on-gender-differences-no-consensus-on-nature-vs-nurture/pst_12-05-17-gender-00-00/

Rider, N. G., McMorris, B. J., Gower, A. L., Coleman, E., & Eisenberg, M. E. (2018). Health and care utilization of transgender and gender nonconforming youth: A population-based study. *Pediatrics, 141,* e20171683. Retrieved from www.aappublications.org/news

Ritchie, S. J., Cox, S. R., Shen, X., Lombardo, M. V., Reus, L. M., Alloza, C., … Deary, I. J. (2018). Sex differences in the adult human brain: Evidence from 5216 UK Biobank participants. *Cerebral Cortex, 28,* 2959–2975. doi: 10.1093/cercor/bhy109

Ruigrok, A. N. V., Salimi-Khorshidi, G., Lai, M. C., Baron-Cohen, S., Lombardo, M. V., Tait, R. J., & Suckling, J. (2014). A meta-analysis of sex differences in human brain structure. *Neuroscience & Biobehavioral Reviews, 39,* 34–50. doi:10.1016/j.neubiorev.2013.12.004

The GenIUSS Group, Williams Institute on Sexual Orientation and Gender Identity Law and Public Policy at UCLA School of Law. (2013). *Gender related measures overview.* Retrieved from https://williamsinstitute.law.ucla.edu/research/census-lgbt-demographics-studies/geniuss-group-overview-feb-2013/

Toomey, R. B., Syvertsen, A. K., & Shramko, M. (2018). Transgender adolescent suicide behavior, *Pediatrics, 142,* e20174218. Retrieved from http://pediatrics.aappublications.org/content/142/4/e20174218

World Health Organization: Genomic Resource Centre. (2018). *Gender and Genetics.* Retrieved from http://www.who.int/genomics/gender/en/index1.html

19

Should Body Mass Index Be Used to Measure Health?

by Kristin L Goodheart, PhD

What does it mean to be healthy and how do healthy people look? A common bias among those living in Western culture is that those who are thin are healthy and those who are fat are not. Western culture values thinness and the medical system uses measurements like weight and body mass index (BMI) to predict health. Diets are often prescribed to encourage weight loss, assuming that weight loss will result in health improvements. However, there is very little evidence to date that shows that BMI is a good measure of health, posing a controversial question: Should BMI be used to make medical decisions and measure health?

Body Mass Index Not Indicative of Health

BMI Measurement of Group. The ratio for BMI was originally created during the mid-1800s by Adolphe Quetelet, a Belgium astronomer, mathematician, statistician, and sociologist. It was called the Quetelet ratio or Quetelet index, specifically human body weight to squared height (Eknoyan, 2008). He developed this ratio in conjunction with his work in "social physics," a branch of science that uses mathematical equations and physics concepts to understand the behavior of human groups. Ancel Keys, an American physiologist who studied the influence of diet on health, began using this ratio in his research beginning in the 1950s. He coined the term "body mass index" in the 1970s. Keys determined that BMI was an appropriate indicator of "relative obesity" for the population, but not appropriate for individual evaluation. Thus, it was a measure that made sense to use in his research to study changes in body size of the population and compare groups across cultures, but not a measure to use for individual purposes.

Health is More than BMI. In addition to the BMI not being developed or intended for individual use, the simplicity of the ratio is limiting. The BMI includes only height and weight in the ratio, so it does not account for age, race, biological sex, weight distribution, or body composition. Additionally, BMI has been used to create ranges to classify people as

Contributed by Kristin L Goodheart, PhD. Copyright © Kendall Hunt Publishing Company

underweight, normal weight, overweight, and obese. Yet, a life insurance company established these ranges, which were selected arbitrarily (Pai & Paloucek, 2000).

In a study using BMI to predict cardiometabolic health, BMI was an inaccurate predictor for nearly 24% of normal weight people, just over 51% of overweight people, and nearly 32% of obese people (Wildman et al., 2008). A similar study was repeated the next decade and showed similar results. Specifically, BMI was an inaccurate predictor of cardiometabolic health for nearly half of overweight individuals, 29% of obese individuals, and 16% of morbidly obese individuals (Tomiyama, Hunger, Nguyen-Cuu, & Wells, 2016).

Normal Weight Does Not Equal Health.   Additionally, research does not support the idea that those in the normal weight category are the healthiest group. Higher weights have been shown to be protective for some health issues, including lung disease and osteoporosis (Edelstein & Barrett-Connor, 1993; Kabat & Wynder, 1992). Additionally, higher weights have been correlated with longer life expectancy. Results of a study comparing the number of deaths in the United States based on BMI found that, compared to the "normal weight" group, obesity was associated with 111,909 excess deaths and underweight was associated with 33,764 excess deaths. Being overweight was associated with 86,094 fewer deaths compared to the normal weight group (Flegal, Graubard, Williamson, & Gail, 2005).

Body Mass Index Indicates Health

Weight and Health are Correlated.   Despite the limitations of the BMI, the current medical system in the United States encourages medical professionals to collect weight and height and determine each patient's BMI, and there are potential advantages to using this measure. Although there have not been studies showing that weight causes various health conditions (Bombak, 2014), there are studies showing a correlation (i.e., connection or relationship) between weight and health (e.g., Kearns, Dee, Fitzgerald, Doherty, & Perry, 2014).

BMI Tracks Change.   Additionally, calculating BMI is quick, easy, low cost, and provides some information about people's bodies and current functioning, similar to other measures like body temperature, blood pressure, and heart rate. Having record of weight and BMI measures could show individual changes over time that might indicate an area of concern or further exploration, such as thyroid dysfunction. Also, although BMI is not a perfect predictor, research has shown that BMI is strongly correlated with other methods for measuring body fat (Gallagher et al., 1996) and is an adequate measure for the majority of the population since "most people are not athletes" (Harvard TH Chan School of Public Health, n.d.). BMI can also be a useful measure to see intentional weight changes over time, which can be helpful in identifying possible eating disorder behaviors.

BMI and Eating Disorders.   Eating disorders are psychological disorders that include having some aspect of dysfunction with food or eating, such as eating uncontrollably, eating very little, being very limited in what is consumed, and compensating for food consumption. The fifth edition of the Diagnostic and Statistical Manual of Mental Disorders (DSM-5; American Psychiatric Association, 2013) recognizes six specific eating disorders: pica, rumination disorder, avoidant and restrictive food disorder, anorexia nervosa, bulimia nervosa, and binge eating disorder. The DSM-5 also includes five types of eating disorders in the other specified feeding and eating disorder category, including atypical anorexia, atypical bulimia nervosa, atypical binge eating disorder, purging disorder, and night eating syndrome. There is also an unspecified feeding and eating disorder classification for all other eating and feeding disorders that do not meet full criteria for a more specific diagnosis, but still interfere with life and negatively affect health. In addition to the psychological distress that accompanies eating disorders, there can also be physical complications or consequences connected to having dysfunctional relationships with food or eating. These physical problems can include heart issues, kidney dysfunction, cognitive impairment, respiratory problems, gastrointestinal issues, and endocrine dysfunction. Eating disorders have the highest mortality rates of all mental disorders, in part because of the medical complications and in part because of the high rates of suicide (Smink, van Hoeken, & Hoek, 2012).

Weight can be an indicator of eating disorders, particularly for those struggling with anorexia nervosa or avoidant and restrictive food intake disorder. However, weight can go unchanged and seem healthy and normal in other eating disorders, such as with bulimia nervosa or binge eating disorder. Thus, eating disorders cannot be diagnosed simply by looking at people, and eating disorders often go undetected as effort is often expended to ensure that loved ones do not suspect the dysfunction and despair that occurs in people's private lives.

In detecting and treating eating disorders, BMI can be used to measure change over time and identify a stable weight range. In some cases, insurance companies request information about BMI to make decisions about the appropriate level of care and to authorize services. Having record of the BMI can be beneficial, as it can help detect rapid weight change and, in some cases, be used to justify medical necessity for care. However, use of the BMI can also be problematic for some struggling with eating disorders. An unfortunate but common misconception, even among health professionals, is that people have to be extraordinarily thin to have eating disorders. Placing too much emphasis on BMI means missing the vast majority of patients with eating disorders, as cases of anorexia nervosa only comprise a small percentage of eating disorder cases and have a lifetime prevalence rate of 0.9% in U.S. women and 0.2% in U.S. men (Smink et al., 2012). Overall prevalence rates of bulimia nervosa (1.6% for U.S. women, 0.1% for U.S. men) and binge eating disorder (3.5% for U.S. women, 2% for U.S. men) are higher than anorexia nervosa, and there are more cases yet of unspecified or other specified eating disorders.

In the same way that insurance companies can approve treatment for people whose weights are extremely low, they can also deny services to people whose weights seem to be healthy based on BMI and associated weight ranges. This is problematic for those who have a high set-point weight, started their weight loss at a higher weight, or have not really experienced much weight change despite significant symptoms and distress. For example, if a woman who is 5 ft 7 in started at 250 lb (BMI = 39.2, "obese") and lost 100 pounds over 6 months by limiting the types of foods she eats and restricting her overall intake, her BMI (23.5) would be toward the top of the "healthy" range. So, she would likely be praised for her efforts and encouraged to continue eating in the way she did to achieve this weight loss. Would she actually be healthy if she were eating the same foods every day, never went out with friends, became fearful of food, felt like she had to exercise at least 2 hours a day to maintain her "healthy" BMI, and became extremely distressed and worried when she ate more than the allotted calories she has decided are appropriate for herself? (Hint: She would probably meet criteria for an eating disorder.) Thus, having a regular measure of BMI could be useful in detecting some eating disorders. However, it is not a perfect measure and, in some cases, might deter a health professional from considering or suspecting an eating disorder.

When people's weights are higher than the "normal" or "healthy" weight range, physicians are encouraged and, in some cases, required to prescribe weight loss. Yet, research has shown that chronic dieting and weight fluctuation is more harmful than maintaining a high weight, and have thus concluded that the safest body size for any given individual is a weight that can be easily maintained (Bosomworth, 2012). One disadvantage to prescribing unfounded weight loss is the potential for developing unhealthy relationships with food, which could eventually lead to the development of eating disorders (Haines & Neumark-Sztainer, 2006).

Certain eating disorders, like anorexia and bulimia, often start as diets, and dieting is common in the United States. At any given moment, 36% of Americans are attempting to lose weight (Sørensen, Rissanen, Korkeila, & Kaprio, 2005). Yet, research has shown that dieting can be both detrimental and ineffective. For example, research has shown that chronic dieting and weight cycling is connected to higher mortality risk (Blair, Shaten, Brownell, Collins, & Lissner, 1993). Most people cannot maintain weight loss long term, specifically, more than 2 years (Neumark-Sztainer et al., 2006). Additionally, dieting has been shown to predict both obesity and eating disorders (Haines & Neumark-Sztainer, 2006; Neumark-Sztainer et al., 2007), and adolescents classified as "obese" are at increased risk of developing anorexia and bulimia (Sim, Lebow, & Billings, 2013). Essentially, people who are prescribed weight loss are asked to obsess about food, exercise, and weight; yet, there is no guarantee that these efforts will result in improved health and could instead be detrimental to their health. Still, health is important to both quality and quantity of life, and it is unlikely that neglecting or avoiding conversations about health and wellness will result in improved health.

Alternatives to Measuring BMI and Prescribing Weight Loss

If prescribing weight loss is not helpful (and potentially harmful) and categorizing people according to BMI provides little value, what are alternatives? One possibility is to adopt a weight-neutral approach to health that challenges people to acknowledge their weight biases and recognize that health can look a lot of different ways (Robison, 2005). Health at Every Size (HAES) is an example of this sort of approach. HAES encourages acceptance of body diversity and eating intuitively. It encourages eating and moving in ways that feel good and that help to nourish and energize people physically, emotionally, and spiritually. It encourages looking at markers other than weight to determine health, such as heart rate, blood pressure, cholesterol levels, feelings of well-being, energy levels, cortisol markers, and adrenal functioning. Additionally, it encourages people to assess their own health and well-being outside of their appearance, such as physical feelings of wellness, overall energy level, overall stress, social connection, spiritual health, and overall life satisfaction (Bacon, 2010).

Some research suggests that cardiorespiratory fitness (CRF) is a better indicator of health than weight. For example, Barry et al. (2014) found that overweight and obese individuals who are fit have similar mortality risks to normal-weight, fit people. Additionally, they found that unfit individuals have two times the risk of mortality compared to fit individuals, regardless of BMI. As a result, they recommended focusing on physical activity and fitness interventions rather than weight loss to improve health and decrease mortality risk. Additionally, research has shown that habits like eating plenty of fruits and vegetables (i.e., five or more daily), regular exercise (i.e., three sessions per week), moderate drinking (i.e., no more than one drink daily for women and two for men aged 21 and older), and avoiding smoking are associated with a significant decrease in mortality, regardless of BMI (Matheson, King, & Everett, 2012). Other interventions encouraging health include promoting body diversity, discussing the dangers and ineffectiveness of diets, promoting behaviors like relaxed eating and enjoyable physical activity in response to natural body cues, and focusing on other areas of life that help create balance like social, emotional, and spiritual matters (Robison, 2007).

Conclusion

There are both advantages and disadvantages to using BMI as a measure of health. On one hand, it is a simple, easy, inexpensive, and noninvasive measure of squared height to weight that can show changes over time and help detect some health issues. On the other hand, the BMI does not give a comprehensive view of health, and well-intended providers could prescribe weight loss to healthy people, which could result in health consequences rather than health improvements. Although BMI can help detect eating disorders, prescribing weight loss can also promote eating disorders. Alternatives to collecting BMI and prescribing weight loss could involve using other measures like heart rate, blood pressure, and cholesterol levels and prescribing health-promoting behaviors like physical activity, eating fruits and vegetables, and limiting or avoiding substances like alcohol and tobacco.

References

American Psychiatric Association. (2013). *Diagnostic and statistical manual of mental disorders* (5th ed.). Washington, DC: American Psychiatric Publishing. Bacon, L. (2010). *Health at every size: The surprising truth about your weight.* Dallas, Texas: BenBella Books.

Barry, V. W., Baruth, M., Beets, M. W., Durstine, J. L., Liu, J., & Blair, S. N. (2014). Fitness vs. fatness on all-cause mortality: A meta-analysis. *Progress in Cardiovascular Disease, 56,* 382–390. doi:10.1016/j.pcad.2013.09.002

Blair, S. N., Shaten, J., Brownell, K., Collins, G., & Lissner, L. (1993). Body weight change, all-cause mortality, and cause-specific mortality in the Multiple Risk Factor Intervention Trial. *Annals of Internal Medicine, 119,* 749–757. doi:10.7326/0003-4819-119-7_Part_2-199310011-00024

Bombak, A. (2014). Obesity, health at every size, and public health policy. *American Journal of Public Health, 104*(2), e60–e67. doi:10.2105/AJPH.2013.30.1486

Bosomworth, N. J. (2012). The downside of weight loss: Realistic intervention in body-weight trajectory. *Canadian Family Physician, 58*(5), 517–523. Retrieved from http://www.cfp.ca/content/cfp/58/5/517.full.pdf

Edelstein, S. L., & Barrett-Connor, E. (1993). Relation between body size and bone mineral density (BMD) in elderly men and women. *American Journal of Epidemiology, 138,* 160–169. doi:10.1093/oxfordjournals.aje.a116842

Eknoyan, G. (2008). Adolphe Quetelet (1796–1874)–the average man and the indices of obesity. *Nephrology, Dialysis, Transplantation, 23,* 47–51. doi:10.1093/ndt/gfm517

Flegal, K. M., Graubard, B. I., Williamson, D. F., & Gail, M. H. (2005). Excess deaths associated with underweight, overweight, and obesity. *Journal of the American Medical Association, 293,* 1861–1867. doi:10.1001/jama.293.15.1861

Gallagher, D., Visser, M., Sepulveda, D., Pierson, R. N., Harris, T., & Heymsfield, S. B. (1996). How useful is body mass index for comparison of body fatness across age, sex, and ethnic groups? *American Journal of Epidemiology, 143,* 228–239. doi:10.1093/oxfordjournals.aje.a008733

Haines, J., & Neumark-Sztainer, D. (2006). Prevention of obesity and eating disorders: A consideration of shared risk factors. *Health Education Research, 21,* 770–782. doi:10.1093/her/cyl094

Harvard TH Chan School of Public Health. (n.d.) Obesity prevention source. Why use BMI? Retrieved from https://www.hsph.harvard.edu/obesity-prevention-source/obesity-definition/obesity-definition-full-story/

Kabat, G. C., & Wynder, E. L. (1992). Body mass index and lung cancer risk. *American Journal of Epidemiology, 135,* 769–774. doi:10.1093/oxfordjournals.aje.a116363

Kearns, K., Dee, A., Fitzgerald, A. P., Doherty, E., & Perry, I. J. (2014). Chronic disease burden associated with overweight and obesity in Ireland: The effects of a small BMI reduction at population level. *BMC Public Health, 14,* 143. doi:10.1186/1471-2458-14-143

Matheson, E. M., King, D. E., & Everett, C. J. (2012). Healthy lifestyle habits and mortality in overweight and obese individuals. *Journal of the American Board of Family Medicine, 25,* 9–15. doi:10.3122/jabfm.2012.01.110164

Neumark-Sztainer, D., Wall, M., Guo, J., Story, M., Haines, J., & Eisenberg, M. (2006). Obesity, disordered eating, and eating disorders in a longitudinal study of adolescents: How do dieters fare 5 years later? *Journal of the Dietetic Association, 106,* 559–568. doi:10.1016/j.jada.2006.01.003

Neumark-Sztainer, D. R., Wall, M. M., Haines, J. I., Story, M. T., Sherwood, N. E., & van den Berg, P. A. (2007). Shared risk and protective factors for overweight and disordered eating in adolescents. *American Journal of Preventive Medicine, 33,* 359–369. doi:10.1016/amepre.2001.07.031

Pai, M. P., & Paloucek, F. P. (2000). The origin of the "ideal" body weight equation. *Annals of Pharmacotherapy, 34,* 1066–1069. doi:10.1345/aph.19381

Robison, J. (2005). Health at Every Size: Toward a new paradigm of weight and health. *Medscape General Medicine, 7*(3), 13. Retrieved from https://www.ncbi.nlm.nih.gov/pmc/articles/PMC1681635/

Robison, J. (2007). Kids, eating, weight and health: Helping without harming. *Absolute Advantage-The Workplace Wellness Magazine, 7*(1), 3–15.

Sim, L. A., Lebow, J., & Billings, M. (2013). Eating disorders in adolescents with a history of obesity. *Pediatrics, 132*(4), e1026–1030. doi:10.1542/peds.2012-3940

Smink, F. R. E., van Hoeken, D., & Hoek, H. W. (2012). Epidemiology of eating disorders: Incidence, prevalence, and mortality rates. *Current Psychiatry Reports, 14,* 406–414. doi:10.1007s11920-012-0280-y

Sørensen, T. I., Rissanen, A., Korkeila, M., & Kaprio, J. (2005). Intention to lose weight, weight changes, and 18-year mortality in overweight individuals without comorbidities. *Public Library of Science Medicine, 2*(6), e171. doi:10.1371/journal.pmed.0020171

Tomiyama, A. J., Hunger, J. M., Nguyen-Cuu, J., & Wells, C. (2016). Misclassification of cardiometabolic health when using body mass index categories in NHANES 2005–2012. *International Journal of Obesity, 40,* 883–886. doi:10.1038/ijo.2016.17.

Wildman, R. P., Muntner, P., Reynolds, K., McGinn, A. P., Rajpathak, S., Wylie-Rosett, J., & Sowers, M. R. (2008). The obese without cardiometabolic risk factor clustering and the normal weight with cardiometabolic risk factor clustering: Prevalence and correlates of 2 phenotypes among the US population (NHANES 1999–2004). *Archives of Internal Medicine, 168,* 1617–1624. doi:10.1001/archinte.168.15.1617

Positive Impact on Engagement. The use of technology in career and technical education classrooms has had positive effects on engagement and increased students' positive attitudes toward the learning activities (Cuendet, Dehler-Zufferey, Ortoleva, & Dillenbourg, 2015). These effects have been noted with TUIs that allow for immediate feedback and multiple repetitions in a short amount of time. It is worth noting that this study did not find that TUIs lead to deeper learning or more advanced skills.

One-to-one initiatives have had positive impacts on instruction and learning. For example, schools with a device for every student can achieve more innovative changes including more active teaching practices and student-centered activities (Lucas, 2018). The devices also allow for more diverse learning activities allowing each student to get the instruction and activities that meet them at their current skills and knowledge level.

Positive Impact on Learning. Technology use in the classroom has consistently shown positive effects on student learning for a wide range of ages and topics (M. Akcayir & G. Akcayir, 2017). One use of technology in education is flipped instruction; this is when the students watch a video of instruction outside of the classroom, and then are able to engage in guided and independent practice in class with the teacher available to provide timely feedback. Schneider and Blikstein (2016) have found that the use of a TUI prior to the flipped instruction prepared students better for future learning, even more so than the use of a TUI after the flipped instruction.

Technology use in secondary classrooms has also had positive impacts on mathematics (Hegedus, Laborde, Armella, Siller, & Tabach, 2017). Technology is mostly used to change the interactions with materials with digital technology allowing for new representations of abstract mathematical concepts, including modeling and noting correlations. Technology also changed the processes in the classroom allowing learners to connect in different ways. Learners were able to connect with one another and see how others are engaging in the material and were able to build on the work of others, which is more consistent with real-world applications. Technology also allowed increased mobility of mathematics instructional materials and provided interactions with materials through multiple modalities (i.e., ʳal, auditory, spatial, etc.).

ʰnology has similar benefits when teachers use it as part of their presentation meth-
ˀr, 2005). It was found that instruction improves when presentation software on a
ˢed making lessons more interactive and spontaneous to meet the students'
ʳe also allowed for electronic inking to bring attention to key concepts and
ᵗions to give more depth to the lessons. Teachers were also able to pro-
ˡes in a time-efficient manner with efficient transitions between

ᴄan be distracting, smartphones used in a BYOD had positive
ᵛironments (Anshari et al., 2017). Students frequently used their
ᵉaching materials and supporting information. Handheld devices

were effective learning aids because of their portability and ability to access multiple sources, as well as providing a comprehensive learning experience. Students also used their smartphones frequently to interact with the teacher outside of class and to maintain group assignments.

The way students interact with technology can have a big effect on learning. TUIs (e.g., simulation devices) have been found to be beneficial with preschoolers. The physical objects help students identify solutions to numerical problems through simple physical interactions and they fostered strategies related to solutions (Manches, 2010). Graphical user interfaces restricted problem solving since items could only be moved one at a time. When the TUI included a color change feature, it helped students recognize numerical changes. Pugnali, Sullivan, and Bers (2017) also found that graphical user interfaces (e.g., traditional computers and tablets) and TUIs (e.g., simulation devices) were effective in teaching computational thinking, though each fosters different types of learning. Both were found equally effective on advanced programming concepts such as repeats (e.g., duplicate actions) and conditionals (e.g., if-then scenarios) and both supported collaborative learning environments where students worked together to solve problems. Tangible interfaces were more effective in teaching sequencing (e.g., putting steps in order) and debugging (e.g., finding errors). This advantage seems related to the developmental reliance of the preschoolers on physical interactions. An interesting difference between GUI and TUI was the sequence of activities for the students. With TUI, students focused first on the stated learning task and then explored further after completing the first task. However, with GUI, students explored the interface first before eventually moving to the task at hand. Tangible had the benefit of staff being able to observe student progress more easily and allowed for more timely feedback and redirection when students were off-task.

Raffaele et al. (2018) found that tabletop TUIs increased student learning by 100%. This was due to the technology allowing active participation from students, responding to instinctive manipulations, and providing immediate feedback.

Tangible technology use in a primary grade (kindergarten through second grade), is predominately used with science content and includes the use of objects, devices, surfaces, and the physical space of the classroom (So et al., 2018). This helps provide increased interaction with materials, uses physical manipulations, and provides the physical digital representational mapping. This has been shown to help students learn spatial relationships, help make invisible concepts visible for the learner, and reinforce abstract concepts.

Teacher perspective of technology in the classroom has an effect on the effectiveness of technology use. Younger teachers are increasingly engaged in digital learning resources (M. Camilleri & A. Camilleri, 2016). It can be argued that as more teachers who see the potential of technology use in the classroom, technology will have a more consistent effect on learning outcomes.

How technology is introduced to teachers has a big impact on their overall acceptance of it as an instructional tool (Tondeau, van Braak, Ertmer, & Ottenbreit-Leftwiche, 2016).

Technology should be introduced in ways that align with teachers' current instructional approaches and a shared vision must be created among stakeholders. Technology is most beneficial in the classrooms of teachers with more student-centric pedagogical beliefs who use more collaborative learning activities and adapt instruction to meet the needs of each student individually. This motivates them to experiment, implement, and refine new approaches to teaching and learning. Technology also has benefits to teachers with teacher-centered pedagogical beliefs who provide more whole-group instruction. However, continued use of technology has the potential to shift beliefs toward more student-centered beliefs. This is best achieved when long-term professional development efforts are in place.

Final Thoughts

As our society becomes more and more entwined with technology and digital spaces, use and experience with technology becomes a social justice issue, as much as a learning one. The reality is that digital literacy is one of the many enablers for participation in our society (Starcic, 2010). If our schools are charged with developing children into adults who can fully and effectively participate in society, then they are obliged to ensure students are familiar and proficient with the technologies of our society.

References

Akcayir, M., & Akcayır, G. (2017). Advantages and challenges associated with augmented reality for education: A systematic review of the literature. *Educational Research Review, 20,* 1–11. doi:10.1016/j.edurev.2016.11.002

Anderson, S. E., Economos, C. D., & Must, A. (2008). Active play and screen time in US children aged 4 to 11 years in relation to sociodemographic and weight status characteristics: A nationally representative cross-sectional analysis. *BMC Public Health, 8,* 366–378. doi:10.1186/1471-2458-8-366

Anshari, M., Almunawar, M. N., Shahrill, M., Wicaksono, D. K., & Huda, M. (2017). Smartphones usage in the classrooms: Learning aid or interference? *Education and Information Technologies, 22,* 3063–3079. doi:10.1007/s10639-017-9572-7

Camilleri, M. A., & Camilleri, A. C. (2016). Digital learning resources and ubiquitous technologies in education. *Technology, Knowledge and Learning, 22,* 65–82. doi:10.1007/s10758-016-9287-7

Cuendet, S., Dehler-Zufferey, J., Ortoleva, G., & Dillenbourg, P. (2015). An integrated way of using a tangible user interface in the classroom. *International Journal of Computer Supported Collaborative Learning, 10,* 183–208. doi:10.1007/s11412-015-9213-3 de Vries, M. J. (2018). Technology education: An international history. In M. J. de Vries (Ed.), *Handbook of technology education* (pp. 73–84). Cham, Switzerland: Springer International. doi:10.1007/978-3-319-44687-5

Depcik, C., & Assanis, D. N. (2005). Graphical user interfaces in an engineering educational environment. *Computer Applications in Engineering Education, 13,* 48–59. doi:10.1002/cae.20029

Hale, L. & Guan, S. (2014). Screentime and sleep among school-aged children and adolescents: A systematic literature review. *Sleep Medicine Reviews, 21,* 50–58. doi:10.1016/j.smrv.2014.07.007

Hegedus, S., Laborde, C., Armella, L. M., Siller, H., & Tabach, M. (2017). Topic Study Group No. 43: Uses of technology in upper secondary education (Age 14–19). *Proceedings of the 13th International Congress on Mathematical Education ICME-13 Monographs,* 579–582. doi:10.1007/978-3-319-62597-3_70

Kurt, S. (2015). Educational technology: An overview. *Educational Technology.* Retrieved from https://educationaltechnology.net/educational-technology-an-overview

Lucas, M. (2018). The use of tablets in lower secondary education: Students' perspectives and experiences. In A. Visvizi, M. Lucas, & L. Daniela (Eds.), *The Future of innovation and technology in education: Policies and practices for teaching and learning excellence* (pp. 127–138). Bingley, UK: Emerald Group Publishing. doi:10.1108/978-1-78756-555-520181010

Manches, A. D. (2010). *The effect of physical manipulation on children's numerical strategies* (Unpublished doctoral dissertation). University of Nottingham. Retrieved from http://eprints.nottingham.ac.uk/11372/1/AndrewManchesFinalThesis2010.pdf

Olivier, W. (2005). Teaching mathematics: Tablet PC technology adds a new dimension. *The Mathematics Education into the 21st Century Project.* Retreived from http://citeseerx.ist.psu.edu/viewdoc/download?doi=10.1.1.108.7453&rep=rep1&type=pdf

Pugnali, A., Sullivan, A., & Bers, M. U. (2017). The impact of user interface on young children's computational thinking. *Journal of Information Technology Education: Innovations in Practice, 16,* 171–193. doi:10.28945/3768

Raffaele, C. D., Smith, S., & Gemikonakli, O. (2018). An active tangible user interface framework for teaching and learning artificial intelligence. *Proceedings of the 2018 Conference on Human Information Interaction & Retrieval - IUI '18.* doi:10.1145/3172944.3172976

Schneider, B. & Blikstein, P. (2016). Flipping the flipped classroom: A study of the effectiveness of video lectures versus constructivist exploration using tangible user interfaces. *Transactions on Learning Technologies, 9,* 5–17. doi:10.1109/TLT.2015.2448093

So, H. J., Hwang, Y. E., Wang, Y., & Lee, E. (2018). Unpacking the potential of tangible technology in education: A systematic literature review. *Education Technology International, 19,* 199–228. Retrieved from https://kset.or.kr:5003/eti_ojs/index.php/instruction/article/view/132

Starcic, A. I. (2010). Educational technology for the inclusive classroom. *Turkish Online Journal of Educational Technology, 9*(3), 26–37. Retrieved from https://files.eric.ed.gov/fulltext/EJ898012.pdf

Tandon, P. S., Zhou, C., Lozano, P., & Christakis, D. A. (2011). Preschoolers' total daily screen time at home and by type of child care. *The Journal of Pediatrics, 158,* 297–300. doi:10.1016/j.jpeds.2010.08.005

Tondeau, J., van Braak, J., Ertner, P. A., & Ottenbreit-Leftwiche, A. (2016). Understanding the relationship between teachers' pedagogical beliefs and technology use in education: A systematic review of qualitative evidence. *Educational Technology Research and Development, 65,* 555–575. doi:10.1007/s11423-016-9481-2

U.S. Department of Education, Office of Educational Technology. (2017). *Reimagining the role of technology in education: 2017 National education technology plan update.* Retrieved from https://tech.ed.gov/files/2017/01/NETP17.pdf

Williamson, D. (2017). *The reading mind: A cognitive approach to understanding how the mind reads.* San Francisco: Jossey Bass.

21

Sex Offender Registration: Does it Increase or Decrease Overall Safety?

by April Terry, PhD

Registries present, "one of the most widely discussed and debated criminal justice policy issues in recent years" (Tewksbury & Mustaine, 2013, p. 95). During the 1990s and 2000s, sex offender registration and offender notification laws were enacted within the United States (Bouffard & Askew, 2017). Due to several publicized gruesome crimes at the time, resulting in legislative mandates, (e.g., Adam Walsh Child Protection Act, 2006; Jacob Wetterling Crimes Against Children and Sexually Violent Offender Registration Improvements Act, 1997; Megan's Law, 1996), the general perception was that sexual offenders were dangerous offenders likely to reoffend (e.g., Sandler, Freeman, & Socia, 2008). This fear influenced the creation of sex offender registration laws, requiring certain convicted sexual offenders to provide contact information to local law enforcement. Sex offender notification laws complemented registration laws by making this information available to the public (Prescott & Rockoff, 2011; Ragusa-Salerno & Zgoba, 2012) while there are also private registries available only to law enforcement. The public tends to perceive sex offender registries as valuable (Kernsmith, Craun, & Foster, 2009; Saad, 2005), as do legislators (Matson & Lieb, 1996; Sample & Kadleck, 2008), and law enforcement (Finn, 1997; Gaines, 2006; Tewksbury & Mustaine, 2013) and even some sexual offenders themselves (Tewksbury, 2006; Tewksbury & Lees, 2007). However, many academics and treatment providers remain skeptical, arguing public registries are costly and ineffective (Bierie, 2016).

Sex Offender Laws Do Not Increase Safety

Sex Offender Registration and Notification (SORN) laws were intended to help law enforcement become more effective at supervising convicted sexual offenders (Prescott & Rockoff, 2011; Terry, 2015), protecting the community, and raising public awareness (Bouffard &

Askew, 2017). Despite widespread implementation, or knowledge of registration databases, only some studies have found minimal support for the impact of SORN laws on incidence of sexual offending (Bouffard & Askew, 2017; Drake & Aos, 2009; Terry, 2015). Specifically, this section outlines three major arguments against the use of public sex offender registries as a means for increasing public safety.

Sexual Offenders do Not Pose a Serious Threat.   First, numerous studies suggest the general public believes sexual offenders pose a significant threat to public safety (Levenson, Brannon, Fortney, & Baker, 2007). However, recidivism rates—or likelihood to commit another offense—among convicted sexual offenders are generally low compared to other offenders. An early review of 42 studies measuring sexual offender recidivism found the sexual offender recidivism rate to be less than 12% (Furby, Weinrott, & Blackshaw, 1989). In Lievore's (2004) examination of 17 studies on sexual offending, it was found that recidivism rates were lower than 10%. As a third example, a meta-analysis of 82 studies conducted by Hanson and Morton-Bourgon (2005) found that only 14% of sexual offenders had committed another sexual offense, and that antisocial orientation was a stronger predictor of re-offense.

Sample and Bray (2003, 2006) conducted a study of different criminal behaviors using a 5-year follow-up. They found the highest recidivism rate of 38.8% to be associated with property offenders compared to a recidivism rate of only 6.5% for sexual offenders. The sexual offenders also had lower rates of general (not sexual in nature) recidivism compared to other offenders. When studying sexual offenders released from prison, they do not pose a serious threat to the community. In one study, roughly 5% of released sexual offenders committed a new sex offense once released. Longer follow-up periods, completed on higher risk sexual offenders, have shown a 15% sexual recidivism rate (Levenson et al, 2007). Studies have consistently found recidivism rates for sexual offenders to be at, or below, the recidivism rates for general offenders. Sample and Bray (2003) concluded that "based on rates of reoffending, sexual offenders do not appear to be more dangerous than other criminal categories" (p. 76).

Potential Victims' Knowledge of Predators.   Second, more than 90% of victims know their attacker and therefore, already have knowledge of the convicted sexual offender (Snyder, 2000). SORN laws assume the logic that if a released sexual offender poses even a slight risk to a potential victim, law enforcement should keep tabs on the person and the community should be notified. This assumes said offenders would opt to seek *new* victims (Prescott & Rockoff, 2011) creating a false sense of security for communities (Bierie, 2016; Craun & Bierie, 2014) due to a lack of realistic knowledge about offending behavior and risks of re-offense (Prentky, 1996). In fact, Websdale (1996) argues that the image of a lurking stranger actually hurts potential victims and their families by creating an inaccurate image of potential sexual offenders.

Whereas previous victims are to be informed of their perpetrator listed on the registry, studies have also looked into nonvictims and their knowledge and use of registry databases.

Studies range from 50% to 90% of participants reporting some knowledge of the existence of public registries with fewer than half ever accessing them (Anderson & Sample, 2008; Harris & Cudmore, 2018). Even those residing closely to a registered sexual offender are generally unaware of the sexual offender's presence (Craun, 2010).

No Significant Reductions in Future Offending.   Third, studies completed before and after the registry went into effect generally show no statistically significant reductions in sexual assault (Prescott & Rockoff, 2011; Tewksbury & Jennings, 2010). Schram and Milloy (1995) were some of the first scholars to compare recidivism rates before and after implementation of Megan's Law. They found no significant difference in a 4.5-year follow-up period. Since Schram and Milloy's 1995 study, several other studies have concluded that SORN laws do not reduce sexual offense recidivism (e.g., Letourneau, Levenson, Bandyopadhyay, Armstrong, & Sinha, 2010; Tewksbury, Jennings, & Zgoba, 2012) or prevent sexual offending in the general community (Ragusa-Salerno & Zgoba, 2012). Zgoba and colleagues (Zgoba, Veysey, & Dalessandro, 2008; Zgoba, Witt, Dalessandro, & Veysey, 2008) measured recidivism, community tenure, and harm reduction of 550 sexual offenders released from correctional facilities pre- and post-Megan's Law implementation. They found no significant differences between the two groups, concluding that despite community support for such SORN legislation, there is little evidence to support these laws as being effective in reducing sexual offending.

Rather than assuming positive outcomes for SORN laws, such laws and regulations may actually increase the financial, social, and psychological burden of released sexual offenders. Evidence suggests that under these conditions, convicted sexual offenders are more likely to recidivate (Prescott & Rockoff, 2011). For juveniles and young adults placed on public sex offender registries for "sexting," their future education and employment opportunities, as well as permanent social stigma, can serve as a barrier to prosocial involvement (Harripersad, 2014; Richards & Calvert, 2009) resulting in a higher risk to recidivate. Additionally, SORN laws have been shown to be related to depression, unemployment, lack of housing, loss of family and social relationships, public shaming, and, at times, violence (Levenson, 2008; Levenson & Tewksbury, 2009; Tewksbury & Mustaine, 2006, 2007).

Sex Offender Laws Do Increase Safety

Community notification laws require government officials to inform the public about the sexual offenders in the community. One suggested goal behind these laws is that when the public has information about a potential threat to safety, they will be motivated to take protective actions to mitigate their risk (Walsh & Cohen, 1998). Under the theoretical position of deterrence, community members feel empowered to provide additional surveillance of suspicious behavior and report it to the police (Pawson, 2002)—thus, deterring and preventing crime. The following section will provide three arguments in favor of SORN laws in increasing safety.

Reductions in Reports of Sexual Offending.   First, some studies have found support for reductions in sexual offending after implementation of SORN laws. Letourneau et al. (2010) studied crime trends and timing in one area of South Carolina. They found SORN laws reduced first-time sexual offenses by 11% from 1995 to 2005. In another study by Prescott and Rockoff (2011), they reported community notification of sexual offenders was associated with a reduction in the frequency of sexual offenses; although, this was not found to reduce sexual offense recidivism among registered sexual offenders.

From a slightly different angle, A. Petrosino and C. Petrosino (1999) evaluated criminal records of sexual psychopaths (n = 136) and found 27% of the sample had a prior conviction that would have met the state's registration requirements before their most recent sex crime. Of the 36 who would have qualified, 12 committed sexual offenses against a stranger. A. Petrosino and C. Petrosino (1999) concluded that a small number of cases could have been prevented if the law had been in effect. In a larger analysis of more than 300,000 sexual offenses, completed in 15 states, scholars found public notification did not reduce recidivism rates but that registration with law enforcement did (Prescott & Rockoff, 2011; Zgoba & Ragbir, 2016). The scholars believed registration reduced the frequency of sexual offenses because it provides law enforcement with information on local sexual offenders. Additionally, findings showed a decrease in crime of local victims (e.g., friends; Prescott & Rockoff, 2011).

(Would-be) Offenders Deterred by the Registration Requirement.   Second, SORN laws might help to reduce sexual offending by providing the community with increased information on sexual offenders—based on the premise of deterrence. Proponents of SORN laws suggest that both general and specific deterrence may arise from implementation of these laws (Drake & Aos, 2009). General deterrence would prevent would-be first-time sexual offenders from committing the crime for fear of not only legal, but also social consequences. A form of public humiliation and shaming is believed to deter some offenders (Pawson, 2002; Schultz, 2014). For those already convicted, they are subjected to specific deterrence due to the monitoring of informed community members who will look for, and report, any suspicious behavior (Schultz, 2014).

Maurelli and Ronan (2013) reviewed archival crime data on forcible rapes for all 50 states from 1960 to 2008. These data were assessed prior to, and after, the passage of SORN laws. They found a decreased rape rate in 17 states following the passage of SORN legislation. Thirty-two states observed no significant decrease in reported rape rates. Maurelli and Ronan (2013) explained the lack of observed declines in the other states as differences in notification and registration practices. Some states have stricter guidelines than others and more active notification practices. This rationale supports the idea of deterrence through increased community and law enforcement awareness.

Help to Reduce Personal Risk of Victimization.   Third, studies have measured how the public responds to availability and access of registration information. Beck and

Travis (2004) surveyed 692 households in Hamilton County, Ohio, using a slight adaption of Ferraro's (1995) Fear of Crime in America Survey. They found a significant relationship between notification and various types of protective behavior adaptations due to an increase in fear prompted by sex offender notification. Those who have accessed the public registry more often report being safety conscious in relationship to sexual victimization (e.g., aware of their surroundings), while 30% to 60% have implemented actual prevention strategies (Anderson & Sample, 2008; Harris & Cudmore, 2018; Lieb & Nunlist, 2008). Prevention strategies include increased monitoring and education of children, sharing information with others, and changing daily routines. Overall, public sex offender registries appear to be somewhat effective at encouraging safety conscious behaviors and prevention measures. Yet, this does not apply to a large number of citizens who do not view the registry and/or are unaware of what preventative measures to take. Encouraging public awareness and use of registries may be warranted; however, this must be balanced with the risk of increasing levels of fear (Napier, Dowling, Morgan, & Talbot, 2018).

Conclusion

> *The purpose of sex offender registries is to deter, shame (McAlinden, 2005), and socially ostracize (Tewksbury & Lees, 2007) as well as track and inform (as cited by Ferrandino, 2012, p. 393).*

Since the implementation of SORN laws, scholars have sought answers on the effectiveness of registration and notification policies. Some have questioned the constitutionality of SORN laws but they persist in the spirit of promoting the public good—risk mitigation against criminal victimization (Bandy, 2011). A growing body of studies suggests that SORN requirements have a weak relationship to sexual offending over time (Bouffard & Askew, 2017). Although no empirical research yet existed when notification laws were passed (Bandy, 2011), Bierie (2016) suggests that, "Continued support despite these [current findings] claims has led some scholars to suggest that proponents are unaware of evidence, indifferent to science, and perhaps driven by emotions" (p. 263). Despite a lack of evidence, state and federal courts have ruled in support for an increase in public safety by means of notification laws. Garland (2001) explains the disconnect between evidence-based research and criminal justice policy as populist and politicized. While fear mongering of sexual offenders continues, citizens will likely stand behind their belief in the effectiveness of SORN laws, (Levenson et al., 2007; Mancini, Shields, Mears, & Beaver, 2010) ensuring that political support will ensue (Logan, 2017). While there is no evidence that SORN laws reduce fear of victimization, some studies have found that they make people feel safer—with safety comes a sense of feeling empowered and able to make informed decisions based on publicly accessible information (Napier et al., 2018). With the exception of this being a "feel-good" policy (Levenson, D'Amora, & Hern, 2007), there is little demonstrable public safety value for SORN (Schram & Milloy, 1995; Zgobaet al., 2008).

References

Adam Walsh Child Protection Act, H.R. 4472 (109th) (2006).

Anderson, A. L., & Sample, L. L. (2008). Public awareness and action resulting from sex offender community notification laws. *Criminal Justice Policy Review, 19,* 371–396. doi:10.1177/0887403408316705

Bandy, R. (2011). Measuring the impact of sex offender notification on community adoption of protective behaviors. *Criminology & Public Policy, 10,* 237–263. doi:10.1111/j.1745-9133.2011.00705.x

Beck, V. S., & Travis, L. F. (2004). Sex offender notification and protective behavior. *Violence & Victims, 19,* 289–302. doi:10.1891/088667004780905697

Bierie, D. M. (2016). The utility of sex offender registration: A research note. *Journal of Sexual Aggression, 22,* 263–273. doi:10.1080/13552600.2015.1100760

Bouffard, J. A., & Askew, L. N. (2017). Time-series analyses of the impact of sex offender registration and notification law implementation and subsequent modification on rates of sexual offenses. *Crime & Delinquency,* 1–30. doi:10.1177/0011128717722010

Craun, S. W. (2010). Evaluating awareness of registered sex offenders in the neighborhood. *Crime & Delinquency, 56,* 414–435. doi:10.1177/0011128708317457

Craun, S. W., & Bierie, D. M. (2014). Are the collateral consequences of being a registered sex offender as bad as we think? A methodological research note. *Federal Probation, 78,* 28–31.

Drake, E. K., & Aos, S. (2009). *Does sex offender registration and notification reduce crime? A systematic review of the research literature.* Washington State Institute for Public Policy. Retrieved from http://www.wsipp.wa.gov/ReportFile/1043/Wsipp_Does-Sex-Offender-Registration-and-Notification-Reduce-Crime-A-Systematic-Reviewof-the-Research-Literature_Full-Report.pdf

Ferrandino, J. (2012). Beyond the perception and the obvious: What sex offender registries really tell us and why. *Social Work in Public Health, 27,* 392–407. doi:10.1080/19371910903126663

Ferraro, K. F. (1995). *Fear of crime: Interpreting victimization risk.* Albany, NY: Suny Press.

Finn, P. (1997). *Sex offender community notification* (Vol. 2, No. 2). Washington, DC: US Department of Justice, Office of Justice Programs, National Institute of Justice. doi:10.1037/e491822006-001

Furby, L., Weinrott, M., & Blackshaw, L. (1989). Sex offender recidivism: A review. *Psychological Bulletin, 105*(3), 3–30. doi:10.1037/0033-2909.105.1.3

Gaines, J. S. (2006). Law enforcement reactions to sex offender registration and community notification. *Police Practice and Research, 7,* 249–267. doi:10.1080/15614260600825448

Garland, D. (2001). *The culture of control: Crime and social order in contemporary society.* Chicago, IL: University of Chicago Press.

Hanson, R. K., & Morton-Bourgon, K. E. (2005). The characteristics of persistent sexual offenders: A meta-analysis of recidivism studies. *Journal of Consulting and Clinical Studies, 73,* 1154–1163. doi:10.1037/0022-006x.73.6.1154

Harripersad, K. W. (2014). *From sexting to sex offender: Adult punishment for teenage hijinks. Florida University Law Review.* Retrieved from https://law.famu.edu/wp-content/uploads/2015/04/Harripersad-Final-Merged_for-EE-1.pdf

Harris, A. J., & Cudmore, R. (2018). Community experience with public sex offender registries in the United States: A national survey. *Criminal Justice Policy Review, 29,* 258–279.

Jacob Wetterling Crimes Against Children and Sexually Violent Offenders Registration Improvements Act, H.R. 1683 (RH) (1997). doi10.1177/0887403415627195

Kernsmith, P. D., Craun, S. W., & Foster, J. (2009). Public attitudes toward sexual offenders and sex offender registration. *Journal of Child Sexual Abuse, 18,* 290–301. doi:10.1080/10538710902901663

Letourneau, E. J., Levenson, J. S., Bandyopadhyay, D., Armstrong, K. S., & Sinha, D. (2010). Effects of South Carolina's sex offender registration and notification policy on deterrence of adult sex crimes. *Criminal Justice and Behavior, 37,* 537–552. doi:10.1177/0093854810363569

Levenson, J. (2008). Collateral consequences of sex offender residence restrictions. *Criminal Justice Studies, 21,* 153–166. doi:10.1080/14786010802159822

Levenson, J. S., Brannon, Y. N., Fortney, T., & Baker, J. (2007). Public perceptions about sex offenders and community protection policies. *Analyses of Social Issues and Public Policy, 7,* 137–161. doi:10.1111/j.1530-2415.2007.00119.x

Levenson, J., D'Amora, D., & Hern, A. (2007). Megan's Law and its impact on community re-entry for sex offenders. *Behavioral Sciences and the Law, 25,* 587–602. doi:10.1002/bsl.770

Levenson, J., & Tewksbury, R. (2009). Collateral damage: Family members of registered sex offenders. *American Journal of Criminal Justice, 34,* 54–68. doi:10.1007/s12103-008-9055-x

Lieb, R., & Nunlist, C. (2008). *Community notification as viewed by Washington's citizens: A 10-year follow-up.* Document no. 08-03-1101. Olympia, WA: Washington State Institute for Public Policy. Retrieved from http://www.wsipp.wa.gov/Reports/240

Lievore, D. (2004). *Recidivism of sexual offenders: Rates, risk factors and treatment efficacy.* Canberra, Australia: Australian Institute of Criminology. Retrieved from https://aic.gov.au/publications/cfi/cfi072

Logan, W. A. (2017). *Sex Offender Registration and Notification.* Academy for Justice, A Report on Scholarship and Criminal Justice Reform, Florida State University, College of Law, Public Law Research Paper No. 833.

Mancini, C., Shields, R. T., Mears, D. P., & Beaver, K. M. (2010). Sex offender residence restriction laws: Parental perceptions and public policy. *Journal of Criminal Justice, 38,* 1022–1030. Retrieved from http://dx.doi.org/10.1016/j.jcrimjus.2010.07.004

Matson, S., & Lieb, R. (1996). *Community notification in Washington State: 1996 survey of law enforcement.* Olympia, WA: Washington State Institute for Public Policy.

Maurelli, K., & Ronan, G. (2013). A time-series analysis of the effectiveness of sex offender notification laws in the USA. *The Journal of Forensic Psychiatry & Psychology, 24,* 128–143. doi:10.1080/14789949.2012.746383

McAlinden, A. M. (2005). The use of shame with sexual offenders. *British Journal of Criminology, 45,* 373–394. doi:10.1093/bjc/azh095

Megan's Law, Pub. L. No. 104-145, 110 Stat. 1345 (1996).

Napier, S., Dowling, C., Morgan, A., & Talbot, D. (2018). What impact do public sex offender registries have on community safety? *Trends & Issues in Crime & Criminal Justice, 550,* 1–19.

Pawson, R. (2002). *Does Megan's law work? A theory-driven systematic review.* London, England: ESRC UK Centre for Evidence Based Policy and Practice.

Petrosino, A. J., & Petrosino, C. (1999). The public safety potential of Megan's Law in Massachusetts: An assessment from a sample of criminal sexual psychopaths. *Crime & Delinquency, 45,* 140–158. doi:10.1177/0011128799045001008

Prentky, R. A. (1996). Community notification and constructive risk reduction. *Journal of Interpersonal Violence, 11,* 295–298. doi:10.1177/088626096011002012

Prescott, J. J., & Rockoff, J. E. (2011). Do sex offender registration and notification laws affect criminal behavior? *Journal of Law and Economics, 54,* 161–206. doi:10.1086/658485

Ragusa-Salerno, L. M., & Zgoba, K. M. (2012). Taking stock of 20 years of sex offender laws and research: An examination of whether sex offender legislation has helped or hindered our efforts. *Journal of Crime and Justice, 35,* 335–355. doi:10.1080/07356 48x.2012.662069

Richards, R., & Calvert, C. (2009). When sex and cell phones collide: Inside the prosecution of a teen sexting case. *Hastings Communication and Entertainment Law Journal, 1,* 35–36.

Saad, L. (2005). *Sex offender registries are underutilized by the public.* Washington, DC: Gallup.

Sample, L., & Bray, T. (2003). Are sex offenders dangerous? *Journal of Criminology and Public Policy, 3,* 59–82. doi:10.1111/j.1745-9133.2003.tb00024.x

Sample, L., & Bray, T. (2006). Are sex offenders different? An examination of rearrest patterns. *Criminal Justice Policy Review, 17,* 83–102. doi:10.1177/0887403405282916

Sample, L. L., & Kadleck, C. (2008). Sex offender laws: Legislators' accounts of the need for policy. *Criminal Justice Policy Review, 19,* 40–62. doi:10.1177/0887403407308292

Sandler, J. C., Freeman, N. J., & Socia, K. M. (2008). Does a watched pot boil? A time-series analysis of New York State's sex offender registration and notification law. *Psychology, Public Policy, and Law, 14,* 284–302. doi:10.1037/a0013881

Schram, D., & Milloy, C. D. (1995). *Community notification: A study of offender characteristics and recidivism.* Olympia, WA: Washington Institute for Public Policy.

Schultz, C. (2014). The stigmatization of individuals convicted of sex offenses: Labeling theory and the sex offense registry. *Themis: Research Journal of Justice Studies and Forensic Science, 2,* 62–81.

Snyder, H. N. (2000). *Sexual assault of young children as reported to law enforcement: Victim, incident, and offender characteristics.* Washington, DC: U.S. Department of Justice, Bureau of Justice Statistics. doi:10.1037/e377732004-001

Terry, K. J. (2015). Sex offender laws in the United States: Smart policy or disproportionate sanctions? *International Journal of Comparative and Applied Criminal Justice, 39,* 113–127. doi:10.1080/01924036.2014.973048

Tewksbury, R. (2006). Sex offender registries as a tool for public safety: Views from registered offenders. *Western Criminology Review, 7,* 1–8.

Tewksbury, R., & Jennings, W. G. (2010). Assessing the impact of sex offender registration and community notification on sex-offending trajectories. *Criminal Justice and Behavior, 37,* 570–582. doi:10.1177/0093854810363570

Tewksbury, R., Jennings, W. G., & Zgoba, K. M. (2012). A longitudinal examination of sex offender recidivism prior to and following the implementation of SORN. *Behavioral Sciences and the Law, 30,* 308–328. doi:10.1002/bsl.1009

Tewksbury, R., & Lees, M. (2007). Perceptions of punishment: How registered sex offenders view registries. *Crime & Delinquency, 53,* 380–407. doi:10.1177/0011128706286915

Tewksbury, R., & Mustaine, E. (2006). Where to find sex offenders: An examination of residential locations and neighborhood conditions. *Criminal Justice Studies, 19,* 61–75. doi:10.1080/14786010600615991

Tewksbury, R., & Mustaine, E. (2007). Collateral consequences and community re-entry for registered sex offenders with child victims: Are the challenges even greater? *Journal of Offender Rehabilitation, 46,* 113–131. doi:10.1080/10509670802071550

Tewksbury, R., & Mustaine, E. E. (2013). Law-enforcement officials' views of sex offender registration and community notification. *International Journal of Police Science & Management, 15*(2), 95–113. doi:10.1350/ijps.2013.15.2.305

Walsh, E. R., & Cohen, F. (1998). *Sex offender registration and community notification: A Megan's Law sourcebook.* Kingston, NJ: Civic Research Institute.

Websdale, N. S. (1996). Predators: The social construction of "stranger-danger" in Washington State as a form of patriarchal ideology. *Women & Criminal Justice, 7*(2), 43–68. doi:10.1300/j012v07n02_04

Zgoba, K., & Ragbir, D. (2016). Sex Offender Registration and Notification Act (SORNA). In C. Calkins & E. Jeglic (Eds.), *Sexual violence: Evidence based policy and prevention* (pp. 33–49). New York, NY: Springer. doi:10.1007/978-3-319-44504-5_3

Zgoba, K., Veysey, B., & Dalessandro, M. (2010). An analysis of the effectiveness of community notification and registration: Do the best intentions predict the best practices? *Justice Quarterly, 27*(5), 667–691. doi:10.1080/07418820903357673

Zgoba, K., Witt, P., Dalessandro, M., & Veysey, B. M. (2008). *Megan's Law: Assessing the practical and monetary efficacy.* Document no. 225370. Washington, DC: U.S. Department of Justice.

22

Is Sexting Best Viewed as a Mating Behavior?

by Scott Ploharz, MS & Carol Patrick, PhD

The term "sexting" first appeared in popular media during the early 2000s to describe the sending and receiving of sexually natured text and picture messages (Hasinoff, 2012). It rose to prominence through news stories painting the behavior as the newest risky and dangerous behavior by teenagers that adults were obligated to stop either through prevention campaigns or legislation. In 2012, the term was added to Webster's dictionary speaking both to the prevalence of the behavior and its increasing role in the everyday lives of individuals (Sexting, n.d.).

Most of the early sexting research was shaped by this media portrayal of sexting as an unwanted and dangerous behavior (Klettke, Hallford, & Mellor, 2014). This research had two objectives: (a) to describe the behavior; and (b) to figure out why individuals chose to engage in it. There were several consistent findings among these early studies. First, sexting is common among young adults with anywhere from 48% to 89% of individuals reporting engagement in the behavior (i.e., Benotsch, Snipes, Martin, & Bull, 2013; Dir, Coskunpinar, Steiner, & Cyders, 2013). Second, sexting is frequently positively associated with engaging in other risky behaviors, such as drug use and other risky sexual behaviors. Finally, sexting exposed individuals to a host of possible negative outcomes (Benotsch et al., 2013; Dir et al., 2013; Ploharz & Baird, 2012; Weisskirch & Delevi, 2011).

These findings have all assumed that sexting is a risky behavior and the results offered support to the view that sexting behavior is primarily a risky behavior that offers limited to no benefits. Early research on sexting has examined its occurrence related to certain personality traits or individual factors; like risk-taking behavior. However, newer research has examined it in light of the possibility that sexting may be a form of mating behavior, which often has inherent benefits and risks. Those two major points of view will be discussed in this chapter.

Sexting as Individual Difference

Risky Behaviors. The correlational relationship between sexting and other risky behaviors has been well established. Individuals who engage in sexting are more likely to use illicit drugs, abuse alcohol, engage in risky sexual behaviors, such as casual sex or having multiple partners, and engage in criminal activity (Benotsch et al., 2013; Ferguson, 2011; Gordon-Messer, Bauermeister, Grodzinski, & Zimmerman, 2012). This relationship has been shown to occur in a variety of populations and is one of the few consistent findings in the literature about sexting. This relationship may suggest that sexting has more in common with risk-taking activities than other less risky sexual activities, such as more traditional flirting and safe sex.

Personality.   Research examining the role of personality in sexting behavior has suggested a positive relationship between the presence of Histrionic personality traits among Hispanic women (Ferguson, 2011). Delevi and Weisskirch (2013) found that sexting was positively related to the personality factors of Extroversion, Neuroticism, and Disagreeableness. These relationships have yet to be replicated with Ploharz and Baird (2012) failing to find any significant relationship between sexting behaviors and any personality traits as measured by the NEO personality model, as well as Ploharz, Baird, and Patrick (2014) finding only partial relationships between sexting and narcissistic personality traits.

Romantic Attachment.   Research has also examined the relationship between adult romantic attachment and sexting. For example, Weisskirch and Delevi (2011) suggested that sexting was positively associated with attachment anxiety and those with higher level of attachment anxiety were more likely to view sexting as a normal and positive part of their relationship. This relationship was partially supported by Drouin and Landgraff (2012) who found that sexting was positively associated with both anxious and avoidant attachment styles. This suggested relationship might mean that sexting is heavily influenced by individual factors operating outside simple sexual behavior and related to long-term romantic relationships.

So, it appears that the research is mixed as to whether personality and individual factors explain sexting. Mating behavior, especially in the short term, has been discussed as a possible explanation for why people risk sexting.

Sexting as Intentional Mating Strategy

Mating Strategy.   Ploharz (2016) suggested an alternative theoretical explanation of sexting behavior; that sexting is best viewed as a flexible, goal-directed behavior used to efficiently and effectively meet an evolutionary goal or need. This alternative theory suggests that sexting is an adaptive behavior used in a way that is consistent with individuals' sexual strategies to meet the goal of reproduction. Central to this view of sexting are the constructs of mating strategy, mate attraction, and mate retention as described in Evolutionary Psychology. Within this construct, individuals are thought to meet the evolutionary goal of finding sexual partners (mate attraction) and keeping those partners (mate retention) through one of two basic strategies, long- or short-term mating (Buss & Schmitt, 1993). Each of these strategies consists of multiple aspects but for our purposes we will examine them at the most basic.

Individuals who utilize a short-term mating strategy are seeking to attract a variety of partners as quickly as possible with little consideration for creating a lasting committed relationship (Buss & Schmitt, 1993). Those using a long-term strategy are not only attempting to attract mates for now, but also for committed relationships that will last an extended period. Any behavior that facilitates, promotes, or enhances individuals' chances of successfully meeting their evolutionary goal is considered adaptive even if there are risks of potential harms (Cosmides, Tooby, & Barkow, 1992). Using this new perspective, that humans utilize a variety of mating strategies to maximize their chances of reproductive success, and that risking a negative outcome can be the right choice if it offers increased chances of evolutionary success, we suggested that sexting is best viewed as an adaptive goal-directed mating behavior, not simply a risky or maladaptive one.

Risk Tolerance in Mating.   Research examining the role of individual mating strategies in sexting behavior has provided some support for the view of sexting as an adaptive mating behavior. When examining the role of individual differences in risk tolerance, Ploharz (2016) suggested that higher levels of risk tolerance in relationship to mate attraction efforts were associated with greater sexting behaviors. Individuals who were more willing to take risks in their efforts to a attract a mate engaged in more sexting, suggesting that individuals were aware of the risks but made a calculated decision to engage due to the likelihood of increased sexual success. However, it was found that there was no significant relationship between sexting behavior and risk tolerance in mate retention. These results suggest that sexting is likely being used as a specific strategy by individuals who have a relatively higher degree of risk tolerance regarding efforts to find sexual partners and are seeking to either attract mates, or pursue short-term sexual relationships.

How sexting is used by those who are currently in a romantic relationship provides further support for the view of sexting as a short-term strategy. Individuals who reported being in committed or dating relationships reported frequently engaging in sexting during the early stages of their relationships; however, the use of sexting decreases substantially after the first 18 months of the relationships (Ploharz & Baird, 2012). Both men and women self-reported that their primary reason for engaging in sexting was to flirt or be sexy, and one third of individuals reported engaging in sex with a new partner for the first time after sexting that partner (Drouin, Vogel, Surbey, & Stills, 2013; Henderson & Morgan, 2011; Ploharz & Baird, 2012). Women reported that sexting had a more positive effect on their relationship than men did, with the largest difference being seen in the reported effect of pictures. These results may suggest that sexting, particularly the use of picture messages, is especially effective for women utilizing a short-term mating strategy or working to attract mates by allowing them to portray themselves as physically attractive or sexually available in a more direct way than was previously possible.

These findings suggest that sexting is being used by individuals to attract potential mates, or to keep partners engaged in the relationship during its earliest stages and that it does so by advertising physical attractiveness and sexual availability. This conclusion is consistent with evolutionary theory about mate attraction strategies which utilize physical attractiveness and sexual availability to obtain sexual partners (Buss & Schmitt, 1993).

Positive Expectations.   The second part of adaptive behavior is flexible engagement in the behavior while aware of the risks to achieve positive outcomes. The reported expectations of those who engage in sexting also suggest that people who choose to send sext messages are expecting positive outcomes, even while they are aware of the possible risks. Dir et al. (2013) examined the role of expectancies, or the self-reported likelihood of specific desired outcomes in the decision to engage in sexting. Individuals were shown to have both positive and negative expectations regarding sexting with higher levels of positive expectancies positively relating sexting and higher levels of negative expectancies being negatively related to sexting. Those individuals who had high negative expectancies engaged in sexting when they also possessed high positive expectancies regarding the behavior. It appears that for many the potential benefits outweigh the possible harms.

Multiple studies have shown that individuals are acutely aware of the risk of potential negative outcomes stemming from sexting (e.g., Dir et al. 2013; Henderson & Morgan, 2011). The most commonly endorsed potentially negative outcome was unwanted message dissemination, or the unintended sharing of messages with others by the recipients. Dir and Cyders (2014) reported that 95% of participants viewed this as a real risk, though in the same study 67% of participants reported sending a sexual message. The high level of sexting participation and perceived risks of sexting suggest that sexting may best be viewed as a goal-directed behavior used by individuals even while they are aware of the potential risks due to a perceived increased chance of sexual or mating success.

Conclusion

The range of findings about personality, attachment, and risky behavior all illustrate the largest challenge in supporting the view of sexting as a mating behavior. To date, there is limited research designed to provide direct supporting or contradicting evidence of the role sexting may have as a mating behavior. This is perhaps the largest issue with the body of evidence addressing the possible adaptive nature of sexting behavior. Much of the support for the mating behaviors view is drawn from reinterpretation of results designed to explore and describe the negative outcomes of sexting and the predictors of the behavior. The view of sexting as a goal-directed adaptive behavior needs further direct study and replication of existing results before it can be confidently supported.

References

Benotsch, E. G., Snipes, D. J., Martin, A. M., & Bull, S. S. (2013). Sexting, substance use and sexual risk behaviors in young adults. *Journal of Adolescent Health, 52,* 307–313. doi:10.1016/j.adolhealth.2012.06.011.

Buss, M. D., & Schmitt, D. P. (1993). Sexual strategies theory: An evolutionary perspective on human mating. *Psychological Review, 100,* 204–232. doi:10.1037/0033-295X.100.2.204

Cosmides, L., Tooby, J., & Barkow, J. (1992). Introduction: Evolutionary psychology and conceptual integration. In J. Barkow, L. Cosmides, & J. Tooby (Eds.), *The adapted mind: Evolutionary psychology and the generation of culture* (pp. 3–15). New York, NY: Oxford University Press.

Delevi, R., & Weisskirch, R. S. (2013). Personality factors as predictors of sexting. *Computers in Human Behavior, 29,* 2589–2594. doi:10.1016/j.chb.2013.06.003

Dir, A. L., Coskunpinar, A., Steiner, J. L., & Cyders, M. A. (2013). Understanding differences in sexting behaviors across gender, relationship status, and sexual identity, and the role of expectancies in sexting. *Cyberpsychology, Behavior, and Social Networking, 16,* 568–574. doi:10.1089/cyber.2012.0545

Dir, A. L., & Cyders, M.A. (2014). Risks, risk factors, and outcomes associated with phone and internet sexting among university students in the United States. *Archives of Sexual Behavior, 44,* 1675–1684. doi:10.1007/s10508-014-0370-7

Drouin, M., & Landgraff, C. (2012). Texting, sexting and attachment in college students romantic relationships. *Computers in Human Behavior, 28,* 444–449. doi:10.1016/j.chb.2011/10.015

Drouin, M., Vogel, K. N., Surbey, A., & Stills, J. R. (2013). Let's talk about sexting baby: Computer-mediated sexual behaviors among young adults. *Computers in Human Behavior, 29,* A25–A30. doi:10.1016/j.chb.2012.12.013.

Ferguson, C. J. (2011). Sexting behaviors among young Hispanic women: Incidence and association with other high-risk sexual behaviors. *Psychiatric Quarterly, 82,* 239–243. doi:10.1007/s11126-010-9165-8

Gordon-Messer, D., Bauermeister, J. A., Grodzinski, A., & Zimmerman, M. (2012). Sexting among young adults. *Journal of Adolescent Health, 52,* 301–306 doi:10.1016/j.jadohealth.2012.03.013

Hasinoff, A. A. (2012). Sexting as media production: Rethinking social media and sexuality. *New Media and Society, 15,* 449–465. doi:10.1177/1461444812459171.

Henderson, L., & Morgan, E. (2011). Sexting and sexual relationships among teens and young adults. *McNair Scholars Research Journal, 7,* 31–39. Retrieved from http://scholarworks.boisestate.edu/mcnair_journal/vol7/iss1/9

Klettke, B., Hallford, D. J., & Mellor, D. J. (2014). Sexting prevalence and correlates: A systematic literature review. *Clinical Psychology Review, 34*, 44–53. doi:10.1016/j.cpr.2013.10.007

Ploharz S. (2016). An evolutionary based evaluation of sexting behavior among college students (master's thesis). Retrieved from FHSU Scholars Repository https://scholars.fhsu.edu/cgi/viewcontent.cgi?article=1014&context=theses

Ploharz, S., & Baird, T. (2012). *Sexting: Individual differences and its effects.* Poster presentation at Rocky Mountain Psychological Association, Denver, CO.

Ploharz, S., Baird, T., & Patrick, C. (2014). *Does narcissistic personality predict sexting?* Poster presentation at Southwestern Psychological Association, San Antonio, TX.

Sexting. (n.d). In *Merriam-Webster online dictionary*. Retrieved from http://www.merriam-webster.com/dictionary/sexting

Weisskirch, R. S., &, Delevi, R. (2011). "Sexting" and adult romantic attachment. *Computers in Human Behavior, 27*, 1697–1701. doi:10.1016/j.chb.2011.02.008

23

Do Emotions Help or Hurt Decision Making?

by Taylor Willits

The experience of emotion is a universal and unique experience of human life. It would be hard to imagine a life, or a decision, that takes place independent of any emotion or feeling. Furthermore, emotions impact our decision in subtle and sometimes unexpected ways. Not only can pre-established emotions influence an individual's decision process, but also the experience of decision making is often an emotional process in itself. As such, research on the impact of emotions on decision making is crucial in order to have an increasingly holistic understanding of human decision making and behavior.

Stemming from research that revealed the cognitive limitations and restricted rationality of human decision makers (Simon, 1972), research on emotion and its impact on judgment and decision making has seen an increase in the past decade. Although still a relatively new topic, emotions are considered by many to have a strong impact on judgments and decisions in a range of settings (e.g., interpersonal, financial, health, etc.; Lerner, Li, Valdesolo, & Kassam, 2015). However, this research has also resulted in competing views on how emotion actually functions to impact our decisions and whether emotion ultimately helps or hinders our judgments and decisions. The goal of this chapter is to address certain findings that have been highly impactful in the emotion and decision-making literature. To provide a more comprehensive review, both supporting and opposing research will be presented for each point.

Pros—Emotions Help Decision Making

Positive Emotions Lead to More Effortful Decision Making. One of the prevailing stereotypes is that emotions lead people to make irrational and self-defeating decisions. But do all emotions lead to such self-defeating behavior? What about emotions which lead to more rational decision making? One study looked at the effect of positive mood on the use of a Decision Support System (DSS) to solve a production-scheduling problem (Djamasbi, 2007). Participants were randomly assigned to a positive or neutral mood group and

Contributed by Taylor Willits. Copyright © Kendall Hunt Publishing Company

participated in 30 trials of a decision task. Effort in the decision task was measured by tracking the number of cues used to make a judgment (more cues result in more informed judgments) and accuracy was measured by looking at the deviation of the participant's solution from the optimal solution. The positive mood group used significantly more cues (exerted more effort) and made significantly more accurate decisions compared to the neutral mood group. This indicated that participants in a positive mood utilized the DSS more effectively than the neutral mood group, resulting in more rational decision processes and accurate outcomes.

Emotions Can Help Buffer Loss Aversion.   An interesting study by Cassotti et al. (2012) examined the impact of positive and negative emotions on a financial decision-making task. The task consisted of either a sure option or a gamble (i.e., risky) option, with each presented in a loss or gain frame. Participants were randomly assigned to a positive emotion group, a negative emotion group, or a control group that was not emotionally primed. Control group and the negative emotion group were both affected by the framing manipulation (i.e., participants chose the risky gamble option more in the loss frame). However, the framing effect was not found for the positive emotion group. More specifically, participants in the positive emotion group were more risk-averse in the loss frame compared to the control and negative emotion group, but no differences were found for the gain frame. Importantly, being in the negative emotion group did not impact the susceptibility to framing compared to the control group. That is, negative emotions did not further increase biased decisions due to framing, and positive emotions actually helped buffer the effects of framing which lead to decreased risk-seeking in a loss frame. These findings indicate that emotions do not necessarily impact risky decision making in a negative manner and may actually decrease decision bias resulting from loss aversion.

Anticipated Emotions Lead to More Vigilant Decision Making.   Anticipated emotions are a function of predicted decision outcomes and can be used to help decision makers predict their future emotions. One of the most well-studied and strongest anticipated emotions in the judgment and decision-making literature is the emotion of anticipated regret. Research has established that anticipated regret does have a substantial effect on decisions, but is the emotion actually helpful to decision makers?

One interesting study by Reb (2008) examined the effect anticipated regret had on the actual decision-making process (rather than just the decision outcome). One of the experiments found that increasing anticipated regret (i.e., the regret condition) led to a 25% increase in the time spent on the decision and a 20% increase in the amount of information searched when choosing among options with risky hypothetical monetary outcomes. Additionally, participants in the regret condition (i.e., feedback on chosen and foregone options) chose the riskier option less often than those in the control condition (i.e., feedback on chosen outcome only). This pattern was replicated in four additional experiments using various decision situations, incentives, manipulations of regret, and dependent variables. For instance, in an experiment in which participants received real money based on their choices in the task, increasing the salience of regret led to a 23% increase in decision duration and a 55% increase in the amount of information collected. Overall, the results from these studies indicate that heightened regret aversion influences decision makers to engage in a more careful, comprehensive decision process. In most instances, slowing down and taking more information into account should result in a better decision, especially for risky decisions.

Cons—Emotions Hurt Decision Making

Negative Emotions Lead to Impulsive Decision Making.   There is a body of research that suggests that negative emotions such as anger and sadness may lead to more impulsive "heat of the moment" decisions. One study suggested that negative affect, or emotional distress, led individuals to prioritize affect regulation (i.e., seeking ways to feel better) which resulted in decreased or failed impulse control (Tice, Bratslavsky, & Baumeister, 2018). In this study, an adaptation of the mood-freezing manipulation first developed by Manucia, Baumann, and Cialdini (1984) was used to make participants believe that their mood was unchangeable. A series of experiments found that emotional distress led to an increased consumption of unhealthy snack food, a decrease in the ability to delay gratification, and an increase in procrastination in participants not receiving the mood-freezing manipulation. However, all of these effects disappeared for participants in the mood-freezing condition. Participants who believed their mood was unchangeable actually decreased their consumption of snack food, delayed gratification more effectively, and preferred to procrastinate with boring rather than interesting distractors. Thus, emotional distress only impacted the self-regulation abilities of participants who believed that pursuing impulsive behavior would change their mood for the better (i.e., reducing distress). These findings indicate that emotionally distressed people indulge their self-defeating impulses in the pursuit of more positive emotion.

Emotions Negatively Bias Risky Decision Making.   One large area of study involves examining the effects of emotions on decisions that involve risk. A prevailing conclusion in the literature is that emotions impact judgments of risk and probabilities, which then impact subsequent decisions. However, there is competing information on whether emotions help or hinder risky decision making. One study by Rottenstreich and Hsee (2001) proposed an effective approach to risky choice in which outcomes had the same monetary values, but different emotional values. The study demonstrated how affect-rich outcomes can change the way probabilities are weighted. For instance, one of the experiments looked at whether participants would prefer to receive $50 in cash or the "opportunity to meet and kiss your favorite movie star." Participants were randomly assigned to a "certainty condition" or a "low-probability" condition (1% chance of winning). In the certainty condition, 70% of participants preferred the cash (affect-poor); however, in the low-probability condition 65% preferred the kiss (affect-rich). The same effects were replicated in another experiment using different prizes. These results indicate that independence of outcomes from probabilities does not hold for different affective values. That is, when making risky decision, preferences depend on the affective reaction associated with each of the potential choices.

Emotional Outcomes can be Overestimated.   Importantly, the value of anticipating emotion relies on the assumption that individual decision makers are able to accurately forecast their future emotions based on certain outcomes. However, individuals may mispredict their own feelings of regret (Gilbert, Morewedge, Risen, & Wilson, 2004). In order to examine a real-world situation with actual consequences, this study examined feelings of regret in a subway station. Passengers were approached and were randomly assigned to a role condition (experiencer or forecaster) and a margin condition (wide or narrow). Experiencers were told that they missed their train by a narrow or wide margin (1 or 5 minutes) and responded with their feelings of regret, whereas forecasters were given a hypothetical situation in which they missed the train with the same narrow or wide margin and responded with their feelings of anticipated regret. Results found that the size of the margin influenced forecasted (anticipated) regret, but not experienced regret. That is, forecasters overestimated how much regret they would feel if they missed the train by 1 minute, but not when they missed the train by 5 minutes. Importantly, this effect was not seen for the similar emotion of disappointment. A follow-up experiment indicated that forecasters predicted more regret than experiencers actually experienced. Additionally, forecasters overestimated how much responsibility they would feel in both the narrow and wide margin conditions, indicating that actual self-blame did not differ between missing the train by 1 or 5 minutes. Overall, these results suggest that future or anticipated regret can be overestimated, and that experienced regret is minimized by our ability to absolve ourselves of responsibility. This misprediction of regret could potentially be costly to decision makers who rely heavily on their anticipation of regret to make decisions.

References

Cassotti, M., Habib, M., Poirel, N., Aïte, A., Houdé, O., & Moutier, S. (2012). Positive emotional context eliminates the framing effect in decision-making. *Emotion, 12,* 926–931. doi:10.1037/a0026788

Djamasbi, S. (2007). Does positive affect influence the effective usage of a decision support system? *Decision Support Systems, 43,* 1707–1717. doi:10.1016/j.dss.2006.09.002

Gilbert, D. T., Morewedge, C. K., Risen, J. L., & Wilson, T. D. (2004). Looking forward to looking backward: The misprediction of regret. *Psychological Science, 15,* 346–350. doi:10.1111/j.0956-7976.2004.00681.x

Lerner, J. S., Li, Y., Valdesolo, P., & Kassam, K. S. (2015). Emotion and decision making. *Annual Review of Psychology, 66,* 799–823. doi:0.1146/annurev-psych-010213-115043

Manucia, G. K., Baumann, D. J., & Cialdini, R. B. (1984). Mood influences on helping: Direct effects or side effects? *Journal of Personality and Social Psychology, 46,* 357–364. doi:10.1037/0022-3514.46.2.357

Reb, J. (2008). Regret aversion and decision process quality: Effects of regret salience on decision process carefulness. *Organizational Behavior and Human Decision Processes, 105,* 169–182. doi:10.1016/j.obhdp.2007.08.006

Rottenstreich, Y., & Hsee, C. K. (2001). Money, kisses, and electric shocks: On the affective psychology of risk. *Psychological Science, 12,* 185–190. doi:10.1111/1467-9280.00334

Simon, H. A. (1972). Theories of bounded rationality. *Decision and Organization, 1,* 161–176. Retrieved from http://innovbfa.viabloga.com/files/Herbert_Simon___theories_of_bounded_rationality___1972.pdf

Tice, D. M., Bratslavsky, E., & Baumeister, R. F. (2018). Emotional distress regulation takes precedence over impulse control: If you feel bad, do it! *Journal of Personality and Social Psychology, 80,* 53–67. doi:10.1037/0022-3514.80.1.53

CPSIA information can be obtained
at www.ICGtesting.com
Printed in the USA
LVHW060551100719
623570LV00001B/1/P